Author ....

Title .....

BACH'S
ORCHESTRA

A CHOIR GALLERY
1732

BACH'S
ORCHESTRA

BY
CHARLES SANFORD
TERRY

LONDON
OXFORD UNIVERSITY PRESS
NEW YORK   TORONTO

Oxford University Press, Ely House, London W. 1

GLASGOW NEW YORK TORONTO MELBOURNE WELLINGTON
CAPE TOWN IBADAN NAIROBI DAR ES SALAAM LUSAKA ADDIS ABABA
DELHI BOMBAY CALCUTTA MADRAS KARACHI LAHORE DACCA
KUALA LUMPUR SINGAPORE HONG KONG TOKYO

ISBN 0 19 315209 6

First edition 1932
Reprinted 1958, 1961, 1966, and 1972

REPRINTED IN GREAT BRITAIN
AT THE UNIVERSITY PRESS, OXFORD
BY VIVIAN RIDLER
PRINTER TO THE UNIVERSITY

CAROLO STRAVBE

MVNERE

QUOD ILLE SEBASTIANVS OLIM EXSEQVEBATVR

NVNC DIGNISSIME FVNGENTI

FOREWORD

BY THURSTON DART

TO the history of musical instruments and their use the scholars of Britain have made a notable contribution. The story begins at least as early as 1695 with a Cambridge enthusiast named James Talbot; his great collection of documents and measurements relating to the instruments of his day remains one of the most important sources of its kind. From the eighteenth century came the treatises, histories, and dictionary articles of such men as North, Grassineau, Hawkins, and Burney; from the nineteenth, the studies of Bunting and Armstrong on the harp and similar instruments, of Rimbault on the organ and pianoforte, of Rockstro on the flute, and many others.

During the last sixty or seventy years the pace has quickened. Ellis, Wood, Jeans, and Lloyd have written on the acoustics of instruments; Hayes, the brothers Hill, and St. George on the viol, the violin, and the bow; Welch, Carse, Blandford, Rendall, Langwill, Halfpenny, and Baines on wind instruments; James, Harding, Sumner, and Boalch on keyboard instruments; Piggott, Moule, Day, Fox Strangways, Robson, Stainer, Farmer, Kirby, Schlesinger, and Picken on non-European instruments. Galpin, Pulver, Donington, and others have prepared textbooks and dictionaries; hundreds of fine craftsmen, working in dozens of workshops, have produced instruments which will endure. To this incomplete review must be added the foundation in England of a flourishing Society, named after Canon Galpin, for the study of the history and use of instruments; and it may be said that the preparation of some of the best exhibitions and catalogues of instruments has taken place under English auspices.

Amongst all this activity Charles Sanford Terry's outstanding book *Bach's Orchestra* has long secured for itself an honoured place. First published in 1932, it is based on a simple and essentially humble point of view which has become increasingly accepted during recent decades. This may be summed up in the phrase 'the composer knew best'. Thousands of professional and amateur musicians from all countries now believe, as Terry did, that Bach was a wise, careful composer with a most discriminating ear; if he chose to write for the bass viol or the harpsichord or the recorder, in preference to the equally available cello or organ or flute, then there is every reason to suppose that his choice was made not capriciously but after deliberate thought. The conclusion seems clear. Bach's music will be best served, first, by discovering his intentions, and then by obeying them as scrupulously as circumstances permit. Terry decided to find out Bach's wishes about instruments by the simple means of examining his scores and the archives of his time. The present book contains the stimulating results of the search.

No one needs to be persuaded that such an approach works well for the music of Mendelssohn or Beethoven or Mozart. We do not find it necessary to touch up the overture to *Ruy Blas*, to re-score for full orchestra Beethoven's septet, or to add parts for trombones, harp, and piccolo to the 'Jupiter' symphony. Yet earlier music is too often regarded as an opponent to be overthrown in a kind of all-in wrestling match, with no holds barred, and the moment we turn to the performance of music composed before 1750 or so our first instinct is usually to behave like Procrustes on a bad day. Handel's delicate web of sound is stretched to cover the Albert Hall; Bach's extraordinarily sensitive pattern of tone-colours is warped and cut away to fit the structure of the modern orchestra. We would do well to remember that few who stayed overnight with Procrustes were able to make a second visit, and that early music is no Theseus.

Terry's book shows clearly that, by comparison with the first half of the eighteenth century, the variety of tone-colours commonly available to a composer has not increased. On the contrary, it is today much smaller. In the orchestra of Bach or Handel a musician could choose, for instance, from two contrasting families of flute-tone (recorders or transverse flutes), two independent families of bowed strings (viols or violins), and three coexisting families of plucked strings (lutes, harps, harpsichords). Of the seven honourable and important families in this list, only three are represented in an orchestra of our own time. Bach composed his sixth Brandenburg concerto as a septet, for a chamber music group drawn from three different instrumental families: two violas, one cello, two fretted bass viols, one violone, and an accompanying harpsichord. It seems to be the unanimous opinion ot most modern conductors that, at the time, Bach cannot really have known what he was doing. They publicly rebuke his implied affront to our more enlightened taste; his chamber septet is played, rather loudly throughout, by an ensemble of twenty or thirty instruments all belonging to a single family (violas, celli, contra-basses); and his expressed desire for the cheerful, necessary jangle of the harpsichord is firmly ignored, since this cannot be anything but another instance of his deplorable insensitivity to nuances of instrumental timbre.

Many feel that such an attitude of mind, to the music of a man respected everywhere as a very great genius, is little better than that of a cannibal. A single reading of Terry's book suggests that conductors may possibly be mistaken in thinking Bach lamentably stupid, inexcusably slipshod, or quite reprehensibly deaf. A second reading of Terry brings reassurance that Bach was a good musician, who meant what he wrote. It also brings high admiration for Terry's exemplary accuracy, as well as for the affectionate respect which permits him to allow Bach to speak for himself. During the last thirty years many scholars have added to our knowledge of Bach and of the instruments he had at his disposal. Yet, so far as I am able to judge, no part of Terry's masterly study needs amending in the light of this more recent work. Most of what he has to say seems even more apt than it can have been twenty-five years ago.

To draw attention to the merits of Terry's book may seem something of an impertinence on the part of a musician two generations his junior. I hope it may not be so considered. To the book and to its author I owe a debt of gratitude for what I have learned over a long period of time about Bach and about the instruments he had in mind for his music. The writing of a foreword can be no more than a token repayment of that debt.

Jesus College,
  Cambridge,
    1958.

POSTSCRIPT

The phrase above 'no part of Terry's masterly study needs amending' sounds—and is—too good to be true. As several correspondents and reviewers have pointed out, the probable chronology of Bach's works has been considerably revised during the last thirty years by the careful work of many scholars from all over the world, and some of Terry's conclusions are therefore no longer to the point. Other scholars have opened up new approaches to Bach's use of such instruments as the harpsichord, the corno da caccia, the fiauto d'echo, and the violone, and a new scholarly edition of his complete works is well under way. In another ten years or so it may well be possible for a second Terry to write a new book on Bach's Orchestra. Until that time, however, the present book would still appear to be the best available guide to the labyrinth. To revise it piecemeal would be premature, laborious, and expensive; to recommend it warmly, warts and all, remains in my opinion the right thing to do.

THURSTON DART

Jesus College,
Cambridge,
1961.

NOTE

BACH'S usage and characterization of his instruments is the major theme of these pages. Of all the Masters whose art has continuing and unabated vogue, he especially spoke through voices silent in the modern orchestra. Some cannot certainly be identified. Of others his prescriptions are unprecise or ambiguous. Thus the subject is approached through obscurities. If I have succeeded in clarifying them, I must attribute it largely to experts in their several spheres who have given me their counsel—Mr. F. T. Arnold, Mr. W. F. H. Blandford, Mr. Gerald R. Hayes, and, above all, Canon Galpin, whose patience is as inexhaustible as his knowledge. But I must not be held to commit them collectively to the conclusions here maintained. My second and sixth chapters, in particular, bristle with arguable topics—for instance, the significance of Bach's 'corno' and 'corno da caccia', from my interpretation of which, *inter alia*, Mr. Blandford dissents. But my debt to one and all is considerable and I warmly acknowledge it.

Closely connected with my main thesis is another, whose relationship has been impressed upon me in the course of my research. Students of Bach's genius are tempted to forget that his cantatas and their like are *occasional* music, whose wider publicity was unforeseen, indeed, unimaginable by their composer. While he held office, in Leipzig or elsewhere, he could repeat them at recurring intervals. But thereafter—oblivion! Another would provide his official quota of original music, and eke it out occasionally from the church's library of dusty manuscript. Into that repository no more than a fraction of Bach's vocal scores found its way. His elder sons divided them, and the eldest dissipated his portion. Only the widow's share returned to the shelves of the Thomasschule, relinquished for a few thalers to relieve her poverty. These circumstances—need it be said?—could not dull Bach's lofty purpose. But they necessarily affected his utterance. Composing for the occasion, he was controlled, and not seldom hampered, by local conditions, particularly in his instrumentation. What those conditions were I have endeavoured to reconstruct in my opening chapter, and the local background has been held in view throughout.

The gist of Chapter III appeared in *The Musical Times* for February 1931. I thank Messrs. Novello for permission to reproduce it. Messrs. Kistner & Siegel have kindly allowed me to include Haussmann's portrait of Gottfried Reiche. Canon Galpin and Mr. Arnold have increased my obligation to them by their close reading of these pages in proof.

C. S. T.

July 1932.

CONTENTS

TABLES

ILLUSTRATIONS

TEXT FIGURES

REFERENCES AND ABBREVIATIONS

The works named below are referred to throughout the pages by
the indicated abbreviations

Adlung = 'Musica mechanica organoedi.' By Jakob Adlung. 2 vols. Berlin: 1768 (facsimile 1931).

Agricola = 'Musica instrumentalis deudsch'. By Martin Agricola. Wittenberg: 1529 (new edition 1896).

Altenburg = 'Versuch einer Anleitung zur heroisch-musikalischen Trompeter- und Pauker-Kunst.' By Johann Ernst Altenburg. Halle: 1795 (facsimile 1911).

Archiv f. M. = 'Die Leipziger Ratsmusik von 1650 bis 1775.' By Arnold Schering. In 'Archiv für Musikwissenschaft', 1921, Heft I.

Arnold = 'The art of accompaniment from a thorough-bass as practised in the seventeenth and eighteenth centuries.' By F. T. Arnold. London: 1931.

Bach = 'Versuch über die wahre Art, das Clavier zu spielen.' By Carl Philipp Emanuel Bach. 2 parts, Berlin: 1753–62 (reprint 1925).

B.-G. = 'Johann Sebastian Bach's Werke. Herausgegeben von der Bach-Gesellschaft in Leipzig.' Leipzig: 1850–1900.

B.-J. = 'Bach-Jahrbuch.' Herausgegeben von der Neuen Bachgesellschaft. Leipzig: 1904– .

Baron = 'Historisch-theoretisch und practische Untersuchung des Instruments der Lauten.' By Ernst Gottlieb Baron. Nürnberg: 1727.

Bojanowski = 'Das Weimar Johann Sebastian Bachs.' By Paul von Bojanowski. Weimar: 1903.

Dolmetsch = 'The interpretation of the music of the seventeenth and eighteenth centuries revealed by contemporary evidence.' By Arnold Dolmetsch. London: 1915.

Eichborn = 'Die Trompete in alter und neuer Zeit.' By Hermann Ludwig Eichborn. Leipzig, 1881.

Eichborn (2) = 'Das alte Clarinblasen auf Trompeten.' By Hermann Ludwig Eichborn. Leipzig: 1894.

Fitzgibbon = 'The story of the flute.' By H. Macaulay Fitzgibbon. London: Revised and enlarged edition 1928.

Forkel = 'Johann Sebastian Bach, his life, art, and work.' By Johann Nikolaus Forkel (1802). Ed. Charles Sanford Terry. London: 1920.

Francœur = 'Traité général des voix et des instruments d'orchestre.' By Louis Joseph Francœur. Paris (?) 1772 (new edition 1813).

Galpin = 'Old English instruments of music, their history and character.' By Francis W. Galpin. 3rd edition. London: 1932.

Gerber = 'Historisch-Biographisches Lexicon der Tonkünstler.' By Ernst Ludwig Gerber. 2 vols. Leipzig: 1790–92.

Götz = 'Schule des Blockflötenspiels nach Lehr und Art der mittelalterlichen Pfeifer.' By Robert Götz. Cöln: 1930.

Grove = 'Grove's Dictionary of music and musicians.' 3rd edition. Edited by H. C. Colles. 5 vols. London: 1928.

Hayes = 'Musical instruments and their music, 1500–1750. II. The viols, and other bowed instruments.' By Gerald R. Hayes, London: 1930.

Heckel = 'Der Fagott. Kurzgefasste Abhandlung über seine historische Entwicklung, seinen Bau und seine Spielweise.' By William Heckel. 2nd edition. Leipzig: 1931.

Hiller = 'Lebensbeschreibungen berühmter Musikgelehrten und Tonkünstler neuerer Zeit.' By Johann Adam Hiller. Leipzig: 1784.

Jordan = 'Aus der Geschichte der Musik in Mühlhausen.' By Dr. Jordan. Mühlhausen: 1905.

Kinsky = 'Musikhistorisches Museum von Wilhelm Heyer in Cöln. Kleiner Katalog der Sammlung alter Musikinstrumente.' By Georg Kinsky. Cöln: 1913.

Kirby = 'The kettle-drums. A book for composers, conductors, and kettledrummers.' By Percival R. Kirby. London: 1930.

Kittel = 'Johann Christian Kittel, der letzte Bach-Schüler.' By Albert Dreetz. Leipzig: 1932.

Mahillon = 'Catalogue descriptif et analytique du Musée instrumental du Conservatoire royal de musique de Bruxelles.' By Victor-Charles Mahillon. Gand: 1893–1922.

Mattheson = 'Das neu-eröffnete Orchestre.' By Johann Mattheson. Hamburg: 1713.

Mersenne = 'Harmonie universelle, contenant la théorie et la pratique de la musique.' By Marin Mersenne. Paris: 1736.

Mozart = 'Versuch einer gründlichen Violinschule.' By Leopold Mozart. Augsburg: 1756.

North = 'Memoires of Musick.' By Roger North (1653–1734). Ed. F. Rimbault. London: 1846.

Piersig = 'Die Einführung des Hornes in die Kunstmusik und seine Verwendung bis zum Tode Joh. Seb. Bachs.' By Fritz Piersig. Halle: 1927.

Pirro = 'L'esthétique de Jean-Sébastian Bach.' By André Pirro. Paris: 1907.

Pirro (2) = 'Johann Sebastian Bach, the organist, and his works for the organ.' By A. Pirro. With a Preface by Ch.-M. Widor. Translated from the French by Wallace Goodrich. New York: 1902.

Praetorius = 'Syntagmatis musici . . . Tomus secundus. De organographia.' By Michael Praetorius. Wolfenbüttel: 1618 (facsimile 1929).

Quantz = 'Versuch einer Anweisung die Flöte traversière zu spielen.' By Johann Joachim Quantz. Berlin: 1752 (new edition 1906).

Roxas = 'Leben eines herrlichen Bildes . . . Grafen von Sporck.' By Ferdinand van der Roxas. Amsterdam: 1715.

Sachs = 'Real-Lexikon der Musikinstrumente.' By Curt Sachs. Berlin: 1913.

Sachs (2) = 'Sammlung alter Musikinstrumente bei der staatlichen Hochschule für Musik zu Berlin. Beschreibender Katalog.' By Curt Sachs. Berlin: 1922.

Sachs (3) = 'Verzeichnis der Sammlung alter Musikinstrumente im Bachhous zu Eisenach.' By Curt Sachs. 2nd edition. Leipzig: 1918.

Schering = 'Musikgeschichte Leipzigs . . . von 1650 bis 1723.' By Arnold Schering. Leipzig: 1926.

Schubart = 'Ideen zu einer Ästhetik der Tonkunst.' By Christian Friedrich Daniel Schubart. Vienna: 1806.

Schweitzer = 'J. S. Bach.' By Albert Schweitzer. 2 vols. London: 1911.

Spitta = 'Johann Sebastian Bach. His work and influence on the music of Germany, 1685–1750.' By Philipp Spitta. 3 vols. London: 1899.

Tappert = 'Sebastian Bach's Compositionen für die Laute.' By Wilhelm Tappert. Berlin: 1901.

Terry = 'Bach: a biography'. By Charles Sanford Terry. London: 1928.

Terry (2) = 'Bach: the historical approach.' By Charles Sanford Terry. London and New York: 1930.

Terry (3) = 'The origin of the family of Bach musicians.' By Charles Sanford Terry. London: 1929.

Terry (4) = 'Joh. Seb. Bach: Cantata texts, sacred and secular.' By Charles Sanford Terry. London: 1926.

Virdung = 'Musica getutscht und aussgezogen.' By Sebastian Virdung. Basel: 1511 (facsimile 1931).

Wäschke = 'Die Hofkapelle in Cöthen unter Joh. Seb. Bach.' By H. Wäschke. Zerbst: 1907.

Walther = 'Musicalisches Lexicon oder Musicalische Bibliothec.' By Johann Gottfried Walther. Leipzig: 1732.

Weissgerber = 'Johann Sebastian Bach in Arnstadt.' By Diaconus Weissgerber. Arnstadt: 1904.

Woehl = 'Musik für Blocknoten . . . Heft I. Blockflötenschule.' By Waldemar Woehl. 2nd edition, Kassel: 1930.

Wustmann = 'Musikgeschichte Leipzigs . . . bis zur Mitte des 17. Jahrhunderts.' By Rudolf Wustmann. Leipzig and Berlin: 1909.

CHAPTER I
THE LOCAL BACKGROUND

AFTER brief service in a chamber orchestra at Weimar, Bach, a lad of eighteen, found himself in the summer of 1703 his own master at Arnstadt, in an occupation laboriously prepared for since his not-distant schooldays at Ohrdruf. In the interval his genius had been surprisingly nurtured by experience. He had heard music at its most active centres, and in all forms then current. In the Particularschule of Lüneburg he had served a society whose musical apparatus surpassed any he so far had known, whose library revealed to him the classics his own art was destined to enrich and supersede. At Hamburg he had heard Opera under Reinhard Keiser, its most prolific and popular composer. Brought up in the severer ecclesiastical tradition, he had found there an orchestra which spoke with independent eloquence, not merely as an accompanist of the human voice, but as its equal partner in the presentation of Biblical and secular drama. At Hamburg, too, the genius of Reinken had made a deep impression on his greatest disciple. At Celle another idiom was encountered. Here, at the Court of its jovial Duke, the gallant music of France was performed by an orchestra of Frenchmen, with the elegant finish and refined technique characteristic of their nation. So, if untoward bereavement expelled Bach from his native Eisenach, it was the happiest stroke in the moulding of his genius that immediately took him thence to his brother's home at Ohrdruf; for his later educative experiences were consequent upon that initial step.

Arnstadt

As organist of the lately restored Bonifaciuskirche at Arnstadt, Bach filled a subordinate position, whose shortcomings were for the moment outweighed by access to an organ entirely his own. In the civic Gymnasium he held no official position, and drew from it its least competent singers. On the civic instrumentalists his call was precarious. Count Anton Günther, seated in Schloss Neideck on the fringes of the town, maintained a Capelle of some twenty players, occasionally heard in the Augustenburg, modelled on the pleasure house of his wife's Brunswick home. To them were added, when need arose, Michael Bach of Gehren, later Sebastian's father-in-law, the Cantor at Breitenbach, and a bassoon player from Sondershausen.[1] Bach, too, no doubt, was employed.

[1] Weissgerber, p. 5.

Following contemporary practice, the Count's musicians also filled domestic or administrative posts in his household. Christoph Herthum, Bach's relative by marriage, combined the posts of Court Organist and Clerk of the Kitchen. The Capellmeister, Paul Gleitsmann, functioned as Groom of the Chamber.[1] The church registers of the period record an inordinate number of Court Trumpeters, who, as elsewhere, were efficient on the other instruments of their craft, 'oboists', and 'lackeys' whose position in the Capelle cannot be determined.[2]

With an orchestra drawn from these sources Bach produced his earliest extant cantata, *Denn du wirst meine Seele nicht in der Hölle lassen* (No. 15), probably on Easter Day (23 March) 1704. But the peremptory orders of the Consistory could not induce him to compose another 'Stück'. For a consuming thirst for instruction drew him in 1705 to distant Lübeck, to hear Dietrich Buxtehude and the famous 'Abendmusiken'. Here he realized fully for the first time the potential contribution of music to the ritual of public worship, and, returning to Arnstadt, awaited with impatience an opportunity to exercise his new convictions elsewhere.

Mühlhausen

The call came in the summer of 1707, when he was elected organist of the noble Blasiuskirche of Mühlhausen. A succession of fires, the most recent of which immediately preceded his arrival, had consumed valuable records of its past history. But one surviving document,[3] dated 6 March 168$\frac{8}{9}$, discloses a musical organization with which we must associate the only cantata positively composed by Bach for church use in his new sphere. *Gott ist mein König* (No. 71) was performed at the Ratswahl service in the Marienkirche on Septuagesima Sunday (4 February) 1708, closely following the festivals of the Virgin Mary and St. Blaise, to whom Mühlhausen's two principal churches are dedicated. The score is laid out in four 'Choirs': (i) three trumpets and drums; (ii) two flutes and violoncello; (iii) two oboes and bassoon; (iv) two violins, viola, and violone. The voices, too, are grouped in a 'Coro pleno' and a 'Coro in ripieno', the former of which Bach's autograph distinguishes as the 'Capella'. Apparently the ripienists were less expert singers—we may liken them to the Leipzig 'Motettenchor', which provided the 'Coro secondo' of the *Mat-*

---

[1] Weissgerber, *loc. cit.*

[2] It has not been possible to obtain more detailed information regarding the Arnstadt players. I must thank Geheimer Studienrat Dr. Grosse for his assistance in the matter.

[3] Jordan, p. 14.

thäuspassion. In the opening chorus they merely shout intermittently, 'Gott ist mein König'. In the second chorus they are silent, and in the final movement only enter at the *Vivace* section to support the Capella's acclamation of Kaiser Joseph and its fervent wishes for 'Glück, Heil und grosser Sieg!'

The score, therefore, demands exceptional resources, vocal and instrumental, whose source is revealed in the document mentioned above. It discloses the existence, as early as 1617, of a local 'musicalische Societät' or 'musicalisches Kränzchen', whose membership embraced the singers and players of the city and surrounding district. Its nucleus comprised those whom its statutes term 'Schulcollegen' and 'Adjuvanten', i.e. the staff of the town-school, and local amateurs whose services assisted the regular singers and players of the civic church choirs. Another category, described as 'Exteri', was evidently drawn from the country-side. That the villages near-by were actively musical we know from Bach's own statement.[1] The 'Societät' was distinct from the lads of the town-school, the official church choristers, though on the instrumental side it included the civic organists and '6 Musici' (Stadtpfeifer). The abnormal score of Bach's Ratswahl Cantata probably was due to its co-operation. If so, we are probably correct in identifying its members with the 'Coro in ripieno', and the 'Capella' with the 'Coro pleno' of school *alumni*.

Weimar

Before the end of the summer of 1708 Bach was installed in ducal service at Weimar, in touch with an orchestral body whose association with him continued over a considerable period (1708–17). His precise situation at the outset is not definitely ascertained. Certainly he entered the Capelle as 'Cammermusicus' (chamber violinist), and subsequently, perhaps after a short interval, was appointed Court Organist. Neither post required him to compose, and as Cammermusicus he was simply a member of the select string orchestra which performed in the Duke's private apartments in Schloss Wilhelmsburg. In March 1714, however, he was promoted to the position of Concertmeister, with the duty of composing cantatas for the ducal chapel.[2] What were his resources for their performance? The singers numbered six boy sopranos and two singers in each of the under parts, twelve in all, a small body, but experienced and efficient. Of the instrumentalists three lists are extant, from which we can deduce the composition of the ducal orchestra. It included three violinists (of whom one

[1] Terry, p. 83.   [2] Cf. Terry, pp. 91–3.

must be supposed a viola player), one violonist, one fagottist, six trumpeters, and one drummer—in all twelve players. Until his death in 1716 (1 December) the director of the musical organization was Capellmeister Johann Samuel Drese, whose son, Johann Wilhelm Drese, acted as his deputy (Vice-Capellmeister), and, to Bach's chagrin, succeeded in 1716 to the higher post. The personnel of the Capelle is recorded in the following Table:[1]

Office	Name	Dates
Capellmeister	Joh. Samuel Drese	d. 1 Dec. 1716.
	Joh. Wilhelm Drese	1716–
Vice-Capellmeister	Georg Christoph Strattner	d. Apr. 1704.
	Joh. Wilhelm Drese	1704–16.
Concertmeister	Joh. Sebastian Bach	2 Mar. 1714–2 Dec. 1717.
Violinists (3)	Joh. Paul von Westhoff	d. 1705.
	Joh. Georg Hoffmann	
	August Gottfried Denstedt ⎱	Entered Capelle before
	Andreas Christoph Ecke ⎰	1714.
Violonist	Joh. Andreas Ehrbach	
Fagottist (1)	Christian Gustav Fischer	d. before 1714.
	Bernhard Georg Ulrich	Entered Capelle before 1714.
Trumpeters (6)	Joh. Georg Beumelburg	
	Joh. Wendelin Eichenberg	
	Joh. Martin Fichtel	
	Joh. Christoph Heininger	
	Joh. Martin Fase	d. before 1714.
	Dietrich Dekker	d. before 1716.
	Joh. Christian Biedermann ⎱	Entered Capelle *circa* 1714.
	Conrad Landgraf ⎰	
Timpanist	Andreas Nicol	

The Duke's conservative disinclination for change, evidenced by his stubborn refusal to release Bach from his service, is illustrated by the composition of the Capelle, whose personnel changed little while Bach was a member of it. The reason was due in part to the fact that, as elsewhere, the Weimar musicians discharged domestic duties in the ducal Court, whose efficient fulfilment probably outweighed deficiencies in their instrumental technique. Westhoff, a violinist of distinction, who had toured widely as a virtuoso, functioned also as 'Cammersecretarius'. Ehrbach was employed as 'Kunstcämmerer' (Superintendent of the Art Museum). Heininger, a trumpeter, was 'Cammerfourier' (Groom-in-waiting). Biedermann, another trumpeter, acted as 'Schloss-Voigt' (Palace Overseer). Denstedt, a violinist, shared the duties of Court Secretary. Of the singers, Andreas Aiblinger, a tenor, held office as 'Secretarius'. Gottfried Ephraim Thiele, a bass, was

[1] Unless the dates indicate the contrary, the persons named were in office during the whole of Bach's service in Weimar.

Court Secretary and Master of the Pages. Christoph Alt, the other bass, was a junior master (Quintus) in the Weimar Gymnasium. The Court chapel, in which Bach's Weimar cantatas were heard, was ill-adapted for concerted music.[1] The building was lofty and narrow, and the organ[2] was placed aloft in a small roof-gallery, whose accommodation was confined and inconvenient for singers and players. The conditions explain the light instrumentation of the Weimar cantatas.[3] All but five of them (Nos. 59, 70, 147, 162, 185) are scored for strings and wood-wind. Even the Easter Day Cantata *Ich weiss, dass mein Erlöser lebt* (No. 160) is not embellished with trumpets and drums, as was Bach's custom at Leipzig. Brass instruments are rarely prescribed—a single trumpet is scored in Nos. 70, 147, 185, and a corno da tirarsi in No. 162. Drums are scored only in the Whit-Sunday Cantata *Wer mich liebet* (No. 59), in association with two trumpets. Even flutes and oboes are rarely called for, and neither trombones nor horns are required.

Cöthen

A new chapter in Bach's professional experience opened in 1717, on his appointment to the post of Capellmeister at the Court of Prince Leopold of Anhalt-Cöthen. The situation was more dignified than the one he vacated. But Cöthen could not vie with Weimar in the scale of its establishment, and the Prince's Calvinist chapel withheld the opportunities the other capital had afforded Bach as a composer. As Capellmeister, he directed an orchestra, chiefly of strings, which entertained its sovereign in the Ludwigs-bau of the Schloss. Its personnel was grouped in three categories: (1) the 'Cammermusici' (chamber musicians), eight in number; (2) four 'Musici', local players retained for occasional employment at a nominal wage; and (3) a corps of trumpeters and drummer, three in all. A copyist—a rare luxury in Bach's experience—completed the establishment, sixteen in all.[4] Six of them had been drawn from Berlin on the dissolution of its Capelle in 1713, and, alone of the chamber musicians, their instruments can be indicated. The following Table names those who served under Bach, 1717-23:

---

[1] See the picture and description of the building in Terry, p. 96.
[2] For its specification see chap. vii, *infra*.
[3] Neither Nos. 21 nor 31 illustrates the resources of the Weimar Capelle. The former was performed at Halle, the second survives as revised in 1731. The Weimar chapel cantatas are Nos. 18, 59, 61, 70, 106, 132, 147, 150, 152, 155, 158, 160, 161, 162, 163, 182, 185, 189, and *Mein Herze schwimmt im Blut*. In these pages the cantatas are generally referred to by their numbers. For their titles cf. Table XXII.   [4] See Terry, p. 119.

Name	Instrument	Dates
Chamber Musicians.		
Josephus Spiess	Violin	
Joh. Ludwig Rose	Oboe	
Martin Fr. Markus	Violin	Left June 1722.
Joh. Christoph Torlee	Bassoon	
Joh. Heinrich Freytag	..	d. 1721.
Christian Ferdinand Abel	Violin and Gamba	
Joh. Gottfried Würdig		
Christian Bernhard Linigke	Violoncello	
Joh. Valentin Fischer	..	Admitted Aug. 1719.
Christian Rolle	..	Admitted June 1722.
Emanuel Heinrich Gottlieb Freytag	..	Promoted Apr. 1721.
Musicians.		
Joh. Freytag, senior		
Wilhelm Harbordt	..	Left Jan. 1718.
Adam Weber		
Emanuel Heinrich Gottlieb Freytag	..	Promoted 1721 (*supra*).
Trumpeters.		
Joh. Christoph Krahl		
Joh. Ludwig Schreiber		
Timpanist.		
Anton Unger		
Copyist.		
Johann Kräuser	..	Left Dec. 1717.
Joh. Bernhard Göbel	..	Admitted Dec. 1717.
Joh. Bernhard Bach ⎱	..	⎰ Admitted and left
Emanuel Leberecht Gottschalk ⎰		⎱ 1718–19.
Carl Friedrich Vetter	..	Admitted Aug. 1719.

To this point, in so far as his extant work is a guide, Bach, as a composer, had not been drawn to purely instrumental music, except for the organ and clavier. But Cöthen afforded scope for no other. With the available literature he was familiar: at Weimar he had studied French and Italian scores with his accustomed thoroughness. But his genius could not rest content with foreign models. His Cöthen years, therefore, produced, especially in the Brandenburg Concertos, absolute instrumental music surpassing any in existence in the variety of its colouring, the freedom of its technique, and the masterliness of its touch.

It has already been remarked that, excepting the players drawn from Berlin and the trumpeters and drummer, there is no direct indication of the instruments the Capelle provided. Bach's compositions, however, reveal those that were available. The three secular Cöthen cantatas—*Durchlaucht'ster Leopold, Mit Gnaden bekröne,* and *Weichet nur*—are lightly scored for strings and flutes or oboes. His instrumental sonatas were written for violin, violon-

cello, flute, and viola da gamba. The last-named instrument was
Abel's, whose son in later years associated with Bach's youngest
son in London. Prince Leopold, too, was a gamba player and may
have joined Abel in the sixth Brandenburg Concerto. The frequent
violoncello parts indicate that Linigke was a player whom Bach
respected, and we can connect Rose with the oboe parts. The
Ouvertures in C and B mi., and all but one of the Brandenburg
Concertos, were within the competence of the Capelle in respect
to the instruments they require. But it supported no horn players,
and the well remunerated visit of two guest 'Waldhornisten' on
6 June 1722 undoubtedly indicates a performance of the Brandenburg Concerto in F, probably the first.

But Bach's Cöthen years were an interlude in the ordered scheme
of his career. His art was to him, before everything, the servant of
religion, and music, in his own words, 'a harmonious euphony to
the glory of God'. Every step in his career, from his first employment at Arnstadt, was guided by one compelling purpose, 'the
betterment of Church music'. Only the inharmonious conditions
of his situation at Weimar, and pique at his exclusion from a post
he reasonably held himself to have earned, had taken him to Cöthen
in 1717. But the high purpose of his life, though checked, was not
stifled. From more than one quarter hands beckoned him to
return to the paths whence he had strayed. In 1723 he yielded to
the appeal, accepted a call to Leipzig, and there for more than a
quarter of a century pursued his life's ideal with unflagging
concentration.

Leipzig

Leipzig's municipal orchestra was adequate neither in size nor
skill for the uses to which Bach put it. It totalled seven professional
players and one apprentice, eight in all. Contrasted with this meagre
supply, his requirements, themselves modest, are on record. For
the due rendering of Church music, he declared in an illuminating
memorandum (August 1730),[1] he needed 'violists', flautists, oboists,
and trumpeters. Under the term 'violist' he included all the
stringed instruments, and with the trumpeters he associated a
drummer. In regard to numbers: he demanded two (preferably
three) first violins, a similar number of second violins, two desks
of violas (four players), two violoncellists, one violone player, two
(or three) oboists, one bassoon player (or two), three trumpeters,
and a timpanist—a minimum of eighteen performers.

Bach's statement is instructive. In the first place, though he

---

[1] Terry, p. 201.

names flutes as necessary, he does not class them as indispensable.
He merely states that their inclusion would bring his orchestra to
a total of twenty players. In fact, since his appointment to the
Cantorship in 1723 they had rarely appeared in his cantata scores.
They occur in only eleven (Nos. 8, 46, 65, 67, 81, 119, 145, 157, 164,
181, 195), whereas at Weimar he constantly prescribed them. The
explanation is found in the memorandum, whence it appears that
he was dependent for flautists on local amateurs—University
'studiosi', or 'alumni' of the Thomasschule. In his first years at
Leipzig he was evidently well served from that source, for all the
eleven cantatas are referred to the period, in which also fall the
Magnificat and both Passions.

In the second place, Bach's enumeration apparently excludes
both horns and trombones. In fact, they are implicit in his fourth
category. For centuries the civic musicians were known as 'the
blowers' ('die Bläser'), responsible for 'Blasmusik', whether
sounded by trumpets, trombones, or horns. To us, accustomed
to the vogue of specialism, the practice appears disadvantageous.
But the explanation is simple. Like others of the kind in Germany,
Leipzig's municipal orchestra was a guild of professional monopo-
lists, and consequently expert in the technique of all the instruments
proper to the discharge of its public duties. The rules of the Saxon
'Instrumental-musicalisches Collegium' (1653) ordain *inter alia*:
'Seeing that an expert musician must profess several instruments,
both wind and percussion, and so be well instructed in them, no
apprentice shall be released under five years or be held competent
to practise his craft' ('Und nachdem ein perfecter Musicant auff
vielen Instrumenten, theils *pneumaticis*, theils *pulsatilibus* unter-
wiesen werden, und darauff auch geübet seyn muss, so soll kein
Lehrknabe unter fünff Jahr frey gesprochen, und dass er seiner
Kunst erfahren, für tüchtig erkennet werden').[1] The relation of
this regulation to Bach's experience at Leipzig will be illustrated
later. Here it only needs to be remarked that the performers of his
trumpet *obbligati* were the same valiant trio for whom he wrote
horn and trombone parts. In the whole range of his music the
three instruments are only once so disposed as to require separate
players. The single instance to the contrary is in the secular
cantata *Der zufriedengestellte Aeolus*, in which three trumpets and
two horns are employed in the same movements.[2]

Thus Bach's Leipzig orchestra was a mixed body of professional

---

[1] Spitta (Germ. edn.), i. 145.

[2] The cornett-trombone combination very infrequently employs four
players.

and amateur players, varying in size and composition according to the means at his disposal. The relative proportions of the two categories, and their contribution to the orchestra, is revealed in the memorandum. In August 1730 the professionals supplied him with two trumpeters (horn and trombone players), two oboists, one bassoon player (the apprentice), and two violinists, seven in all. Bach styles the latter respectively '1 Violine', '2 Violine', indicating the leaders of the firsts and seconds. Regarding the parts for which he had to look elsewhere, he names two first violins, two second violins, two violas, two violoncellists, one violone player, and two flutes. At the first and second violin desks he therefore had two amateurs and one professional leader, six in all. The number was customary: his predecessor Kuhnau had asked in 1704 to be provided with a box large enough to hold six violins for carriage from church to church.[1] Outside the professional body Bach also needed two viola players, two violoncellists, one violonist, and two flutes. All of these, he explains, were provided occasionally ('zum Theil') by University 'studiosi', but generally ('meistens') by *alumni* of the Thomasschule. From the latter source his second violins generally ('meistens'), and his viola, violoncello, and violone players invariably ('allezeit'), were recruited 'for lack of more expert players' ('in Ermangelung tüchtigerer *subjectorum*'). We can therefore deduce that his amateur first violins and flautists were undergraduates of the University. Most frequently, we may suppose, they had proceeded thither from the Thomasschule.

It must not be inferred that Bach's orchestra regularly and normally numbered twenty, or even eighteen, players. For it associated exclusively with the 'Coro primo' or 'grosse Cantorei' of his singers, which performed the Sunday cantatas and occasional concerted music. In 1730 it numbered seventeen choristers, and as many in 1744. Seventeen may therefore be accepted as its normal strength.[2] Small in number, it was also unevenly balanced. In 1744 it comprised five sopranos, two altos, three tenors, and seven basses. The weakness of the melodic part explains its frequently strong instrumental backing in Bach's scores, especially in the Chorals. The choir was certainly inadequate to associate with an orchestra that outnumbered it. Excepting festal occasions, we can conclude that Bach's instrumentalists rarely exceeded ten or twelve players, besides the organ. If so, his dependence on non-professional aid was not so urgent as must otherwise have been the case. For it is not to be supposed that the professional players were only on duty when the Sunday cantata contained a part for

[1] Spitta, iii. 303.   [2] Cf. Terry (2), p. 51.

their principal instrument. Indeed, Altenburg[1] advised a trumpeter to make himself efficient on the fiddle. Johann Schneider,
Bach's pupil, and organist of the Nikolaikirche, explicitly directed
his horn and oboe players in certain movements of a wedding
cantata of his composition to put down those instruments and
take up their violins. A similar usage obtained in the orchestral
concerts which began to be a feature of Leipzig's musical activity
in the same period,[2] Bach's players undoubtedly observed the
convention.

Thus, on Sunday mornings, at the chief service of the day
(Hauptgottesdienst), the choir gallery of St. Thomas's or St.
Nicholas's accommodated a body of about thirty performers for the
rendering of the cantata. On festal occasions the number would be
larger, but not considerably. The choir was not usually augmented,
save for occasional 'Adjuvanten' in the under parts. In the
orchestra trumpets (or horns) and drums were added to the
instruments normally heard. But their presence did not necessarily
enlarge the personnel. On special occasions, however, Bach could
increase his forces considerably. In the *St. Matthew Passion*, for
instance, the inclusion of his 'Coro secondo', or 'kleine Cantorei',
of twenty voices brought the tale of his singers to nearly forty;
and, since he used two orchestras, each of at least twelve
players, singers and instrumentalists together totalled about sixty.
Nowhere else does he demand so large a 'Kirchenorchester',
though some of his secular cantatas made heavy calls on his
resources, and for an obvious reason: they were written for open-
air performance.

The arrangement of Bach's singers and players in church is
apparently revealed by a closely contemporary (1710) print, which,
in some particulars, confirms the speculations of the preceding
paragraph.[3] It shows the choir gallery of the Thomaskirche during
the performance of a 'Stück' (cantata) in the Cantorship of Johann
Kuhnau, Bach's immediate predecessor. The organ is on the west
wall, and the performers are grouped on either side of and behind
the organist seated at the manuals in the middle of the picture.
On his left is the violonist, and next to him a lute player, an
instrument the cembalo superseded, and of which Bach made little
use in his church music. In front of these players a quartet of
strings is observed, two violins and two violas, and on their left,
immediately behind the organist, the timpanist faces his kettle-
drums. In the foreground the Cantor beats time with a roll in his

hand. On his left is a group of three, two playing natural trumpets,[1] the third, a horn player, with the bell of his instrument held upward, as was customary. In all, the players number ten, and are stationed generally on the Cantor's left, facing the singers, who are ranged on his right in three groups of four, twelve in all. Their costumes show that they are not separated in parts (soprano, alto, tenor, bass), but that each quartet is a complete vocal unit, the bass in each acting as group-conductor, and taking the beat from the Cantor. Including the organist, the performers number twenty-three.

As an indication of Bach's disposition of his forces, and of his place among them, the picture is unreliable. The gallery of St. Thomas's was far smaller than it is to-day, and its front was filled by the imposing case of the Rückpositiv.[2] The singers and players were grouped round the harpsichord, which probably stood midway between the organ and Rückpositiv. As the frontispiece to his *Musicalisches Lexicon*, published in 1732, Joh. G. Walther, Bach's Weimar friend, used a picture of what we may perhaps identify as the organ gallery of the civic church in that town.[3] The conductor stands close to the organist, on the left of the console, and therefore in a position to control the most powerful voice in his orchestra. Immediately behind him are the continuo players and strings, with the brass instruments in the rear. The singers are not visible, but their position is indicated by the attitude of the conductor, who faces them across the intervening harpsichord. He has a roll of music in either hand. Johann Bähr, Bach's contemporary and acquaintance at Weissenfels, remarks that conductors varied in their methods: some stamped with their feet; others, their feet being employed, beat time with their head; some used one hand, some both hands; one waved a roll of paper, another grasped a roll in each hand; and some used a stick.[4] Of Bach as a conductor we have his son Carl Philipp Emanuel and his pupil Agricola's statement that he was precise and particular, and preferred a lively *tempo*.[5] Gesner, under whom as Rector he served for a short time, is more descriptive. He seats Bach at the keyboard, whence 'he controls this one with a nod, another with the rhythm of the measure, a third with a directing finger'.[6]

Since Bach occasionally used the harpsichord and organ, displacing the regular player of the latter, he would adopt a position as conductor which would give him quick access to both keyboards,

---

[1] They are holding their instruments below the boss and so control only one position.   [2] Cf. *infra*, p. 12.   [3] See the frontispiece to this volume.
[4] Spitta, ii. 325.   [5] Terry, p. 267.   [6] *Ibid.*, p. 107.

and at the same time enable him to control his singers and players. The conductor's position in Walther's frontispiece was admirably chosen for these purposes, and we may accept it as Bach's habitual place. The disposition of his choir and orchestra are indicated on the following plan, which makes their numbers accord with the facts set forth in an earlier paragraph:

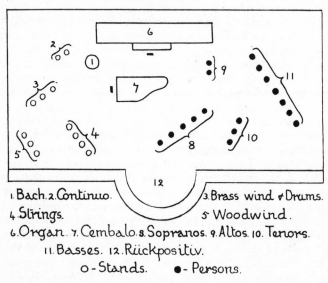

1. Bach. 2. Continuo.   3. Brass wind & Drums.
4. Strings.   5 Woodwind.
6. Organ. 7. Cembalo. 8. Sopranos. 9. Altos. 10. Tenors.
11. Basses. 12. Rückpositiv.
        o - Stands.   ● - Persons.

It would be agreeable to recover the names of the privileged company who for a quarter of a century introduced Bach's masterpieces to an indifferent world. We can only guess, though with some certainty, those of his voluntary helpers. Senior among them was Joh. Gotthelf Gerlach, who left the Thomasschule in 1723, became organist of Leipzig's New Church, and eventually succeeded Bach as conductor of the Collegium Musicum (University Musical Society). His contemporaries Joh. Gabriel Rothe, later Cantor in Grimma, and Christ. Gottlieb Gerlach, afterwards Cantor of his native Rochlitz, who left the school respectively in 1723 and 1726, must also have been useful in Bach's early years at Leipzig.[1] His nephew Joh. Heinrich, son of his Ohrdruf brother, left the school in 1728 in his twenty-first year. Later he became Cantor at Oehringen and was competent to requite his uncle with his service. Towards the middle of Bach's Cantorship, his favourite, Johann Ludwig Krebs, left the school (1735) and

[1] They both proceeded to the University, Gerlach in 1727, Rothe in 1725.

proceeded to the University. The part he played in Bach's unhappy quarrel with the prefects in 1736[1] proves that he continued to assist his former master. In 1737 he became organist at Zwickau. Gottlob Heinrich Neicke and Joh. Ludwig Dietel are also associated with this period of Bach's Cantorship. They left the school in 1733 and 1735 respectively, proceeded to the University, and were Cantors in after-life. Christoph Nichelmann left the school in 1733. His association with Bach's family was close: Bach's eldest son Wilhelm Friedemann was his master for the clavier,[2] and Philipp Emanuel helped to secure his appointment as second cembalist to Frederick the Great. Another alumnus of this middle period was Christ. Friedrich Schemelli, with whose father Bach collaborated as musical editor of the so-called 'Schemelli Hymnbook' (1736). The younger Schemelli left the school in 1734, matriculated at the University in 1735, and eventually succeeded his father as Cantor at Zeitz. We may not include in this problematical list of auxiliaries Joh. Gottfried Böhme, afterwards Cantor at Tragheim (?), whose stay in the Thomasschule was brief. He entered it in 1732 and left it 'privily' ('clanculum') in 1733, complaining that the tasks of the ordinary curriculum impeded his progress in music![3] Joh. Gottfried Kade, who entered the school in his fourteenth year, and left it (1745) when he was twenty-three, had the greater opportunity to be of service, seeing that he found employment in St. Nicholas's School as Tertius[4] and Cantor. Joh. Wilhelm Cunis, who left the school in 1747 and proceeded to the University, afterwards Cantor in his native Cölleda, was another probable helper. Bach's talented sons undoubtedly aided him, and in the closing years of his Cantorship two others of his name may be recorded in this company: Joh. Ernst Bach, an Eisenach cousin, who came to Leipzig in 1737 and was eventually expelled for taking French leave of absence,[5] and a more reliable relative, Joh. Elias Bach, who entered Bach's household in 1738, served him affectionately till 1742, and left to become Cantor of Schweinfurt. That, regularly or on occasion, some or all of these deciphered Bach's bold manuscript on their playing-desks we can be sure.

No dubiety exists as to Bach's professional players: their names are tabulated on p. 14.

With the addition of the anonymous apprentice-bassoonist, the first seven names on the Table are those of the professional players Bach took over from his predecessor. They represented two

[1] Cf. Terry, chap. viii, *passim*. [2] Gerber, ii. 26.
[3] B.-J. 1907, p. 71. [4] i.e. third master. [5] B.-J. 1907, p. 73.

Name	Kunst-geiger	Stadt-pfeifer	Died[1]	Principal Instrument
Gottfried Reiche	1700–6	1706–34	9 Oct. 1734	1st trumpet.[2]
Heinrich Christian Beyer	1706–48	..	21 Sept. 1748	2nd violin.[2]
Christian Rother	1707–8	1708–37	25 Oct. 1737	1st violin.[2]
Christian Ernst Meyer	1707–30	..	Apparently left Leipzig	? 3rd trumpet or 3rd oboe.[4]
Joh. Cornelius Gentzmer	1708–12	1712–51	25 Oct. 1751	2nd trumpet.[2]
Joh. Caspar Gleditsch	1712–19	1719–47	22 May 1747	1st oboe.[2]
Joh. Gottfried Kornagel	1719–53	..	14 Sept. 1753	2nd oboe.[2]
Joh. Friedrich Caroli	1730–38	..	1 March 1738	? 3rd trumpet or 3rd oboe.[4]
Ulrich Heinrich Ruhe	..	1734–87	11 June 1787	1st trumpet or 1st violin.[3]
Joh. Friedrich Kirchhof	..	1737–69	20 May 1769	oboe or flute.[3]
Joh. Christian Oschatz	1738–47	1747–62	13 Jan. 1762	oboe or flute or 2nd trumpet.[3]
Carl Friedrich Pfaffe	1748–53	1753–73	3 Mar. 1773	trumpet.[5]
Andreas Christoph Jonne	1749–62	1762–84	28 June 1784	? violin.[6]

separate, and not invariably harmonious, corporations. The civic office of Stadtpfeifer (town-piper, town-musician) in Leipzig dated from 1479, when the municipality instituted Master Hans Nagel and his two 'sons' (probably apprentices: 'Gesellen', 'Lehrlinge') at a yearly wage of forty gulden and their uniform. They functioned on occasions of public ceremony, but derived their chief emolument from weddings, at which they alone were privileged to perform, receiving fees according to the station of the spouses. A silver-gilt shield denoted their office.[7] Their instruments were the trumpet, Zink (cornett), and trombone.[8] But their monopoly did not remain unchallenged. In the course of the sixteenth century competitors invited public patronage and threatened their pecuniary interests. The challengers were known as 'Feldtpfeifer und Trommelschläger' (drum- and fifers), who so far had served other uses, acting as town-criers, and summoning the citizens to military duty. But in 1550 a civic ordinance permitted 'a drummer and his fifer' to perform at weddings. Conflict between the rival bodies consequently threatened, and was averted by an amicable

---

[1] The dates are those of burial. I am obliged to Dr. Reinhard Fink for extracting them from the church registers.

[2] Named in Bach's memorandum of August 1730.

[3] So described in the 'Tabula musicorum der Löbl. Grossen Konzertgesellschaft, 1746–48'. Cf. *Archiv f. M.*, p. 50.

[4] Meyer held one of the posts named by Bach as vacant in August 1730. His successor Caroli, no doubt, received it. Probability indicates the trumpet or oboe as their principal instrument.

[5] Succeeded Gentzmer as Stadtpfeifer. Gentzmer probably had succeeded Reiche as principal trumpeter in 1734.

[6] Perhaps took Beyer's place. [7] Wustmann, p. 31. [8] *Ibid.*, p. 33.

agreement concluded in 1587.[1] By then the number of Stadtpfeifer stood fixed at four, and that of their competitors at two pairs of drums and two fifers. The eight now (1587) arranged themselves in four groups to serve in alternation at ceremonies for which their instruments were required, leaving to the Stadtpfeifer exclusively the duty of assisting the music in the churches.

Thus was constituted an orchestra whose activities persisted till Bach's period, and beyond. But whereas the Stadtpfeifer continued to profess the instruments proper to 'Blasmusik', the Feldtpfeifer and Trommelschläger succumbed to the vagaries of public taste. In 1595, responding to the citizens' preference for the newer 'Hausmusik', the Council licensed two fiddlers to perform at weddings.[2] In 1603 we hear of 'public fiddlers', and by 1607 they are definitely 'town fiddlers' ('Stadtgeiger'), with their number fixed at three,[3] as in Bach's period. The Stadtpfeifer, however, retained their traditional privileges. They enjoyed the monopoly of all weddings celebrated 'in der Stadt', and surrendered to their rivals only the meaner sort ('die schlechten Hochzeiten vor den Thoren'), along with the less distinguished, and therefore less profitable, of two weddings fixed for the same day and hour 'in der Stadt'.[4] Again, in 1607, when the Kunstgeiger[5] were at length permitted to participate in the music of the two principal churches, the concession was restricted to association with the 'Coro secondo' or 'kleine Cantorei', reserving to the Stadtpfeifer their traditional right to accompany the 'Coro primo' or 'grosse Cantorei'.[6] But their separation could persist no longer than the character of 'die Musik' permitted. During the Cantorship of Johann Kuhnau (1701–22), Bach's immediate predecessor, the newer cantata style decisively prevailed. It demanded for its due performance a mixed orchestra of wind and strings. 'Stadtpfeifer' and 'Kunstgeiger' accordingly coalesced to assist the 'Coro primo' in the performance of the weekly 'Musik' in that one of the two churches privileged to hear it, leaving the 'Coro secondo', Bach's 'Motet Choir', to sing the old-style music a cappella or accompanied by the organ in the other.[7] At the same time, and for the same reason, the

---

[1] *Archiv f. M.*, p. 19.   [2] Wustmann, p. 155.
[3] B.-J. 1907, p. 34; Wustmann, p. 156.
[4] *Archiv f. M.*, p. 20. Weddings served by the Stadtpfeifer and Kunstgeiger were known respectively as 'grosse oder blasende Hochzeiten' and 'geigende Hochzeiten'. (Cf. *ibid.*, p. 26.) For the practice in Bach's time see *infra*, p. 21.
[5] The term was first used officially in 1626 (B.-J. 1907, p. 34).
[6] Wustmann, p. 156.
[7] In several motet-like choruses Bach reverts to the older tradition, and reinforces the voices with cornett and trombones.

restriction of the two professional bodies to a particular category
of instruments, wind or strings, fell into desuetude. Evidence is
lacking to determine when the change was accomplished. But in
Bach's time, as the Table on page 14 reveals, the Stadtpfeifer were
recruited from the Kunstgeiger. Indeed, for half his period of
service at Leipzig, his leader of the first violins was a Stadtpfeifer.

The Kunstgeiger, however, remained inferior in status and
income, and, though privileged and official, lived in surroundings
of discomfort and penury. Bach's appointment in 1723 was almost
coincident with an ordinance which, to some degree, bettered
their lot. In 1721, towards the close of Kuhnau's Cantorship, they
had approached the civic Council with a statement of their
grievances. They complained that, unlike themselves, the Stadtpfeifer lived rent free in official lodgings, received a weekly wage
of eighteen groschen, were exclusively engaged at University
graduations of doctors and masters, received gratuities from well-
to-do citizens to whom they offered New Year serenades, were
employed at the theatre ('haben sie die Comödie zu blasen')
during the three annual fairs, attended public banquets and the
Whitsuntide shooting matches, and were preferentially employed
at weddings.[1] The facts were correctly stated. Since 1599 the
most regular duty of the Stadtpfeifer was to sound fanfares from
the Rathaus tower twice daily.[2] Their weekly wage consequently
had been increased from fifteen to eighteen groschen, with an
allowance for clothing. Till 1717 they paid no local taxes. They
lived in a common lodging in the Stadtpfeifergässlein—to-day
the Magazingasse—and for their participation in church music
received, since 1633, ten thalers. Their 'Neujahrsgeld' brought
them two florins six groschen. Moreover, a Stadtpfeifer's widow
was privileged to remain a half-year in the house after her husband's
death, enjoying his official income and half the fees ('accidentia')
his successor might earn in that period.[3] In their effort to share
these privileges the Kunstgeiger were only partially successful.
Their exclusion from all but the meaner weddings continued.
On the other hand, they were granted an official lodging, which,
after 1725, they shared with the Stadtpfeifer in the Stadtpfeifergässlein. In 1740 they again petitioned for a closer approximation
of their status to that of their house-neighbours. But in vain;
the time was not ripe for such a break with tradition.[4]

[1] B.-J. 1907, p. 35.
[2] Specimens of these 'Abblasen' are given by Schering, p. 276.
[3] *Archiv f. M.*, p. 21. Since 1665 a Kunstgeiger's widow had the same
privilege as to income.   [4] *Ibid.*, p. 23.

Such was the situation when Bach came to Leipzig in 1723. The Stadtpfeifer provided him with four players, the Kunstgeiger with three, and the 'Geselle' added an eighth. The smaller body still viewed the other with envy, and regularly ascended to its ranks. Of the thirteen musicians who served under Bach only two reached Stadtpfeifer rank direct. For, notwithstanding their designation, the Kunstgeiger were not competent on stringed instruments only. Kuhnau, in 1709, reported that 'the Stadtpfeifer, Kunstgeiger, and apprentices, eight in all' ('die aus 8 Personen zusammen bestehenden Stadt Pfeiffer, Kunst Geiger und Gesellen') supplied him with two trumpeters, two oboists or cornettists, three trombonists, and one bassoonist.[1] It must not be concluded that none of the eight was a string player, though Kuhnau complained that such were hard to find. In 1730, as has already been shown, the two bodies gave Bach only two violinists. For the rest of the strings, he, like Kuhnau, depended on 'studiosi' and 'alumni'.[2] The easy transformation of a Kunstgeiger into a Stadtpfeifer, and his general competence to handle the so-called 'Stadtpfeiferinstrumente'—the trumpet, Zink (cornett), horn, trombone, bombard, dulcian, with some facility on the flute, oboe, and strings—is illustrated by the fact that in Bach's time a Kunstgeiger was not subjected to an examination before promotion to the higher post.[3] Two illustrative cases occurred during his Cantorate. In 1745 the Council directed him to settle the conflicting claims of two players to fill the next vacancy among the Stadtpfeifer—Johann Christian Oschatz, already a Kunstgeiger, who alleged that the Council had promised him promotion, and Carl Friedrich Pfaffe, trumpeter Gentzmer's apprentice 'cum spe succedendi' (with the prospect of succession). Oschatz was excused examination on the ground that his competence had been already established in 1738, when he was admitted a Kunstgeiger. Pfaffe submitted himself to trial, and on 24 July 1745 received from Bach a testimonial to his competence 'on the various instruments a Stadtpfeifer must profess, namely, the violin, oboe, traverso [flute], trumpet, horn, and other [wind] instruments' ('auf jedem Instrumente, so von denen Stadt Pfeifern pfleget gebrauchet zu werden, als Violine, Hautbois, Flute Travers., Trompette, Waldhorn und übrigen [Blas] Instrumenten').[4] Five years later a candidate failed to pass the test 'on the three principal instruments, namely, (1) the trumpet, (2) the horn, and (3) the oboe' ('auf den drey Haupt Instrumenten, als 1. Trompete, 2.

---

[1] Spitta (Germ. edn.), ii. 859. [2] *Supra*, p. 9.
[3] *Archiv f. M.*, p. 37. [4] *Ibid.*, p. 44.

Waldhorn, und 3. Hautbois'), without practical knowledge of
which, his examiners added, no one, 'however many extra instruments he may study, can pass muster as a Stadtpfeifer' ('ob er
gleich noch so viel neben Instrumente verstünde, ohnmöglich
vor einem Stadt-Pfeiffer passiren kan').[1] A third case is recorded
in 1769, when Johann Friedrich Doles examined two candidates
for a vacant post as Stadtpfeifer. Both were required to play the
violone part of a concerted Choral, a simple Choral on all four
trombones, a violin trio, a concerted Choral on the Zugtrompete
(tromba da tirarsi), and either a horn or an oboe and flute concerto![2]

These examples sufficiently indicate the all-round proficiency a
Stadtpfeifer was expected to display. On the other hand, they
provoke doubts as to his competence in the technique of them all.
In his report on the less worthy of the candidates in 1769—Joh.
Gottl. Herzog, a Kunstgeiger since 1763 and for twenty years
(1773-93) a Stadtpfeifer—Doles commented on his bad oboe tone,
inability on the Zugtrompete, inaccurate reading, lack of technique
as a trombonist, and uselessness as a violonist! None the less, a
Stadtpfeifer laid down his office only at his death. None ceased
to function until he was physically incapable, when he supplied a
deputy, who established a sort of claim to succeed him. Of those
in office when Bach came to Leipzig in 1723 one already had
served under two Cantors, and the experience of all went back to a
period when the 'status musices', as Bach called it, was far different
from that of his own generation. Kuhnau wrote contemptuously
in 1709 of his 'couple of Stadtpfeifer apprentices' ('etwa ein Paar
Stadt Pfeiffer Gesellen').[3] 'Discretion', Bach remarked of his
professional players in 1730, 'forbids me to offer an opinion on
their competence and musicianship. I merely observe that some
of them are *emeriti*, and others not in such good *exercitium* as
formerly.'[4] Even a non-professional critic in 1748 suggested that
'more accuracy' ('grössere Accuratesse') in their playing would be
agreeable.[5] It may be doubted whether Bach ever heard his scores
interpreted with even approximate excellence. How much more
fortunate was Handel in London!

It would appear that their instruments were generally as anti-
quated as the players. Kuhnau, soon after his appointment,
invited (1704) the Council's attention to the fact that the church's
trombones were battered and useless from long service. He asked
for a new 'choir' of four—discant, alto, tenor, bass—and also for a

[1] *Archiv f. M.*, p. 45.   [2] *Ibid.*, p. 45.
[3] Spitta (Germ. edn.), ii. 859.   [4] Terry, p. 202.   [5] *Archiv f. M.*, p. 44.

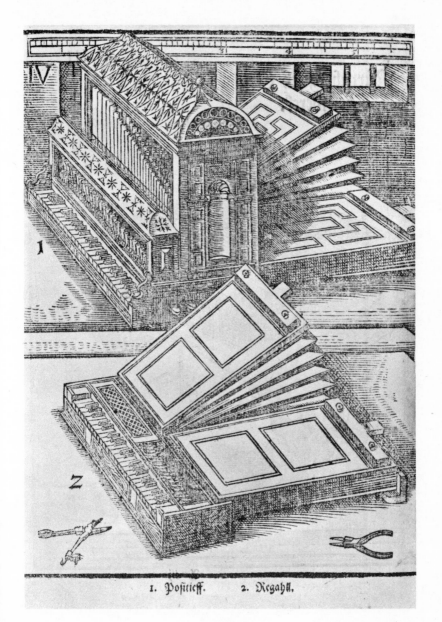

1. Positieff.   2. Regahl.

POSITIV AND REGAL
(*Praetorius*)

colascione,[1] which, though indispensable, he was forced to borrow. He failed to obtain it. Five years later he again begged for one, and also reported that the School violin was damaged beyond the means of the School funds to repair it. As a case for the church violins[2] had not been provided, he asked that nails might be driven into a board in the choir gallery, in order that there might be no excuse for leaving the instruments in jeopardy on the floor. He added that the harpsichords in both churches were in such disrepair that they needed to be patched every time they were used.[3] In 1747 the pipes of St. Thomas's organ were so full of dust and rubbish that many of them would not speak![4]

Both churches possessed their own instruments. When Schelle entered on his Cantorship in 1678, St. Thomas's owned a spinet, violone, octave bombard, bass bombard, fagotto, timpani, two *viole da braccio*,[5] and two violins.[6] The accounts show that there were also available: a flute, a 'choir' of trombones, and two trumpets. The drums, though ten years old in 1678, were not renewed till 1686![7] When Kuhnau took office in 1701, he found in St. Thomas's a violone, fagotto, spinet, five bombards, six trumpets, three trombones, and two recently acquired violins. St. Nicholas's owned a violone, fagotto, bombard, three trombones, two old violins, two violas, and two new violins. An official violoncello was not at Bach's disposal till 1729.[8] The preponderance of wind instruments is evident. An inventory for 1723 has not survived. But it is not doubtful that Bach inherited a collection of instruments which already had done honourable service. For instance, the cembalo in St. Thomas's had been in use since 1672 and was in a ruinous condition. It was not replaced till 1756, six years after his death![9] The School was not equipped with a cembalo, but a Positiv had been installed in 1685. In 1739 Bach begged for a new instrument, and was refused. It was erected and tuned to Cammerton during the Cantorship of his second successor (1756).[10] In St. Nicholas's a cembalo was not available in 1693, when the church's accounts show that it shared St. Thomas's instrument. But Kuhnau's reference in 1709 to 'the large *clavicembali* in both churches' ('in beyden Kirchen befindlichen grossen Clavi-

---

[1] A species of lute. Mattheson (p. 279) calls it 'ein kleines Lauten-mässiges mit 5. einfachen Sayten bezogenes und fast wie die Viola di Gamba gestimmtes Instrument (D. G. c. f. a. d.).' Having regard to its exotic character, Kuhnau's demand is strange. [2] *Supra*, p. 9.
[3] Spitta (Germ. edn.), ii. 853 f. [4] *Ibid.*, ii. 870.
[5] In Bach's time the name indicated the ordinary viola.
[6] B.-J. 1907, p. 38.
[7] *Archiv f. M.*, p. 34. They belonged to the two churches in common.
[8] Schering, p. 114. [9] Schering, p. 112. [10] B.-J. 1907, p. 41.

cimbeln')[1] shows that the defect had by then been made good, apparently by the generosity of a private donor.[2] The accounts of the School and the two churches for the period of Bach's Cantorship frequently record the repair of the instruments. But there is the barest indication that any new ones were acquired while he was in office. Zacharias Hildebrand received payment for repairing St. Nicholas's clavicembalo in 1732–3, and for restringing and tuning it in the following years till 1740. Otherwise the accounts reveal no expenditure upon musical instruments. Similar items appear in St. Thomas's accounts, which incidentally reveal that Carl Philipp Emanuel Bach was employed to tune its clavicembalo in 1731–2 and 1732–3. In the year 1729–30 two violins, one viola, and one violoncello were purchased, with their appropriate bows, and in 1739–40 a new 'Pedal-Clavier' was acquired from Johann Scheibe. For school practice a 'large' violone[3] was bought at an auction in 1735–6.[4] But otherwise the instruments that served Kuhnau did duty for Bach without replacement or augmentation—their inventory is repeated with monotonous reiteration annually to 1750:[5]

'*An Musicalischen Instrumenten*

1 *Regal*, so alt und ganz eingegangen.
1 *dito ão* 1696 angeschaffet.
1 *Violon ão* 1711.
1 *Violon ão* 1735, in der *Auction* erstanden [omitted 1723–34].
2 *Violons de Braz*. 2 *Violinen ão* 1706 repariret.
1 *Positiv* in die Höhe stehend von 4 Registern und Tremulanten, gelb mit Golde angestrichen *ão* 1685 angeschafft.
1 *Positiv* in *Form* eines Thresores mit 4 Handhaben, welches ein gedacktes von 8 Fuss Thon hat.
1 Dergleichen von 4 Fuss.
1 *Principal* von 2 Fuss, ist *ão* 1720 angeschaffet worden, um bey denen Hauss Trauungen zu gebrauchen.'

It is therefore evident that Bach was dependent on private owners for many of the instruments he employed. The necessity probably accounts for his own large and varied collection. Besides claviers, it included three lutes, a small spinet, two violins, a violino piccolo, three *viole da braccio*, one viola da gamba, two violoncellos, and one violoncello piccolo. That Bach was extraordinarily selective in his search for orchestral colour is admitted. But it is evident that his scoring was restricted by the accessibility

---

[1] See Praetorius, Plate VI, at p. 160.   [2] Schering, p. 112.
[3] Mr. Hayes conjectures that the adjective indicates a double-bass violin.
[4] I am obliged to Dr. Reinhard Fink, who searched the records on my behalf.
[5] Spitta (Germ. edn.), ii. 774.

of particular instruments at the moment he required them. The difficulty did not present itself in regard to wind instruments, for the Stadtpfeifer and Kunstgeiger had their own, or were provided with them to fulfil their civic duties. Reiche, for instance, Bach's chief trumpeter, also possessed a Zugtrompete and Waldhorn. His colleague Gleditsch, Bach's principal oboist, owned a Zink or cornett.[1]

In Leipzig, as in other German towns of the period, the principal and regular duty of the Stadtpfeifer was to blow the 'Abblasen' or 'Turmblasen' daily at 10 a.m. and 6 p.m. from the balcony of the Rathaus tower in the Marktplatz. At festival seasons, and on occasions of civic and academic solemnity, Chorals also were sounded by trombones or cornetts from the church towers.[2] But, for the necessary augmentation of their income, the town's musicians relied particularly on the *accidentia* derived from weddings. These were held in church with or without a Wedding Mass ('Brautmesse'); it might be either 'a whole Mass' (ganze Brautmesse) or 'a half Mass' (halbe Brautmesse).[3] The former took place at four o'clock in the afternoon, the latter at ten o'clock in the morning. At a full Mass both Stadtpfeifer and Kunstgeiger performed; at the morning function only the latter were employed. The poorer citizens, and such as desired to evade the expense of a musical ceremony, were married at eight o'clock in the morning. Some, who misliked the hour and implication of so early a ceremony, held their weddings elsewhere, and roused the ire of the local musicians thereby cheated of their fees.[4] The fee for a full Mass varied according as the bridal pair were received with music on entering church, or processed in silence ('in der Stille'). If music was provided at the wedding banquet which followed, the musicians received an additional fee. At half Masses the Kunstgeiger monopolized the wedding and the breakfast after it. The Cantor only attended a full Mass and received a fee of two thalers and a measure of wine. Their scoring indicates that all Bach's extant Leipzig wedding cantatas were performed at a full Mass. At the wedding banquet that followed, the Cantor with his 'Coro primo' was not infrequently invited to provide a cantata. Bach's 'Coffee Cantata', *O holder Tag, Vergnügte Pleissen-Stadt*, and *Weichet nur, betrübte Schatten* were composed for the purpose. His daughter Lieschen was married in St. Thomas's at a half Mass on 20 January 1749,[5] and it is probable that the 'Three Wedding

---

[1] *Archiv f. M.*, p. 34.   [2] Schering, pp. 271, 278, 285.
[3] Cf. *Archiv f. M.*, p. 31. Schering, p. 91.
[4] Cf. Terry, p. 180.   [5] *Ibid.*, p. 257.

Chorals', from the score of which drums and trumpets are absent, were sung on the occasion.

Funerals, which chiefly augmented the Cantor's salary—Bach estimated their annual contribution to his income as considerable[1] —brought no grist to his instrumentalists. For funerals were no longer conducted with the musical pomp still permitted to decorate weddings. Instead, memorial services were held at a short interval after the funeral, when a sermon was preached and music might be sung. Five of Bach's motets were composed for such occasions. But they were sung *a cappella*, and only one of them received orchestral accompaniment. It was performed in memory of an academic dignitary in the University chapel (Paulinerkirche), a building not subject to the civic rule which forbade instruments to be heard in the churches on such occasions. Another composition of this character is the *Trauer-Ode*, also composed for the University Chapel, and, like the Motet, provided with orchestral accompaniment. Both ceremonies were controlled by the University, and to the score of neither work were the distinctive 'Stadtpfeifer-instrumente' admitted. On the other hand, Bach's motet *O Jesu Christ, mein's Lebens Licht* is scored for them, for what occasion is not known. Certainly it was not performed in a Leipzig church, but probably at the grave-side.

[1] Terry, p. 205.

CHAPTER II

TRUMPET, HORN, CORNETT, TROMBONE

The Tromba

BACH'S younger contemporary, Johann Ernst Altenburg, son and pupil of a famous trumpeter, concisely particularizes his instrument. 'Our ordinary trumpet,' he writes,[1] 'known by the Romans as *Tuba*, by the French as *Trompette*, and by the Italians as *Tromba* or *Clarino*, is familiar as a musical and military, in particular a cavalry, instrument. Its tone is mettlesome, penetrating, clear, somewhat shrill in the high notes, but strident in its lower register. It rings out above all others, and justifies its title— "Queen of instruments". Mattheson characterized it as "resonant and heroic", and Schmidt as "exultant". It is usually made of hammered silver or brass, in six sections forming three tubular lengths, expanding funnel-wise towards the bell-end, and fitted with a mouthpiece proportionate with its narrow tubing.'

With rare exceptions Bach gives the trumpet its Italian name— *Tromba*. Only in the Arnstadt (No. 15) and the three Leipzig cantatas (Nos. 24, 48, 167) does he particularize the *Clarino*, and the *Principale* only in No. 15. The distinction is one of compass, to which players formerly rigidly adhered. Francœur, in his treatise published in 1772,[2] gives the compass of the clarino ('le premier Dessus') as from *g'* to *c'''* inclusive, and that of the principale ('second Dessus') as from *c* to *d''*. But these limitations ceased to be regarded, and by Bach were not observed. For that reason the terms 'Clarino' and 'Principale' occur so seldom in his scores, though, when both instruments are prescribed, as in cantata No. 15, the limitations of their registers are considered. For the same reason he disregards the convention which required the principale's part to be in the alto C clef. His trumpet parts are normally written in the treble G clef: the only exceptions are in cantata No. 15, where he uses the soprano C clef for the third trumpet; in cantata No. 63, where the third and fourth trumpets respectively are in the soprano and alto C clefs; and in cantata No. 119, where the fourth trumpet is scored in the soprano C clef. In all four cases the instrument accepts the register of the principale.[3]

What were the appearance and mechanism of Bach's 'Tromba'? The popular notion is confused by the so-called 'Bach Trumpet', invented by Julius Kosleck and used at Joachim's performance of the

---

[1] P. 9. [2] P. 66. [3] See Table I.

B minor Mass (*Hohe Messe*) in Eisenach, at the unveiling of the Bach Statue, in September 1884. Improved by Walter Morrow, it was formerly used for the trumpet parts in Bach and Handel scores. A smaller instrument in D, first made by Mahillon, is now employed. Bach's 'Tromba' was not a straight instrument with pistons, of the coach-horn or 'Aida' type, but an eight-foot tube bent in three parallel branches, uniform in bore throughout, but expanding in

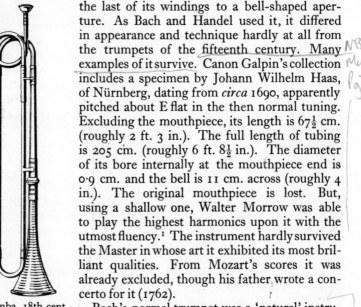

the last of its windings to a bell-shaped aperture. As Bach and Handel used it, it differed in appearance and technique hardly at all from the trumpets of the fifteenth century. Many examples of it survive. Canon Galpin's collection includes a specimen by Johann Wilhelm Haas, of Nürnberg, dating from *circa* 1690, apparently pitched about E flat in the then normal tuning. Excluding the mouthpiece, its length is $67\frac{1}{2}$ cm. (roughly 2 ft. 3 in.). The full length of tubing is 205 cm. (roughly 6 ft. $8\frac{1}{2}$ in.). The diameter of its bore internally at the mouthpiece end is 0·9 cm. and the bell is 11 cm. across (roughly 4 in.). The original mouthpiece is lost. But, using a shallow one, Walter Morrow was able to play the highest harmonics upon it with the utmost fluency.[1] The instrument hardly survived the Master in whose art it exhibited its most brilliant qualities. From Mozart's scores it was already excluded, though his father wrote a concerto for it (1762).

Tromba, 18th cent., length 65 cm.

Bach's normal trumpet was a 'natural' instrument, equipped neither with slides, valves, nor pistons: Its fundamental note varied according to the length of tubing; the Berlin collection contains examples in C, D flat, D, E flat, F, F sharp (probably for a flat pitch G). Another in high A flat is in the Heyer Collection at Leipzig. But the trumpet in D was most generally used.[2] Its natural scale, i.e. the notes it normally produced, was as follows in terms of the key of C:

[1] I owe the information to Canon Galpin. In 1895 Morrow demonstrated 'Clarinblasen' before the Musical Association on instruments lent and exhibited by Mr. W. F. H. Blandford. See the *Musical Times* for July 1895.

[2] The Heyer Collection exhibits an example (No. 1824) by Joseph Schmied, of Pfaffendorf, 1772. It is pitched to the E flat of its period (not F, as in Kinsky, p. 195). On doubtful authority it is said to have been used for the trumpet part in the second Brandenburg Concerto. See Richard Hofmann's article in B.-J. 1916.

The open tube gives the fundamental (1) and its octave (2), notes of poor quality infrequently prescribed: within the lowest two octaves c,–c' the third harmonic is the only note of practicable utility. In the third octave c'–c'' the series gives a pure fourth (4), major third (5), minor third (6), minor third (7), and major second (8). In the fourth octave c''–c''', by increased lip-tension

Mouthpieces (from left to right): Clarino, Tromba, Principale, Waldhorn.

and wind-pressure, the player sounds the harmonic scale. There is no reason to suppose these high harmonics, which modern technique deems unduly exacting, to have presented abnormal difficulty to Bach's players. His trumpet parts frequently soar to the eighteenth harmonic (d'''), and, in a single case (cantata No. 31), to the twentieth (e''') on the trumpet in C. Altenburg[1] actually takes the harmonic scale up to g''' and beyond!

So extended a compass could not be conveniently covered by a single instrument of uniform capacity. Hence the player was assisted by appropriate mouthpieces; that of the clarino was shallow and saucer-shaped; the principale's was larger, deeper, more cup-shaped. By this means it was practicable and convenient, when a 'choir' of trumpets was employed, to allot to each a particular section of the harmonic scale. Clarino I took charge of the

[1] P. 69.

harmonics from *g′* and upwards.[1] Clarino II slightly overlapped it
over the octave *g′–g″*. The principale covered the lower section
from *c* to *d″*. Bach, however, was at no pains to observe this convention. His first trumpet frequently descends to *c′*, sometimes
falls below the second trumpet,[2] and even touches *g*.[3] The average
compass of his second trumpet is *c′–a″*, but on occasion it rises
to *c♯‴* and *d‴*. His principale's normal range is *c′–g″*, and its
extreme compass (in the *Magnificat* and *Aeolus*) *a–b″*. In the two
scores in which he uses a fourth trumpet he employs a true principale: its compass is *g–g′* in the first (cantata No. 63) and *g–c″* in
the second (cantata No. 119). In both cases it sounds only the third,
fourth, fifth, sixth, and eighth harmonics[4] and generally supports
the rhythm of the drums.

The wide range of Bach's trumpet parts may invite the suggestion that, at least for the high clarino, two players were employed,
a concertist and ripienist, of whom the former reserved himself
for the upper harmonics. No practical difficulty opposed the
accommodation. But its assumed necessity is founded on a mis-
apprehension of the circumstances. In Bach's experience the
compromise was neither feasible nor necessary. His resources were
too limited to permit the allocation of two players to a part within
the competence of one, and the difficulties the modern player
encounters were not apparent to musicians schooled by long
tradition in the technique his scores demanded.

It has already been stated that trumpets were available in every
key. But Altenburg[5] remarks that a 'Concerttrompeter' required
only three, or at most four, in G, F, D, and B flat. For movements
in A major, the G or 'English' trumpet, raised to the higher key
by means of a 'Sordun',[6] was available; for G major, the same
without the mute; for F major, the F or 'Field' or 'French' trumpet;
for E major, the same lowered a semitone by a shank ('Setzstück');

---

[1] Altenburg writes (p. 95): 'Wir verstehn unter Clarin oder unter einer
Clarinstimme ungefähr das, was unter den Singstimmen der Discant ist, nem-
lich eine gewisse Melodie, welche grösstentheils in der zweygestrichenen Oktave
[*c″–c‴*], mithin hoch und hell geblasen wird.'

[2] Cantatas 74, 197, *Christmas Oratorio*, Pt. VI, Sinfonia in D.

[3] Cantatas 20 and 31.

[4] Excepting four notes in bars 33–34 of cantata No. 119 (No. 7: Coro).

[5] P. 85.

[6] Altenburg (p. 86) defines the 'Sordun' (Surdun: Sordin): 'Das Surdun oder
der Sordin, hat seinen Namen von Surdus, das ist: schwach oder gedämpft.
Eigentlich ist es ein von hartem und festem Holze rund ausgedrehetes Instrument, das zwar an sich selbst keinen Klang von sich giebt; wenn es aber unten in
die Trompete gesteckt wird, so giebt es ihr nicht nur einen ganz andern, fast
einer Oboe ähnlichen Klang, sondern erhöhet ihn, wenn er gut gedrechselt ist,
auch um einen ganzen Ton.' To play in A, he therefore directs the player to
use a G trumpet 'und stoffe den Sordun hinein'.

for E flat major, the same crooked down a tone; for D major, 'the German Cammerton D trumpet'; for C major, the same crooked down a tone.[1] Altenburg remarks on the non-existence of a 'short' B flat trumpet for music in that key, and recommends the performer to play an octave lower, on the 'long' instrument. Bach approved Altenburg's suggestion. In cantatas Nos. 5, 46, and 90 he prescribes a trumpet in B flat, but its notes lie between $b\flat$–$b\flat''$ in each of the three scores. After his appointment to the Leipzig Cantorate in 1723 his usage preferred the trumpet in D. Prior to that date he had exclusively employed the tromba in C.[2]

The addition of three, sometimes four, trumpets and drums constituted Bach's festival orchestra. They are rarely lacking in his Christmas, Easter, Whit-Sunday, and festival church music, and are invariably heard in his secular cantatas of public and gratulatory character. To all of them the trumpet communicates stately exhilaration, invariably in the choruses, occasionally in the arias and recitatives.[3] Yet, when Bach came to Leipzig in 1723, the trumpet had been for less than twenty years a licensed intruder in church music; his predecessors, Knüpfer and Kuhnau, rarely used it.[4] Into his normal orchestra of strings and wood-wind it seldom intrudes. It is obbligato in so few as sixteen arias. It adds a note of triumph to the concluding Choral of the Easter cantata No. 31. Infrequently it is woven into the orchestral texture of a chorus; jubilantly, as in the first movement of the Easter cantata No. 66:

> Rejoice now, ye faithful!
> Be mirthful and joyful!

On the eve of Advent, in the first chorus of No. 70, it sounds the watchman's call:

> Watch ye! pray ye!
> Ready be, night and day!
> Soon upon the clouds ye'll see
> God to judge all mortals coming.

---

[1] Altenburg (p. 12) distinguishes as German the 'chortönige C-Trompete' and 'kammertönige D-Trompete'; as French, the 'kammertönige F-Trompete'; and as English, the 'kammertönige G-Trompete'. For the Italian 'gewundene' trumpet, or tromba da caccia, see *infra*, p. 48.

[2] The second Brandenburg Concerto is the only exception to the statement. The trumpet there is in F, consistently with Bach's habit of putting the instrument in the key of the movement. This was in accordance with custom. Altenburg (p. 83) writes: 'Da ich nun bereits erwähnt habe, dass die Trompete . . . nur diatonisch modulirt, und höchstens in G dur, wegen des hohen fis cadenziren kann, so muss daher der Blasende, wenn er mit andern Instrumenten zugleich einstimmen will, seine Trompete darnach einrichten, dass sie zu der Tonart, woraus das Stück geht, genau harmonire.'

[3] See Table I.

[4] Cf. Schering, p. 151. Its use was licensed by a 'Trompetermandat' of 1706 (*ibid.*, p. 297).

In cantata No. 76 the Psalmist's paean constrains Bach to add a seraphic trumpet to the chorus of exultation. In the opening chorus of cantata No. 126 it rallies the Church against her pressing foes:

> Hurl them down headlong, foeman so haughty!
> Confound their scheming, bring them to naught!
> May hell's abysses yawning devour them!
> Make their plots wither, sternly o'erpower them!

So sings a bass voice in the aria. Bach reacts to this belligerent command, and the trumpet in the first chorus sounds its challenge to the enemies of the Word. In the second movement (coro) of the Easter cantata No. 145 jubilant trumpet figures acknowledge the festival's promise of salvation. Again, in the opening chorus of No. 147 the trumpet brilliantly acclaims the Saviour. In No. 148, for the Seventeenth Sunday after Trinity, it obeys the injunction of the opening chorus to praise and worship God. In this category, cantata No. 181 must also be mentioned. Like No. 126, it is an anthem for Sexagesima and illustrates the prescribed topic—God's Word. As always when that thought is present, Bach's perceptive mind pictures a citadel beleaguered, but impregnable. So, in the final chorus he sounds a flourish of victory, to which the trumpet adds triumphant music over a continuo that marches with inexorable rhythm and confidence.

With similar discrimination and restraint Bach associates the trumpet with a solo voice, usually a bass. In cantata No. 70, for the Twenty-Sixth Sunday after Trinity, the theme of the Second Advent informs the text, especially in the bass recit. and aria of Part II. In the first, the trumpet sounds the appropriate Advent melody, 'Es ist gewisslich an der Zeit'. In the aria

> Welcome Resurrection morn!
> Peal out, ring out, Judgement call!

the trumpet peals a sternly urgent summons above the agitated strings and continuo—

> Heaven and earth in wrack are falling!

With similar significance it is heard in the alto aria of No. 20, and in the bass aria of No. 127, for Quinquagesima—

> When loud and clear the trumpet calleth,
> And when the frame of earth to atoms falleth.

Bach here writes agitated descending passages for the strings, above which sound the clamorous trumpets of the Judgement. In cantata No. 128 the bass aria acclaims the risen Christ:

> Up, up, ye trumpets, call!
> Tell forth to one and all,
> Jesus on high is throned!

As a vehicle of praise the trumpet is also much used by Bach, as though he borrowed from the angels the inspired instrument of their adoration. In the familiar bass aria in Part I of the *Christmas Oratorio*:

> Mighty Lord and King supernal!

how brilliantly the trumpet acclaims the Eternal Majesty! Two soprano arias of cantata No. 51 are accorded a trumpet obbligato:

> Praise ye God, all men, adore Him!
> Heaven and earth, His praises sing!

and particularly the brilliant 'Alleluia' of the second aria. Similarly, in the bass aria of the Christmas cantata No. 110:

> Ye strings, well tuned to sing devotion,
> Your praise up-roll ye as an ocean
> To God enthroned in pomp on high!

Bach adds oboes to his choir and the trumpet peals above them all. It sounds, again, in the bass aria of cantata No. 147:

> Of Jesu's wounds my soul is singing
> A song of praise and loud thanksgiving.

Easter joy pervades the bass aria in cantata No. 145 and explains the trumpet's intrusion, though the actual words do not directly invite it. Nor do those of the bass aria of No. 75:

> My doubting heart is stilled;
> For Jesu's self doth love me,
> And with his flame surrounds me.

Here the trumpet proclaims the victory of faith over doubt. It utters a militant call in the bass aria of cantata No. 5:

> Disperse, ye lords of hell!
> I mock your proudest might!

Also in the bass aria of No. 76:

> Avaunt, ye godless crew!

And again in the bass aria of cantata No. 90:

> In anger and fury the Judge will avenge Him,

where the trumpet is the flashing sword of the Avenger. In the alto aria of No. 77 it voices the authority of the Law.

An obvious conclusion is invited. Bach's trumpet is never irrelevant, never purely orchestral, but the expression of a definite mood, a detail in a picture keenly visualized.[1]

---

[1] Bach's employment of a 'choir' of trumpets is considered in Chapter III.

The Tromba da tirarsi (Zugtrompete)

Bach's tromba parts do not rigidly exclude certain notes normally alien to the instrument's natural scale. For the eleventh harmonic he writes *f♮″* and *f♯″* indifferently, as was usual before the adoption of hand-stopping or a similar device. Infrequently he slips in *b′* as a passing note in rapid passages, or in positions where it is unstressed. He also occasionally writes the following notes:

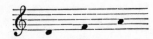

But these ultra-harmonic notes are used so rarely, and with such careful avoidance of stress, that their presence does not necessarily indicate another instrument than the natural trumpet. On the other hand, the diagram on page 25 shows three notes in the octave *c′–c″* to have been absolutely outside its scale:

Since these notes are definitely ultra-harmonic, their presence in a part bearing the indication 'Tromba' is reliable proof that it was not written for the natural trumpet. Whether they could be produced on it by 'faking' need not be discussed. Bach deemed them beyond its ability, and excluded them from parts undoubtedly written for it.[1] They must therefore be associated with another instrument. In cantatas Nos. 5, 20, 77, Bach names it 'Tromba da tirarsi', a term apparently not found outside his scores.[2] In cantata No. 46 he offers the alternative 'Tromba o Corno da tirarsi', and in cantatas Nos. 67 and 162 prescribes a 'Corno da tirarsi'. These definite indications are found in fourteen movements, in eight of which the instrument reinforces the melody of a Choral 'col Soprano', and in one other plays the Choral melody obbligato. Its compass in these Choral movements falls mainly in the octave *e′–e″*. But its full range is in no way behind the natural trumpet's, since, in three of the fourteen movements, it functions in an obbligato with the freedom and fluency of that instrument.

What kind of instrument was this trumpet, which could accomplish all and more than the natural tromba? In what respect, if at all, did it differ from the corno da tirarsi? As its name (Tr. da

[1] Whenever the tromba is associated with the drums the natural instrument was certainly used.
[2] The instrument was in use in Leipzig in 1769. See *supra*, p 18.

tirarsi) indicates, it was equipped with a slide. Editing cantata No. 5 for the Bachgesellschaft in 1851, Moritz Hauptmann supposed it to have been the discant (alto) trombone. Some fifty years earlier (1795) Altenburg[1] had already remarked its constructional resemblance to that instrument: 'The Zug-trompete, generally used for playing the Chorals from church towers'—a significant detail—'re-sembles the alto trombone, since, during the act of blowing, its slide-action conveniently pro-duces the lacking harmonics.'[2] Mahillon, writing in 1880,[3] inclined to Altenburg's opinion. There exists, however, in the Berlin Hochschule für Musik, the unique example of an instrument which exactly fits Bach's definition and is cap-able of fulfilling the purposes to which he put the tromba da tirarsi.

The Berlin Zugtrompete (slide trumpet) has the appearance of an ordinary natural trumpet. But, unlike the latter, its mouthpiece is pro-longated by an inner tube, which, at the player's will, slides out and in within the topmost of the instrument's parallel branches. The length of its slide is 56 cm. (22·050 in.). The tubing, apart from the slide, is 143 cm. (roughly 56 in. =4 ft. 8 in.) long, and the conical length of the instrument is 57 cm. (roughly 1 ft. 10½ in.). Thus, with the slide drawn to its fullest extent, the trumpet measures roughly 112 cm. (3 ft. 8 in.) from mouthpiece to bell. Its internal diameter at 25 cm. of length is 12·8 mm. (under half an inch), and at the bell-end 98 mm. (roughly 4 in.).[4] The instrument is in D[5] of its

Zugtrompete, 1651, fully extended, length 112 cm.

period, was made by Hans Veit of Naumburg, and bears the date 1651 engraved on the bell.

The possibility must not be overlooked, that in the Berlin Zugtrompete we have a simple device for tuning the tromba down from D to C without crooking. On the other hand, the Berlin example is generally competent in the uses to which Bach puts his

[1] P. 12.
[2] Mr. W. F. H. Blandford is of opinion that Altenburg had in mind some model with a double 'trombone' slide.   [3] Vol. i. 281.
[4] I am indebted to Dr. Curt Sachs for these measurements.
[5] On its measurements, Mr. Blandford makes it intermediate between E natural and E flat diapason normal.

tromba da tirarsi. When the slide is pushed home it becomes a natural tromba, indeed is more easily played, owing to the narrower bore of the tube receiving the slide. No doubt it was difficult for the player to hold the mouthpiece to his lips with his left hand, while his right moved the instrument up or down the slide. But rapid movements were not necessary. Experimenting with a slide on his Haas trumpet, Canon Galpin found that it has three positions: (1) When 5 inches of the slide are withdrawn, the pitch is lowered from *d'* to *c♯'*, with a corresponding fall throughout the scale. (2) When 10½ inches of the slide are exposed, the pitch falls two semitones, from *d'* to *c'*, and by an equal interval all over. (3) When the slide is at 17 inches, the fall of yet another semitone follows, and *d'* becomes *b* natural. These positions indicate considerable movements of or along the slide, first of 5 inches, then of 5½ inches, and again of 6½ inches, owing to the slide operating in a single, and not, as with the trombone, a double tube.[1] For that reason the instrument may have been held sloping downwards with greater convenience, a position which might account for Altenburg likening it to the alto trombone.

Canon Galpin's experiment permits us to apply the technique of the Berlin Zugtrompete to Bach's tromba da tirarsi parts. As the Table on page 191 reveals, he uses the latter chiefly to sound the melody of a Choral, in movements whose *tempo* is moderate and their notes sustained. Slide movements consequently would be deliberate. For instance, the concluding Choral of cantata No. 5, in which, along with the first violins and two oboes, the tromba da tirarsi is 'col Soprano',[2] could be played thus on Veit's trumpet in D:

---

[1] At the concerts of the Paris Société de Musique d'autrefois a Zugtrompete is in use, a slide being adapted to the tromba, as in the Berlin example. While agreeing that Veit's trumpet proves that a distinct form of Zugtrompete existed, Mr. Blandford is of opinion that the collection of parts attributed to it in Table II, *infra*, is too complex for a single instrument of Veit's pattern, even aided by extra mouthpieces. Certainly deeper instruments similarly constructed would be handled with difficulty.

[2] The figures 0, 1, 2 indicate respectively the open notes with closed slide and its first and second shifts. The *bb'* throughout must be slightly sharpened.

I o — — 2 — — o 2 — — o 2

Or take the concluding Choral of cantata No. 20, where also the tromba da tirarsi, with other instruments, is 'col Soprano' in C:

2 o 1 2 o — — — 2 — o 1 2 — —

— 1 o 1 2 — — 1 o 2   o — 1 2 —

1 — o — — — 2 1 o — 2

These examples demonstrate the ease with which a player using the Zugtrompete could produce the ultra-harmonic notes of Bach's tromba da tirarsi Chorals. And its obbligato parts are both few in number and present no greater difficulties. In the bass aria of cantata No. 46 only a single note, though persistent and emphatic, lies outside the normal harmonic series of the instrument. In cantata No. 103 (tenor aria), again, the slide is called into action only in bars 19–22. In cantata No. 24 (coro) the part is dotted with extra-harmonic notes, and, at bars 27 and 35, repeated a'''s and f'''s, but they occur in the least florid passages and do not require rapid movements of the slide. The concluding Choral of cantata No. 24 is peculiar in its use of the alto clef for repeated low f's and a's.

As has already been remarked, the tromba da tirarsi is generally associated by Bach with Chorals, either as a support to the voices in the melody,[1] or (as in cantatas Nos. 12 and 24) to supply an obbligato above it, or (as in cantatas Nos. 10, 12, 48, 75, 77, 137, and 185) to sound the Choral melody itself as an obbligato in a chorus, or duet, or instrumental movement. But in three move-

[1] All of the Choral melodies in which the instrument is simply indicated as 'col Soprano' could be played on an instrument in C. But to obtain the best notes, and to obviate considerable shifting of the slide, instruments in B♭, A, and high D may also have been used. In the above example a' must be slightly sharpened throughout.

ments—two arias and one coro—his slide trumpet serves the purposes to which Bach elsewhere puts the natural instrument.
In the bass aria of cantata No. 46 the trumpet adds a detail of terror to the storm which overthrows Jerusalem—

> Long since a tempest hath been brewing,
> At last the storm in fury breaks,
> And havoc dire and awful makes.
> Thy sin and pride commingled
> God's angry fires have kindled,
> And doomed thee evermore to ruin.

In the tenor aria of cantata No. 103 the trumpet contributes a note of exhilaration to a movement of utter gaiety:

> Away with care, O troubled mortal!
> Ne'er give thyself to sighs and woe!
> No more to sorrow ope the portal,
> Nor let hot tears of anguish flow!
> Lord Jesu, Thou wilt come to save me;
> O rapture sweet beyond compare!
> Thy promise doth with longing fill me;
> Come, take my all into Thy care.

An apparent incongruity presents itself in the third movement (Coro) of cantata No. 24. The words, 'Whatsoever ye would that men should do unto you, even so do unto them' (St. Matthew vii. 12), hardly invite a trumpet to the score. But the German text begins with the word 'Alles', a word to which Bach invariably accords spacious treatment: 'Alles nun, das ihr wollet, das euch die Leute thun sollen, das thut ihr ihnen.'[1] In the present case he actually repeats the word six times before proceeding with the text, and the whole movement is pervaded by a spirit of vivacious animation, which tells us he was thinking less of the duty of neighbourliness than of the initial suggestion of multitude.

The Corno da Tirarsi

Bach's scores prescribe not only a 'slide trumpet' but also a 'slide horn'. In cantata No. 46 they are alternative, though the prescription 'Tromba o Corno' might indicate variant names of the same instrument, did not cantatas Nos. 67 and 162 mention the corno da tirarsi alone. What, then, was the 'Corno' da tirarsi?
Unlike the slide-trumpet, of which an example is extant, there is no other evidence than Bach's nomenclature that a slide-horn

---

[1] See, for example, the opening chorus of *Alles nur nach Gottes Willen* (No. 72); the soprano-bass duet 'Alles was von Gott geboren' of No. 80; and the 'Alles was Odem hat' section of the motet *Singet dem Herrn*.

was known to his generation. Praetorius gives no indication of such an instrument, and Bach's predecessors in the Leipzig Cantorate did not use one. But Tables II, V, VI show that in his church cantatas the 'slide horn' occurs as frequently as the ordinary instrument. In the majority of cases it sustains the melody of a Choral. Otherwise, but rarely, it furnishes an independent obbligato. Its parts differ neither in compass nor character from those of the slide-trumpet; indeed, without Bach's indication it would be difficult to decide which he intended.[1] The facts suggest that his prescription 'Corno da tirarsi' does not indicate an actual instrument, but some device or adjustment for producing horn tone.[2]

Consider, for example, the 'Choral Cantatas' written *circa* 1740–4, thirteen of which are included in Table II. They are built on a uniform plan: their opening chorus elaborately treats a Choral, whose melody is generally sustained by the sopranos in unison with a trumpet (cantatas Nos. 10 and 48) or a horn (cantatas Nos. 26, 62, 78, 96, 114, 115, 116, 124, 125). They all conclude with a Choral, in which the melody is similarly supported, in three cases by a trumpet (cantatas Nos. 10, 48, 126), in ten by a horn (cantatas Nos. 3, 26, 62, 78, 96, 114, 115, 116, 124, 125). We infer from these figures that Bach preferred horn tone to trumpet tone for this particular purpose, owing, no doubt, to its closer blending with the human voice. But what instrument did he use? Not one of the parts indicated above was playable on the natural horn. But all of them were practicable on the Zugtrompete, which, by substituting the appropriate mouthpiece, could produce horn tone as well. Thus, in cantatas Nos. 24 and 167, a very shallow-cupped mouthpiece would give the sharp, penetrating clarino tone the score prescribes. In cantatas Nos. 14, 16, 89, 107, and 109, where Bach indicates the corno da caccia, a short conical cup-like mouthpiece would communicate to the Zugtrompete its peculiar mellow tone. A tromba mouthpiece, having a slightly deeper cup than the clarino's, would produce a more ringing tone than the latter, while the long conical cup of the Waldhorn would impart the characteristic cooing tone of that

---

[1] Cf. B.-J. 1908, p. 141, where Dr. Curt Sachs identifies Bach's 'Corno da tirarsi' with the Zugtrompete discussed in the preceding section, an opinion he has since rejected.

[2] I owe the suggestion to Canon Galpin. Admittedly, no historical evidence supports it. On the other hand, none refutes it, nor, so far, has one more plausible been advanced. Mr. Blandford doubts the skill of players exposed to this test; but the trumpeters also played the horn and trombone (*supra,* p. 8).

instrument. Thus, at pleasure, the Zugtrompete could become a corno da tirarsi, or a corno da caccia da tirarsi, by the device which enabled it as easily to act as a tromba da tirarsi or a clarino da tirarsi.[1] The addition 'da tirarsi' completes the direction 'Tromba', 'Corno', 'Corno da caccia' only in six cantatas (Nos. 5, 20, 46, 67, 77, 162). Elsewhere the music itself is the only guide to Bach's selection. And here an interesting point presents itself. In 1769, nineteen years after Bach's death, Johann Friedrich Doles, his second successor in the Leipzig Cantorate, examined two candidates for a vacancy in the ranks of the Stadtpfeifer. Of one he wrote: 'He cannot manage the concerted Choral on the Zugtrompete, and has to do the best he can on an alto trombone' ('Mit dem concertirenden Choral konnte er auf der Zugtrompette gar nicht fortkommen und musste er es auf der Altposaune versuchen, so gut es gehen wollte'). On the other he reported: 'He played the simple Choral well on the discant, alto, tenor, and bass trombones' ('Den simplen Choral auf der Discant- Alt- Tenor- und Bass-Posaune . . . hat er gut geblasen').[2] The inference is clear: in simple four-part Chorals the trombone was customarily used; the Zugtrompete in the elaborate choruses with which the Choral Cantatas begin. If, as is probable, this was the practice in Bach's time, we are confirmed in the conclusion that the tromba da tirarsi (as in the first chorus of cantata No. 5), the corno (as in the first chorus of cantata No. 8), and the corno da caccia (as in the first chorus of cantata No. 16), were all represented by the Zugtrompete equipped with appropriate mouthpieces. As regards the simple Chorals, we must either conclude that Doles had ceased to follow his great predecessor's example, or, as is more probable, that the trombone was occasionally used instead of the Zugtrompete. One thing is evident: the Zugtrompete was *not* identical with the alto trombone.

The Cornett

For sustaining Choral melodies Bach was not restricted to the tromba and corno da tirarsi. In eleven cantatas[3] he prescribes a cornett, and employs it in every case but two to sound the Choral

[1] Canon Galpin points out that, provided the mouthpieces were practically of the same diameter internally, the inside shape of the cup would make no difference to the player, though it affected his tone. Altenburg, chap. ix, enlarges on the mouthpiece technique. The interchange of mouthpieces was facilitated, it must be recognized, by the fact that every player professed all the 'Stadtpfeiferinstrumente'.

[2] *Archiv f. M.*, p. 45. On Bach's neglect of the discant (alto) trombone see *infra*, p. 40.   [3] See Table III.

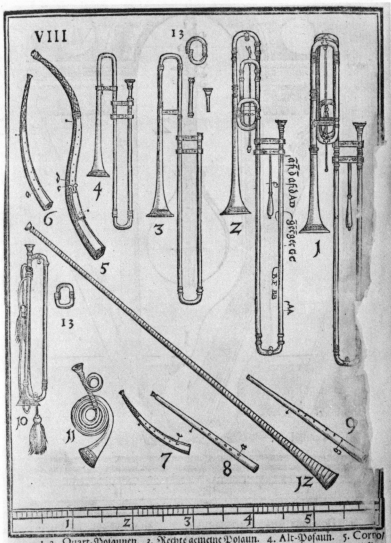

TRUMPET, CORNETT, TROMBONE, JÄGER-TROMPETE

(*Praetorius*)

cantus.[1] The instrument, one of the oldest, was already obsolescent.
Known in England as the Cornett, in Italy as the Cornetto, in
France as the Cornet à bouquin, and in Germany as the Zink, it
was used in two forms, the straight and the curved. The former
(cornetto diritto, c. muto, gerader Zink, stiller Z.) was in one piece,
mouthpiece and tube. The curved variety (c. curvo, krummer
Zink) was made of two pieces of wood, planed to an octagonal
shape, slightly curved, bound together in black leather with metal
clasps, and fitted with a shallow mouthpiece (its only resemblance
to the modern cornet) of horn, hard wood, or ivory.[2] Straight or
curved, the instrument was pierced with six holes on the upper
surface for the fingers, and one underneath for the thumb. Made
in different sizes, the cornett, according to Praetorius,[3] sounded
the chromatic scale over a normal compass of two octaves $a-a''$,
and, like the trombones, formed a complete 'choir' of instruments,
the lowest[4] of which (cornetto torto, cornon, great Zink) sounded
from d upwards. Bach made no use of these various forms. The
compass of his cornett parts—from d' to a''[5]—shows that he wrote
for the ordinary Zink—the 'recht Chor Zink' of Praetorius—
whose compass ranged from a to a''.

The cornett had a brilliant tone. In his *Harmonie universelle*
(1636) Marin Mersenne likened it to 'a ray of sunshine piercing
the gloom and darkness, when heard among the voices in some
cathedral or chapel' ('un rayon de Soleil, qui paroist dans l'ombre
ou dans les tenebres, lors qu'on l'entend parmy les voix dans les
Églises Cathedrales, ou dans les Chapelles').[6] Roger North, a
hundred years later, declared in Bach's lifetime: 'To say the truth,
nothing comes so near, or rather imitates so much, an excellent
voice, as a cornet-pipe,'[7] a eulogy which explains its vogue with
Bach and other composers. Mattheson, North's contemporary,
lamented its decreasing use, remarking its value in church music.[8]
Its decline was in some measure due to the onerous tax it laid on
the lungs of the player. North observed that 'the labour of the lips
is too great, and it is seldom well sounded'. It survived in·Germany
after it had passed from use elsewhere, but barely survived the
dawn of the nineteenth century. Writing in 1806, Schubart[9]

---

[1] It is perhaps open to question whether Bach desired clearly to distinguish
between 'corno' and 'cornetto' in these movements.
[2] See Praetorius, Plate VIII, at p. 36. [3] P. 36.
[4] Excluding the Serpent.
[5] In cantata No. 118 he carries it exceptionally to d''' on the 'little Zink'.
[6] Bk. V, p. 274. [7] P. 79. [8] P. 269.
[9] 'Es ist aber so schwer für die Brust zu blasen, weil der Hauch nur durch
eine ganz kleine Oeffnung hinein gebracht wird, dass sich schon mehr als ein
Zinkenist, Schwindsucht und Tod damit zugezogen hat. Schwerlich gibt es

surmised that German lung-power had deteriorated, since so few Zink players were to be found.

The cornett, being a Stadtpfeifer instrument, has no place in Bach's scores before 1723, and is associated chiefly with the cantatas of his latest period. Almost invariably it supports the sopranos in a Choral melody, associated always, excepting cantatas Nos. 133 and 135, with trombones.[1] It is never obbligato in Bach's usage, though the opening chorus of No. 133 suggests that he shared Mersenne's admiration of its quality. The cornett there is 'col Soprano'. The accompanying instruments are the strings and two *oboi d'amore*, the second of them in unison with the viola. The words—the first stanza of Caspar Ziegler's 'Ich freue mich in dir'—dwell on the thought of Jesus as the Brother of man:

How sweet the word doth sound!
(*Ach, wie ein süsser Ton!*)

sing the voices. Bach pointedly prolongs the word 'Ton' over three bars and a half. The cornett and sopranos sustain it on *c♯″*, the oboe d'amore and viola on *c♯′*, while the under voices thrice ejaculate 'Ach, wie ein süsser Ton!' 'One need but read the words', remarks Pirro,[2] 'to realize that Bach contrives a rare and charming effect, intending that the voices shall not idly sing the words "Ah! quel doux ton!"' In cantata No. 135 the cornett is restricted to the concluding Choral, the *canto fermo* being in the bass of the opening chorus. In the remaining nine cantatas the instrument acts as the discant of a choir of trombones.

The Trombone

Praetorius[3] names four instruments of the trombone family:
(1) The *Alto* or *Discant-Posaun* (*Trombino: Trombetta picciola*), in D.
(2) The *Gemeine rechte Posaun* (*Tuba minor: Trombetta: Trombone piccolo*), in A.
(3) The *Quart-Posaun* (*Tuba major: Trombone grando: Trombone majore*), sounding a fourth or fifth (*Quint-Posaun*) below the preceding.
(4) The *Octav-Posaun* (*Tuba maxima: Trombone doppio: Trombone all'ottava basso*), in A, sounding an octave below the second of the series.

---

ein die Gesundheit so angreifendes Instrument wie dieses. Das mag wohl Ursache seyn, warum sich so wenige Menschen bis zur Meisterschaft darauf legen' (p. 317).
[1] The cornett displaced the discant trombone owing to its more brilliant and effective tone.
[2] Pirro, p. 242.   [3] P. 31. See his Plates VI and VIII at pp. 36 and 160.

The Octav-Posaun was rarely used, Praetorius adds. It was made in two forms; either its length was twice that of the Gemeine rechte Posaun, or (the recent invention of Kunstpfeifer Hans Schreiber) the fitting of an extra bend between the bell and the slide enabled the dimensions of the instrument to be conveniently shortened. Of the discant (an octave above his No. 3) Praetorius remarks,[1] that, though agreeable for playing a melody ('mit welcher ein Discant gar wol und natürlich geblasen werden kan'), it was too insignificant in tone for concerted music ('wiewol die *Harmony* in solchem kleinen *Corpore* nicht so gut').[2] No. 2 of Praetorius's series can be identified with the tenor B flat trombone in modern use,

for he gives ⟨music⟩ as its lowest note. So, accepting his

indications of their pitch relatively to the Gemeine rechte Posaun, we deduce that his

Quart-Posaun, being a fourth lower, was in F;
Quint-Posaun, being a fifth lower, was in E flat;
Octav-Posaun, being an octave lower, was in B flat;
Alto-Posaun, being an octave higher than the Quart- or Quint-
Posaun, was in F or E flat.

We may reasonably put the working compass of the four trombones in Bach's period as follows, in actual sounds:

1. Discant in B flat   .   .   .   .   .   .   *eb–bb″*
   (The notes below *c′* are very poor and *a″* and *bb″* are
   difficult.)
2. Alto in F   .   .   .   .   *bb,–f″*
   (The notes below *f* are poor; *eb″* and *f″* are difficult.
   Alto in E flat a tone lower.)
3. Tenor in B flat   .   .   .   .   .   .   *eb,–bb′*
   (The low notes are fairly good; *a′* and *bb′* are difficult.)
4. Bass in F .   .   .   .   *b,,–f′*
   (The low notes are fairly good; *e′* and *f′* are difficult.
   Bass in E flat a tone lower.)

Bach's scores reveal his preference for a 'choir' of three or four trombones. The prescription of a single instrument is very exceptional. In cantata No. 3 a bass trombone strengthens the Choral melody voiced by the basses. In the duet of cantata No. 4 both voices are supported in a free treatment of the Choral melody, the soprano by a cornett, the alto by an alto trombone. In cantata

---

[1] The reason for its supersession by the cornett has been stated on p. 38 *supra*.
[2] Mr. Blandford observes that Breughel's picture 'Hearing', in the Prado, painted before 1625, shows a trombone with two crooks or 'tortils' between the bell and the slide. We may have here a picture of Schreiber's invention.

No. 96, in whose opening chorus the altos sing the Choral *cantus*, they are reinforced by an alto trombone and a horn. In the opening chorus of cantata No. 135 the Choral *cantus* is given to the continuo, and a bass trombone helps to sustain it. Elsewhere Bach scores for either a quartet of trombones or for a cornett and three trombones.

The discant trombone is not among the instruments mentioned in the preceding paragraph. Nor does Bach often prescribe it, even in the concluding simple Chorals, where, according to the usage of 1769,[1] it was customarily employed. Evidently Bach shared the opinion of Praetorius regarding its quality, which has been quoted on an earlier page. Taking 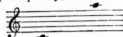 as its effective compass, we can deduce its employment only in cantatas Nos. 2, 21, and 38, where it is associated in every case with an alto, tenor, and bass trombone. Elsewhere and invariably Bach prefers the cornett to complete his quartet.[2] It follows that, in the majority of cases, his prescription 'Trombone I' indicates the alto trombone in F, e.g. in cantatas Nos. 4, 23, 25, 28, 64, 68, 96, 101, 118, and 121. The tenor B flat must be inferred as 'Trombone III' in cantatas Nos. 2, 21, and 38, in which the discant instrument has the soprano part, but as 'Trombone II' in cantatas Nos. 4, 23, 25, 28, 64, 68, 101, 118, 121, where a cornett has the discant. The bass trombone in E flat or F is the 'Trombone IV' of cantatas Nos. 2, 21, 38, and the 'Trombone III', generally in F, of cantatas Nos. 4, 23, 25, 28, 64, 68, 101, 118, and 121. Its usage in cantatas Nos. 3 and 135 has been recorded in the preceding paragraph.

Unlike the horn, proper to the pageantry of Courts, the trombone was a Stadtpfeifer instrument, adapted for civic ceremonial. Bach's employment of it was timid and consistent. As an independent obbligato instrument it has no place in his scores. Even if his text invites him to display it—e.g. in the bass recit. of cantata No. 70, where the voice sings of the 'Posaunen Schall' at the Second Advent—he prefers the trumpet, having in mind the mundane associations of the other instrument.[3] And he employs it infrequently. It is prescribed in so few as fifteen cantatas, and nowhere else in his music.[4] With one exception, the fifteen belong to the Leipzig period. For neither the Weimar nor Cöthen Capelle was

---

[1] *Supra*, p. 36.   [2] See Table IV.
[3] The obbligato in Handel's 'The trumpet shall sound' is said to have been formerly played on the alto trombone. Either the story is untrue, or the experiment was an exhibition of misdirected skill.   [4] See Table IV.

equipped with an instrument alien to Court ritual. Cantata No. 21, the single pre-Leipzig score which includes a trombone, was composed for Halle, where, as later at Leipzig, 'Stadtpfeiferin-strumente' were accessible. Even at Leipzig Bach rarely prescribed it. Of the fourteen cantatas of that period, ten belong to the last decade of his activity as a composer (1734–44), and in the preceding decade (1723–33) trombones are found in only four.[1] The fact may indicate that the instruments themselves were un-serviceable: Kuhnau, in 1704, described the church's set as battered and useless.[2]

But a more probable reason can be offered for Bach's infrequent use of the trombone. In every score in which it is found it is used in association with a Choral or a chorus of the older motet form. Excepting three cases, it never sounds independently of the voices, but simply reinforces the vocal parts. In the first of these, cantata No. 25, a quartet of three trombones and cornett adds a harmonized Choral to the orchestral scheme. In the second, cantata No. 118, a similar quartet provides the instrumental accompaniment. In the third, cantata No. 135, a single trombone strengthens the continuo in the *cantus* of the Choral on which the chorus is founded. Saving these exceptions, Bach's trombones merely reinforce the vocal parts. Moreover, seven of the fourteen Leipzig scores in which they are found belong to his last series of Choral Cantatas, and their usage in that period seems to indicate the deficiencies of his choristers, for which, it must be admitted, he was himself in some measure

Trombone, 17th cent., length 108 cm.

responsible. At least, it is clear that Bach connected the trombone, like the cornett, with the older 'Status musices' rather than the new. Of its orchestral capabilities, which Mozart and Beethoven were soon to reveal, there is in his scores no glimmer of recognition.

The Horn (Corno: corno da caccia)

Bach's 'Corno', like his 'Tromba', is a problem the lexicons confuse and do not resolve. Riemann (*s.v.* Horn) groups as ex-changeable the 'Naturhorn, Waldhorn, Corno di caccia, Cor de chasse, French horn'. 'Grove's' list of alternatives is as generous.

[1] Nos. 4, 23, 25, and 64.　　　　　　　　[2] *Supra*, p. 18.

Miss Kathleen Schlesinger, whose erudite articles distinguished the classic Eleventh, but are characteristically excised from the latest, self-styled 'humanized', *Encyclopaedia Britannica*, places in a single category 'The French horn (*Fr. cor de chasse* or *trompe de chasse, cor à pistons*; Ger. *Waldhorn, Ventilhorn*; Ital. *corno* or *corno di caccia*)'. Adopting, as almost invariably, their Italian style, Bach names either a 'Corno' or a 'Corno da caccia', and once, in cantata No. 14, a 'Corno par force'. All three indicate a 'natural' horn, a simple coiled tube operated without keys, valves, or slides. Whether his varying nomenclature indicates two types of horn is a preliminary problem to be faced.

The earliest form of the corno da caccia was the 'Jagdhorn' or 'Jägerhorn' figured by Praetorius (Plate XXII), elementary specimens of which, known as 'Hiefhörner' or 'Hifthörner', were only capable of sounding rhythmic signals to the huntsmen. This early type was never wound in circles large enough to surround the body, was less slenderly tubed than its improved successor, and terminated in a bell not exceeding seven inches in diameter. As an orchestral instrument it was of no value, and was not so employed. It underwent considerable improvement in the seventeenth century, however, and, at about the period of Bach's birth (1685), a new type, recently invented in France, and distinguished as the 'French horn', so interested the Bohemian dilettante Franz Anton Count von Sporck (1662–1738)[1] that he caused his musicians to learn the instrument and introduced it, certainly before 1715,[2] into Germany, where it was generally known as the 'Waldhorn' or, much enlarged, as the 'Parforcehorn' (*corno par force*).[3]

Thus the Waldhorn was a novelty when Bach's career as a composer was about to begin. Handel used it in his 'Watermusic' (? 1717) in honour of George I, at the period when Bach was entering on his service at Cöthen. But Germany was not behindhand in appreciating its qualities for other uses than the characteristic fanfares of operatic hunting scenes or calls to arms in dramatic situations. Reinhard Keiser particularly was adventurous in experiments at Hamburg, where Mattheson penned a eulogy which proves that, in that active centre, if not elsewhere, the Wald-

---

[1] Shortly before his death Sporck received from Bach the parts of the B minor 'Sanctus'.

[2] Gerber is usually quoted for the statement. Mr. Blandford, however, finds contemporary evidence in Sporck's *Life* by Ferdinand van der Roxas (Friedrich Rothscholz) published in 1715.

[3] See Plate XXI in Sachs (2).

horn was in service before 1713. 'The stately mellow-sounding Waldhorn', he wrote,[1] 'has come a good deal into vogue of late . . . partly because it is less raucous than the trumpet, partly because it is more easily handled. . . . It produces a rounder tone and fills out the score better than the shrill and deafening *clarini*.' It generally superseded the *Jagdhörner* (few specimens of which have survived) in the ceremonious uses associated with the latter, and at the same time commended itself to composers, who, from the first

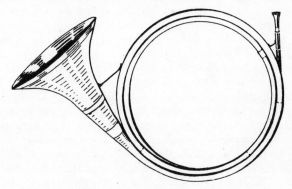

Waldhorn, 18th cent., length 58 cm.

decade of the eighteenth century, if not earlier, added it appreciatively to their orchestra.

In the first decade of the eighteenth century Hamburg was the musical capital of Germany, and we should err in supposing its musical apparatus to have been completely available elsewhere. Its adoption of the Waldhorn, consequently, cannot certainly indicate contemporary use of the instrument by the smaller communities to which Bach devoted his earliest service. Till his arrival in Leipzig the horn is named only twice in his scores. He prescribed one in his Weimar secular cantata *Was mir behagt* (1716), and again, five years later at Cöthen, in the first Brandenburg Concerto, in F (1721). In both he named it 'Corno da caccia', and in both prescribed it for performance by other players than his own—the earlier for the Weissenfels Capelle, the later for that of Brandenburg. Consequently, even if his 'Corno da caccia' was a Waldhorn, its prescription in those two works does not prove that it was at his disposal at Weimar and Cöthen.

[1] P. 267.

After his arrival at Leipzig, Bach's indications are no longer uniform. Twice in 1724 (cantatas Nos. 16 and 65), once in 1729 (No. 174), twice in 1733 (*Hohe Messe* and *Hercules*), thrice in or about 1735 (Nos. 14, 128, 143), and thereafter not at all, he prescribes, as at Weimar and Cöthen, a 'Cors de chasse,' a 'Corno da caccia', a 'Corne da caccia'. But in one of his earliest Leipzig cantatas, No. 40, performed on 26 December 1723, he for the first time writes 'Corno' *tout court*. In 1724, 1725, 1726 it appears again in his scores, and, after an interval, in 1730?-31-32-34. Finally, eight more examples fall in the last years of his activity as a composer.[1]

Was the 'Corno' a different instrument from the 'Corno da caccia'? Its parts in Bach's scores afford no assistance to an answer. His 'Corno' is crooked to seven keys—D, F, G, A, B flat, D (high), F (high), sounding a minor seventh, perfect fifth, perfect fourth, minor third, and major second below their parts in C, and a major second and perfect fourth above it. He uses his 'Corno da caccia' in similar keys—C (sounding an octave below), D, F, G, and B flat. Nor is there appreciable difference in the compass of the parts allotted to the two, nor do they exhibit differences of technique by which they can be distinguished. One or the other term, however, certainly indicates the Waldhorn, or French horn, first heard by Count von Sporck at Paris in 1680,[2] known also as the 'Corno par force', a term Bach uses, on a single occasion, in 1735 (cantata No. 14). The fact that the 'Corno' first appears in his Leipzig scores favours the opinion that the word was his equivalent for the Waldhorn. On the other hand, since the variety of Waldhorn used in the chase bore indifferently in France the names 'cor de chasse' and 'Trompe de chasse', the former of which Bach himself uses both in its French form and Italian equivalent (*corno da caccia*), it is maintainable that by that term, and not the more concise 'Corno', the Waldhorn is indicated. In that case, Bach's nomenclature must distinguish not the older Jagdhorn and more recent Waldhorn, but the Waldhorn in its original form as an instrument of the chase, and the Waldhorn modified in tone and structure for other purposes. Such modifications, however, were improbably within Bach's experience. Mr. Blandford remarks that even the French were not equipped with the orchestral horn until the decade following Bach's death, and that the change of tone was associated with the adoption of an embouchure different from that used by horn players in the time of Bach and Handel, who placed the mouthpiece on the lower lip; while, in the horn

---

[1] See Tables V and VI.   [2] Gerber, ii 547.

embouchure, two-thirds of the mouthpiece lies on the upper lip, and the rim, narrower than that of a trumpet mouthpiece, is sunk in the red part of the under lip. Such, in concise outline, is the problem, a positive solution of which may not be attainable. A decided judgement, however, can be expressed on one or two very relative points. In the first place, the nature of Bach's horn parts forbids one to suppose that he ever used the obsolete Jagdhorn of Praetorius' time. In the second place, Mattheson's eulogy of the 'lieblich' Waldhorn certainly indicates an agreeably mellow tone which distinguished it from the hunting horn it immediately superseded. In the third place, the view that 'Corno' and 'Corno da caccia' indicate the same instrument is contradicted by Bach's practice. If there is one thing clearly revealed in his scores, it is his meticulous indication of instrumental *tone*. Hence we have sound reason for supposing that the terms 'Corno' and 'Corno da caccia' distinguish the mellow tone Mattheson associated with the Waldhorn, and the more strident tone of the traditional Jagdhorn, which the newer instrument had not yet supplanted at those princely Courts, e.g. Weimar and Cöthen, where the horn was still an instrument of the palace. It is certainly significant that Bach's use of the 'Corno' exactly coincides with the cessation of his courtly service, and with the beginning of his career in a community in which the ceremonial hunting horn had not a similar vogue. That he was ever familiar with the refinements of the orchestral horn is not suggested. But that he could have had at his disposal not only the 'lieblich' Waldhorn, but also the large coiled Jagdhorn, is evident from the existence of such a horn in the Heyer Collection, dated 1740 and specifically associated with church usage.[1] Its tone differed from the Waldhorn's, and since in outward form the two instruments were indistinguishable, the difference, no doubt, arose from their mouthpieces, the Waldhorn's deeply conical, the Jagdhorn's shallow and conical, and its tube cylindrical throughout its whole extent, to the point where it widens to form the bell.

To the hypothesis that Bach's 'Corno' was the Waldhorn and his 'Corno da caccia' the Jagdhorn further support is afforded by his evident characterization of the latter. In his use of it his reaction to the feudal conventions of his generation is evident. The author of a recent disquisition[2] has advanced the wayward

[1] The instrument (No. 1664 of the Heyer Collection), in D or E flat, by Johann Werner, is inscribed 'in die Kirche zu Priesnitz gehörig' (Kinsky, p. 185).
[2] Rutland Boughton, *John Sebastian Bach* (London, 1930).

thesis that Bach's music breathes a spirit of revolt against his social environment. In fact, he was as stout a conservative as his contemporary, Samuel Johnson. However stubborn he could show himself on occasion, when confronted by authority menacing his freedom as an artist, he accepted the ritual of Germany's petty Courts as readily as the Lutheran *Formula Concordiae.* Hence his use of the corno da caccia was governed by approving experience of its ceremonial associations. On such domestic occasions as those for which the 'Peasant Cantata' (*Mer hahn en neue Oberkeet*) or *Aeolus* were composed, the 'Corno' satisfied him. But for Duke Christian's 'Tafelmusik' (*Was mir behagt*), or for the *Hercules* music in honour of Saxony's Crown Prince, the corno da caccia was imperative; its notes by long tradition were the salute of princes.

Nor does Bach restrict this deference to his secular scores. The naïve literalness so prominent in his character invited him to salute the Lord of lords with the same instrumental voice. The familiar bass aria of the *Hohe Messe*, 'Quoniam tu solus Dominus', is an instance. The words acknowledge the sovereignty of Christ, throned with the Father in Heaven; the horn obbligato is an obeisance to his Kingship. In cantata No. 16 it sounds again; for the theme is the same—a free version of the *Te Deum laudamus.* And again in No. 65, an Epiphany anthem:

> Three kings from the East, as long foretold,
> Did come with myrrh, with incense, with gold,
> Alleluia! Alleluia!

Bach remembered the Introit proper to the festival: 'Ecce advenit dominator Dominus, et regnum in manu ejus, et potestas et imperium'—God's majesty implicit in the Child's infant frame. So the horn again pays conventional homage. With similar purpose the instrument is scored in No. 128, for Ascension Day:

> I see Christ through the starlight
> In brightness passing sunlight
> Enthroned as God's dear Son.

The same theme—the majesty of God—inspires cantata No. 143, an anthem for the New Year, to whose orchestral accompaniment, and here only, Bach adds three *corni da caccia* and drums. Its bass aria, 'The Lord is Sovereign everywhere', exceeds the 'Quoniam tu solus' in the elaborateness of its ceremonial courtesy. The horns echo and re-echo their familiar 'call':

Cantata No. 174 affords another example. Two *corni da caccia* are prescribed in the opening Sinfonia, a movement borrowed from the third Brandenburg Concerto written eight years earlier. But, to pay homage to 'the Highest', the horns are an addition to the original score.

Bach's 'Corno' was not identified in his mind with similar associations. He uses it purely for its orchestral value, and rarely outside his choruses and Chorals. On the infrequent occasions when it has pictorial significance, it decorates a pastoral and not a ceremonious scene. For instance, in the opening chorus of cantata No. 112:

> The Lord my Shepherd deigns to be.

Again, in the opening chorus of No. 1:

> How brightly shines yon Morning Star,
> Whose beams shed blessing near and far!

Again, in the tenor aria of No. 40, composed for the second day of the Christmas festival, whose Gospel (St. Luke ii. 15–20) relates the visit of the shepherds to the Manger. And again in the bass aria that opens cantata No. 88. The text is from Jeremiah xvi. 16: 'And after will I send for many hunters, and they shall hunt them from every mountain.' The horns sound a sonorous summons to the mountain-side.

Cantata No. 118 requires particular consideration. It is a motet for S.A.T.B. with wind accompaniment—a cornett, three trombones, and two instruments Bach names 'Lituus'. The music was composed for an open-air funerary ceremony, perhaps at the grave-side. But what was the 'Lituus'? Praetorius[1] defines it as the 'Krummhorn',[2] an instrument with a long English tradition.[3] Bach's Weimar friend, Johann G. Walther, describes it as a Zink, but remarks that formerly the name denoted the 'tuba curva' or 'Heerhorn'.[4] Dr. Max Schneider, editing the motet for the Neue Bachgesellschaft, supposed it to be a 'Flügelhorn' (or 'Bügelhorn'). But the problem is solved by the more recent publication[5] of a catalogue of musical instruments preserved at Ossegg (Bohemia) in 1706. It mentions two 'litui, vulgo Waldhörner'. Bach's instruments are in high B flat, sounding $bb-a''$, a rare instance of his employment of horns in that key. And nowhere else does he

---

[1] P. 40.
[2] The range of the parts in cantata No. 118 is the best evidence that the instrument was not a Krummhorn.
[3] Cf. Galpin, p. 164.   [4] B.-G. xxiv, p. xxiii.   [5] B.-J. 1921, p. 96.

use the term 'Lituus'. His use of it clearly is related to the fact that the cantata is the only one he scored exclusively for 'Stadt-pfeiferinstrumente'.

It has already been remarked that Bach did not use the corno da caccia at a higher pitch than B flat. But the trumpet part in the second Brandenburg Concerto suggests that he may have scored that work for the high Jagdtrompete, a trumpet coiled like the horn. Eichborn[1] quotes a late seventeenth- or early eighteenth-century writer who distinguished the trumpets of his period in four classes: (1) the German or 'ordinar-Trommete'; (2) the French, higher than the German; (3) the English, higher than the French; and (4) the Italian or 'gewundene' (circular) trumpet. Altenburg also places the 'gewundene' trumpet in a 'Zweyte Klasse', distinct from the German, French, and English trumpets. 'In this connexion', he writes,[2] 'the so-called "Invention" or Italian trumpet merits the highest consideration; for, owing to the frequent windings of its tube, its form is particularly convenient. It is much used in Italy and has the same trumpet *timbre* as those of the other class.' ('Hier verdient die sogenannte Inventions- oder italienische Trompete den ersten Rang, weil sie, wegen der öftern Windung, auf eine bequeme Art invertirt ist. Sie sind vorzüglich in Italien gebräuchlich, haben den nemlichen Trompetenklang, wie die vorigen [i.e. the *trombe* of the "Erste Klasse"], und sind von verschiedener Grösse.') So these Italian trumpets were coiled horn-wise, not folded like the tromba. An example can be seen in E. G. Haussmann's portrait of Gottfried Reiche,[3] Bach's most accomplished Stadtpfeifer. It represents him holding one in his right hand, with four coils of tubing. After taking exact measurements Mr. Blandford concludes that it was in D, at a pitch rather below diapason normal, with a C crook. In his left hand Reiche holds the manuscript of one of his 'Abblasen'. Its compass is from *bb* to *bb″*:

---

[1] Eichborn (2), p. 22.   [2] P. 12.
[3] See the illustration at p. 48, and Praetorius, Plate VIII, at p. 36.

GOTTFRIED REICHE
(*From the portrait by E. G. Haussmann*)

Few specimens of this high tromba da caccia survive. The Heyer
Collection, now in the University of Leipzig, exhibits one 'in Des'
(=D in the pitch of its period), described in the Catalogue (No. 1819)
as less blaring than the D-tromba, with a compass to a''''. It is a
Leipzig instrument, made by Heinrich Pfeifer, and dated 1697.[1]
Another example, apparently in D, was loaned to the exhibition of
musical instruments at South Kensington in 1872; it bears the
date 1688 and was made by Wilhelm Haas of Nürnberg.[2] The
Brussels Conservatoire has one in E, by the Vienna maker Michael
Leichamschneider, dated 1713. Mahillon[3] conjectures that it was
pitched to the F of its period.

[1] Pfeifer was distinguished as a trombone maker. He was appointed 'Thomas-
türmer' in 1680 and died in 1718, aged 66. Cf. Schering, p. 295.

[2] It is now in the Hohenzollern Museum at Sigmaringen. Mr. Blandford is
not disposed to group it with the Pfeifer and Reiche specimens.

[3] Vol. ii. 381.

CHAPTER III

THE TIMPANI

PRAETORIUS[1] names three varieties of drum—(1) the 'grosse Heerpaucken', kettle-shaped, copper-framed, proper to the ceremonial of Courts and the discipline of war; (2) 'Soldaten Trummel', or side-drum, associated with the transverse or Swiss pipe; and (3) the 'klein Paucklin', or little drum, used by the French and Dutch, which a man could beat with his right hand while supporting a three-holed pipe at his mouth with the left—the pipe and tabor of the Morris Dance.[2]

The timpani or 'Heerpaucken', originally military (cavalry) drums, were admitted to the concert orchestra before Bach's birth (1685), and from an earlier period were fitted with a tuning mechanism. In Sebastian Virdung's[3] illustration the parchment is held taut by a surrounding circlet of metal, and its tension is regulated by ten screw-joints operated by a detachable key. Praetorius,[4] in the following century, illustrates them with six screws. But rapid changes of tuning were impossible, and by Bach and his contemporaries were not attempted.

Bach usually indicates the instrument under the name 'Tamburi', a word which strictly connotes the big drum or 'Trommel'. The rare exceptions are cantata No. 100, where he writes 'Tympalles'; the revised (D major) *Magnificat*, in which he uses the form 'Tympali'; and cantata No. 191, where he writes the contraction 'Tymp.'. Only in the memorandum addressed to the Leipzig Council in August 1730[5] he employs the German 'Pauken', probably reflecting that those he addressed would find another word unintelligible!

Bach's use of the timpani was governed by a convention scrupulously observed. They sounded, according to his contemporary Altenburg,[6] 'the fundament or bass of the trumpet's heroic music'. The two instruments even shared their technical terms, e.g. 'einfache Zungen' (single tonguing), 'doppel Zungen' (double tonguing). Hence, in Bach's tradition, the timpani were an ingredient of 'Blasmusik' (music for wind instruments) and, apart from it, claimed no place in his scores. In his orchestral music they are found only in the Violin Sinfonia in D[7] and the two *Ouvertures* in that key.[8] They are scored in both the Oratorios, but neither of the *Passions*; in the *Hohe Messe*, but not in the four shorter

---

[1] P. 77.   [2] See Praetorius, Plates IX and XXIII, at pp. 54 and 64.
[3] P. 25.   [4] See his Plate XXIII, at p. 54.   [5] Terry, p. 201.
[6] P. 25.   [7] B.-G. xxi (1)   [8] B.-G. xxxi (1).

Masses; in the *Magnificat*, *Sanctus* in C,[1] thirty-four church cantatas, and seven secular works—in all, forty-nine separate compositions.[2] They are associated invariably with seasons of festal mood or public ceremony. Only four of the church cantatas in which they occur are not definitely of that character (Nos. 21, 69, 100, 137). No. 21, however, was performed under exceptional conditions at Halle in 1713,[3] and the festal scores of the other three (for the Twelfth and Fifteenth Sundays after Trinity) are probably accounted for by the nearness of those Sundays to the Ratswahl (Inauguration of the Council) service, for which they probably served again. At Leipzig the instruments were shared by the two principal churches, being transported from one to the other as occasion required.

The drums are never found in Bach's orchestra except in association with (a) three (rarely four) natural trumpets;[4] or (b) two natural horns (Waldhorn); or (c) three natural *corni da caccia* (Jagdhorn). The first category far outnumbers the others: the *Corni-Timpani* combination is found in only four scores (cantatas Nos. 79, 91, 100, 195); the *Corni da caccia-Timpani* group in one (cantata No. 143). Being inconsistent with the Motet form, drums have no part in Bach's *Cornett-Trombone* category.

The larger and lower of the two orchestral drums was styled the 'G drum', though, as in Bach's usage, its pitch might be raised to *a,* or lowered to *f,*. The smaller and higher instrument was distinguished as the 'C drum', though, as in Bach's scores, it frequently sounded *d* and occasionally *bb,*. The larger instrument was placed at the player's right hand, and the smaller on his left. A black cloth ('ein schwarzes Tuch'), spread over the parchment, muted the tone when occasion required.[5]

Owing to their close association with a 'choir' of trumpets, the drums were normally tuned in fourths in the eighteenth century. They were thereby enabled, in Altenburg's words, 'to sound the Fundament or Bass' ('das Fundament oder den Bass machen'). In old trumpet marches the fourth trumpet part was often written in fourths to allow it to be played on the drums if necessary.[6] Bach, however, does not always adopt the conventional tuning. Invariably his drums are transposing instruments, scored in C in the bass clef. But their tuning varies with the instruments with which he associates them. When scored with trumpets he tunes

them in fourths: and generally puts the movement

---

[1] B.-G. xi (1). [2] See Table VII. [3] Terry, p. 101.
[4] The Weimar cantata No. 59 is the sole exception. Only two trumpets are in the score. [5] Cf. Altenburg, p. 127. [6] Kirby, p. 12.

into the key of D major.[1] In but thirteen cases C major is the tonic key. The only other exception to D major normality is the *Magnificat* in its first form. Bach wrote it originally in E flat, tuning his drums in fourths, tonic, and (lower) dominant. Why he chose this exceptional key is not clear. It was unsuited to the conditions at Leipzig, for whose churches a revised version in D was subsequently prepared. As festival music the E flat score is unique in its tonality.

The association of drums and horns is found in four scores—cantatas Nos. 79, 91, 100, 195. Here the three trumpets of the *Trombe-Timpani* category are replaced by two natural horns (Waldhorn: Corno) in G (the key of the movement), and the drums are tuned in fifths (dominant and tonic): The absence of a third horn is observable. Bach never admits more than two natural horns to his scores. His tuning of their associated drums in fifths instead of fourths must be attributed to the fact that the tonic G could not be sounded on the smaller C drum.[2] Also, by putting it on the larger and lower 'G drum', the upper in some degree supplied the third trumpet (principale) of the *Trombe-Timpani* category. The *Corni da caccia-Timpani* group occurs in a single cantata (No. 143). The three horns here are in B flat (the key of the movement), and the drums are tuned in fourths, sounding the tonic and (lower) dominant: A tuning in fifths (dominant and tonic), though practicable, was obviously not preferable, since it diminished the resonance.

In all three categories Bach's treatment of the drums is uniform. Their pitch remains unchanged throughout the entire work. If a movement modulates into a key incongruous with their original tuning, they and their associated 'choir' are silent till the initial key returns. The drummer had merely to count his bars, unhampered by the need to adjust his instruments to changing tonality. An example may be taken from the early cantata No. 15. The terzetto which opens Part II begins in F major and ends in E minor, with two intervening sections in C major (the key of the cantata). In the C major sections alone the drums and trumpets are sounded.

With the rarest exceptions[3] Bach never assigns an obbligato or

---

[1] See Table VII.
[2] The limitations of tuning in the eighteenth century were respectively *bb.*– and *f.*–*c* for the smaller and larger drum.   [3] See *infra*, p. 54.

solo part to the drums, but restricts them to those passages in which their associated trumpets or horns are also sounding. Instances to the contrary are so infrequent, that one might declare it his rule for the drums not to sound unless all the voices of the 'choir' above them are simultaneously speaking. Like Altenburg, he viewed them as the peculiar fundament, or Toccato, of 'Blasmusik', and allowed them to speak only as members of that body.

Bach's reticent use of the drums was largely due to fear lest they should seem over boisterous on an ecclesiastical platform. This is evidenced not only by his disinclination to give them a solo part—a point discussed later—but also by deliberate neglect of their more elaborate and noisy 'beatings'. Altenburg[1] indicates the 'Schlag-Manieren' (beatings) in use in 1768, less than twenty years after Bach's death. They number twelve:

1. Viertel (Crotchets). 2. Halbe Takte (Half-bars). 3. Ganze Takte oder Schläge (Whole bars or beats).

4. Achtel oder einfache Schläge (Quavers or single beats).

5. Einfache Zungen (Single tonguing). 6. Doppel- oder gerissene Zungen (Double or rapid tonguing).

7. Tragende Zungen. 8. Ganze Doppel-Zungen.

9. Doppel-Kreuzschläge (Double cross beats). 10. Triolen (Triplets).

11. Wirbel (Roll). 12. Doppel-Wirbel (Double roll).

[1] P. 129.

Bach's scores only afford examples of the first five. Demisemi-quaver beats occur infrequently—for instance, in the final move-ment of cantata No. 71. Professor Kirby states that the roll (Wirbel) was not much used in the period. Bach frequently indicates it (e.g. the opening chorus of the *Christmas Oratorio*). More generally he uses the measured *tremolo*, as throughout cantata No. 80. Whether he desired semibreves and minims to be rolled when the *tr.* above them was omitted, it is not possible to say. Almost surely a drummer would roll a long closing note. But the scores of the two *Ouvertures* in D seem to indicate that Bach required the notes to be struck and sustained unless the roll was indicated. Indeed, since he used the instrument with fairly slack parchments, a held note without rolling would have ample resonance.

Such being Bach's standpoint, it is not surprising that the infrequent examples of a drum obbligato are, with one exception, found in his secular music. The first occurs in the opening chorus of *Vereinigte Zwietracht der wechselnden Saiten*, composed in 1726. The text invites it:

> Sweet voices harmonious of strings softly playing,
> Ye thundering drum-rolls exultant and clear,
> Hither draw listeners, coaxed by the sound!

The drums (bar 30), in an otherwise silent orchestra, acknowledge the reference in a simple rhythmic figure:

Timpani in D.

It is worth observing that, while Bach's drums here perform a rhythmic beating where an actual *roll* is invited, the voices and continuo, with exaggerated energy, picture an object gyrating in curves!

The second example of a drum obbligato occurs in the opening chorus of *Tönet, ihr Pauken*.

Here the drums actually open the movement, more familiar as the first chorus of the *Christmas Oratorio*. The writer has expressed the opinion[1] that the music was originally written to the Oratorio text, a conclusion Bach's treatment of the drums appears to

[1] See the *Musical Times*, Oct.–Dec. 1930, Jan.–Mar. 1931.

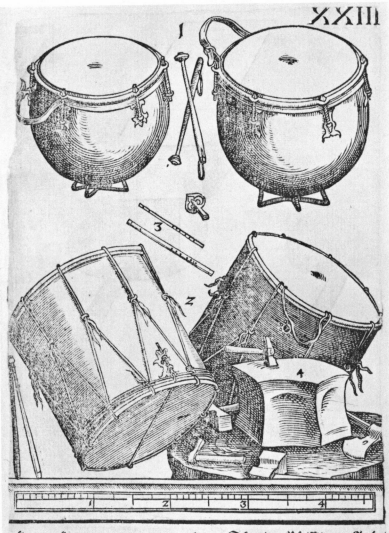

XXIII

Heerpaucken. 2. Soldaten Trummeln. 3. Schweitzer Pfeifflin 4. Amboß

DRUMS
(*Praetorius*)

challenge. Certainly the opening drum-solo and following trumpet-
calls are more obviously appropriate to the command 'Tönet, ihr
Pauken! erschallet, Trompeten!' than to the Oratorio text, which
mentions neither drums nor trumpets. But the words 'Christians,
be joyful!' to which the Oratorio chorus is generally sung in English,
do not correctly translate the original 'Jauchzet, frohlocket!'
'Jauchzet' invites a mood of unrestrained exhilaration, to which,
in Bach's view, the drums seemed peculiarly appropriate. For, in
the second movement of cantata No. 120, the repeated and imperative injunction 'Jauchzet!' moves him there also to insert an
obbligato for the drums (see p. 56).

It has already been observed that the conventional tuning of
the drums in fourths was due to their association with the trumpet

CORO.

'Chor', in that it enabled them to double or replace the fourth trumpet in a part sounding the tonic and (lower) dominant. We detect this convention in cantatas Nos. 63 and 119, in which the drums are associated with four trumpets. Here are the two related parts in the first chorus of the Christmas cantata No. 63, composed in 1723:

CORO.
Tromba IV in C.

In cantata No. 119, also composed in 1723, the correspondence is less close, but conspicuous. Here are the two parts in the opening chorus:

CORO.
Tromba IV in C.

Naturally Bach introduces the drums chiefly in choruses, where they complete his festival orchestra. But, associated always with a 'choir' of trumpets or horns, they are occasionally heard in other movements, to whose texts he held them appropriate. In the church cantatas they are present in six arias. In the alto aria of No. 71 they appropriately proclaim the 'mächtige Kraft' of the Mühlhausen Council, in whose honour the cantata was composed. In the Michaelmas cantata No. 130 they accompany the bass aria:

> With writhing fury Satan stands,
> Fresh mischief patiently he plans.

Satan's name always summoned to Bach's vision one of two pictures. Either he saw, and delineated, a sinuously beguiling serpent, or the fallen archangel in arms against the faithful legions. In this aria he paints a stirring battle-piece. The blare of trumpets, the tuck of drums, ring out from the first bar to the last. In the New Year cantata, No. 143, he scores the bass aria 'Der Herr ist König ewiglich' with three *corni da caccia* and drums. As in the 'Quoniam tu solus sanctus' of the *Hohe Messe*, he here naïvely indicates the Saviour's royal dignity by introducing the hunting horn, typical of the pastime of the Courts with which he was familiar. Here its proud flourishes are enhanced by the insistently beating drums. In the Whit-Sunday cantata, No. 172, the invocation to the Trinity in the bass aria

> Blessed Holy Trinity,
> God of might and glory!

invites a display of pomp which Bach's trumpets and drums heartily afford. In the early Easter cantata, No. 15, they are consonant with the season rather than with the words of the two arias into which they are introduced. The comment applies equally to the two duets (cantata No. 59 and the *Easter Oratorio*) in which drums and trumpets are found. To the truculent trio of No. 15 they are wholly appropriate.

The drums add their voice to a single recitative. It occurs in the Ratswahl cantata, No. 119, in a movement for bass heavily scored. The text is a patriotic invocation of Leipzig:

> How bravely stand'st thou, city blest!

Bach gives the sentiment the proudest decoration, befitting the presence of the civic Council on the day which inaugurated its year of office.

In the secular cantatas, Bach normally reserves the drums for the spirited choruses which flowed so easily from his fluent pen. But they accompany the vigorous bass aria 'Zurücke, zurücke' in

Aeolus, and the bass recit. 'Ja! ja! die Stunden' in the same cantata. In the latter, Aeolus summons the Winds in one of the most vivid storm-pieces in musical literature. The trumpets shriek, the drums rattle their thunder, the strings and flutes discharge lightning! A less tempestuous commotion occurs in *Preise dein' Glücke*, in the bass recit. 'Lass doch, o theurer Landesvater', where a reference to the menace of French hostility, when 'alles um uns blitzt und kracht', rouses the drums to another coruscation of fury.

Though the German drummers of Bach's generation were reputed particularly expert, his scores made no unusual demands upon their skill. As with Handel, the instrument was chiefly rhythmical in his usage. He prescribed only two drums, whose tuning, as already shown, remained unaltered throughout an entire work, however lengthy, and they remained silent when its tonality deserted the original key. His 'beatings' are straightforward and without complications, and the parts are rarely annotated with dynamic or other markings. Very occasionally he indicates *forte*, *piano*, *staccato* (e.g. in the better known Ouverture in D). And he rarely phrases.[1] But his orchestra was a permanent body, schooled by frequent oral instruction in his requirements.

[1] See the 'Gloria' of the *Hohe Messe* and the opening choruses of cantata No. 130, *Phoebus und Pan*, and *Schleicht, spielende Wellen*.

CHAPTER IV
THE FLUTES

The Blockflöte, Flûte à bec, Flûte douce

THE monopoly it enjoyed till the middle of the eighteenth century permitted the Blockflöte, disdaining its rival, to be known without qualification as 'the flute' (Flöte; flûte; flauto). Bach invariably names it so (Flauto; Fiauto), adding the classifying 'à bec' in only one of his scores.[1] The term is derived from the feature which distinguished the instrument from the modern variety—the whistle or fipple (whence 'fipple flute') mouthpiece, that allowed the player to hold the instrument vertically, as the clarinet and oboe in present usage. Praetorius names it 'Blockflöte' or 'Plockflöte', because its upper aperture was partially obstructed, leaving a narrow channel through which the wind passed from the player's lungs. Comparison with its noisier fellow gave it the name 'flûte douce', and to its weaker volume of tone it owed the definition 'flauto d'èco', a term Bach uses in the fourth Brandenburg Concerto in G, where two flutes discourse with a solo violin. As the 'Recorder' it had a long English tradition.[2]

The size of the instrument varied according to pitch. But generally it formed a cylindrical, or cylindrical and partly spheroconical, tube, originally in one piece, latterly jointed, most frequently made of wood, pierced with seven lateral holes in front, and having one for the thumbs behind. Its *timbre* was softer than the transverse flute, and the lack of overtones gave it a tenuous quality which commended it to Bach for the uses to which he put it. It needed delicate manipulation, for some of its notes, naturally impure, required correction by breath pressure or fingering. But it blended equally well with the voice and strings, and Bach employed it, though sparingly, throughout his active career; it is first found in his scores in 1708 and appears in his latest cantatas c. 1740. Owing to the fact that the transverse variety superseded it in the period when modern instrumental technique was beginning, it underwent little modification or improvement during its currency, and passed out of use in the form in which it had been known since the sixteenth century. It survives in its main feature only in the English and French

---

[1] Clavier Concerto in F. See Table VIII.
[2] Cf. Galpin, chap. viii.

flageolets, the so-called 'penny-whistle', and the flutework of the organ.[1]

The *Blockflöten* formed a considerable family of one-key instruments. Praetorius[2] cites eight varieties, twenty-one of which were needed to complete the band of flutes so popular in the sixteenth and seventeenth centuries.[3] He enumerates the following:

1. Klein Flöttlin in *g''*
2. Discant   ,, *d''*
3. Discant   ,, *c''*
4. Alto   ,, *g'*
5. Tenor   ,, *c'*
6. Basset   ,, *f*
7. Bass   ,, *bb'*
8. Gross Bass ,, *f'*

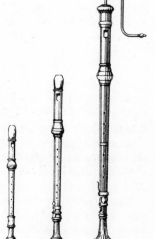

Discant, Tenor, and
Bass Blockflöte,
18th cent.

With an effective compass of two octaves and one note, which an expert player could extend some four or five notes upwards, the Blockflöte of Bach's generation was available in various keys, discant, alto, tenor, and bass. Those in general use were the

1. Discant sounding *a'–a'''*
2. Discant   ,,   *g'–g'''*
3. Discant   ,,   *f'–f'''*
4. Alto   ,,   *eb'–eb'''*
5. Alto   ,,   *d'–d'''*
6. Alto (Tenor),,   *c'–c'''*
7. Tenor   ,,   *bb–bb''*
8. Bass   ,,   *f–f''*

To these must be added high discants (*flauto piccolo*) in *f''*, *d''*, *c''*, *bb'*, the first and second of which Bach employs in cantatas No. 96 and No. 103 respectively. But the compass-chart in Table VIII shows that he made little use of any but discants Nos. 1–3. Only in one score (cantata No. 13) the instrument descends to *c'*. In two others (cantatas No. 39 and No. 152) it touches *d'*. Its lowest note averages *f'*. As a general statement it may be said that an alto flute served when the compass fell below that note to *e'*, *d'*, *c'*, and a discant for parts whose lowest note was *a'*, *g'*, and even *f'*, except when that note occurred frequently or was stressed,

[1] Cf. Dolmetsch, p. 457.   [2] Pp. 21, 33; see his Plate IX at p. 64.
[3] Cf. Praetorius, p. 13.

conditions which demanded an alto instrument. Table VIII does not indicate such differences of compass as permits a definitive allocation. But, in those infrequent cantatas in which three flutes are prescribed,[1] it may be safely concluded that the third is an alto. The 'Bass' and 'Gross-Bass' mentioned by Praetorius had already passed out of use, being found too soft in tone. Bach employed neither of them. Nor can we anywhere detect his usage of the bass f–f''. The tenor bb–bb'' may have been used in cantata No. 25, but not elsewhere. Thus, in Bach's scores the Blockflöte is essentially a soprano instrument.

Observing a convention whose practical utility is not apparent in his own case, Bach wrote for the Blockflöte in the French violin

G clef set on the bottom line   Players accustomed

to the normal G clef for the transverse flute must have been confused by the practice. Certainly Bach's Blockflöte tends to soar higher than the other variety. But the difference is not considerable, nor is it adequate to explain his use of the two clefs. At an earlier period, however, the French clef had an obvious advantage; for, as Praetorius shows, the Blockflöte discants were then keyed to higher pitches. Bach evidently preserved a convention for which his own music made no urgent call.

The Blockflöte, being a one-key instrument, normally sounded the notes as written in its peculiar clef. The player selected the one most conveniently keyed for the music before him. But in Bach's scores are six cases in which the flute part is transposed:

    1. Cantata No. 18. Excepting a few bars, in which they are silent, the flutes throughout are in octaves with the first and second violas. The latter are scored in the alto C clef in the key of the work (G minor). The former are keyed in A minor in the French violin G clef, transposing down a whole tone. Consequently on the stave the notes are identical (see p. 65).

The significant point here is, that Bach does not, as we should expect, score the flutes for the alto C in the key of the movement, but transposes their part for the tenor B flat. It is improbable that the former instrument was not available. Hence we must conclude that Bach deliberately chose the tenor in order to secure the uniform notation already remarked.[2] For, as it stands, the flute part sounds right, whether in the French G clef, as written, or (an

[1] Nos. 25, 122, 175.

[2] The argument is not affected by the possibility that the high discant in B flat rather than the tenor B flat was used here. The former would relieve the sombre colour of the score.

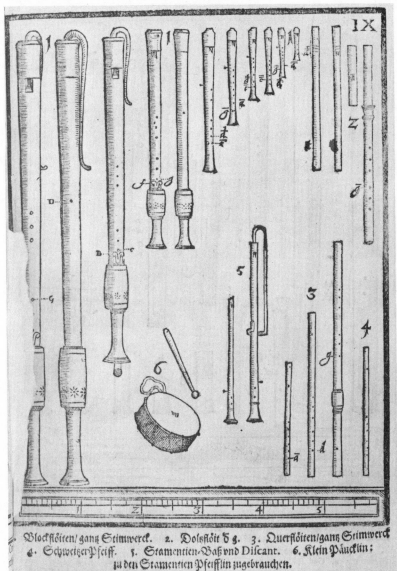

FLUTES
(*Praetorius*)

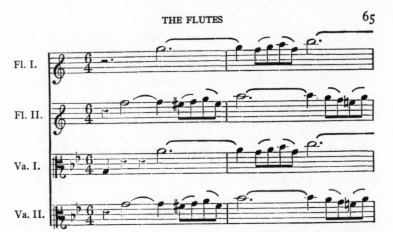

octave lower) in the alto C clef, which an inexperienced player
could readily visualize or substitute. It has been shown in an
earlier chapter that Bach was dependent on unprofessional players
for his flute parts. His practice here is therefore readily explained.
It emphasizes the fact, often overlooked, that his scores do not
always reveal his preferences, but rather the inadequate material
at his disposal.

2. Cantata No. 103. The opening chorus is in B minor
(S.A.T.B., continuo, strings, oboe d'amore I and II). The Blockflöte piccolo is scored in D minor and transposes down a minor
third. Since the pitch of the Leipzig organ does not account for
the interval of transposition, we must suppose that Bach's player
was accustomed to the discant in *f'*. Fingering *f''* on the piccolo,
he here sounds *d''*, the lowest note on the smaller instrument.

3. Cantata No. 106. The work is in E flat major (S.A.T.B.,
continuo, viola da gamba I and II). The flutes are in F, sounding
a major tone below the part as written. The occasion for which the
work was composed is not certainly determined. Probably it
was composed for a service in commemoration of the Weimar
Rector, Philipp Grossgebauer, in 1711. In that event it was performed in the Stadtkirche. That it was not intended for the ducal
chapel is proved by the fact that a tone, and not a minor third,
separates the pitches of the flutes and organ.[1]

4. Cantata No. 152. The short work is in E minor (S.B., continuo, viola da gamba, viola d'amore, oboe). The flute is in G
minor, transposing down a minor third, to suit the high pitch
(Cornett-Ton) of the Weimar organ.

[1] Cf. *infra*, chap. vii.

5. Cantata No. 161. All the movements in which the flutes participate are in C major (continuo, organ, strings, S.A.T.B.). The flutes are in E flat, transposing down a minor third.

6. Cantata No. 182. The movements in which the flute is employed are in G major and E minor (S.A.T.B., strings, continuo). The flutes are in B flat, transposing down a minor third.

It is noteworthy that, excepting No. 103, all the cantatas named above belong to Bach's Weimar period. The ducal Capelle was not equipped with flautists,[1] and Bach had to look elsewhere for players. Consequently he rarely used the instrument. Indeed, beyond the five instances already given there is no certain evidence of his use of either flute there. For both cantatas No. 142 and No. 189, attributed to those years, are of doubtful authenticity, which the present argument further undermines. Bach's transposition of the flute parts was due to the high pitch of the organ in the ducal chapel, and the fact that the parts stand a minor third higher than the ordinary Cammerton indicates that it was tuned to Cornett-Ton.[2]

The high discant (*flauto piccolo*), in *d″* and *f″*, is found in only two scores, and those among the latest—cantatas No. 103 and No. 96. In both it occurs in a single movement (Coro), and in both reinforces, or is reinforced by, another instrument at the octave: in No. 96 it is 'col Violino piccolo', in No. 103 'col Violino concertante o Flauto traverso'. In both we discern Bach's intention to mitigate the shrillness of the little instrument, and in both its employment is evidently related to the words. In No. 103 it is appropriate to Luther's text of St. John xvi. 20, on which the chorus is built. In No. 96 the lines

> He is the Star of Morning,
> Whose beams declare the dawning,
> When other stars do pale.

prompt Bach, invariably moved to make a picture, to suggest the distant spaces of the sky. Yet these were not his first opportunities to use the little discants, whose belated employment indicates how alertly experimental his genius·remained to the end.

The earliest example of Bach's usage of the Blockflöte merits attention, since it adds a detail to our knowledge of the conditions attending the first performance of the cantata in which it occurs. The cantata, No. 71, is scored for trumpets, drums, flutes, violoncello, oboes, bassoon, strings, and organ, arranged in four 'Cori', of which two—(1) trombe–timpani and (2) strings, as well as the

---

[1] *Supra*, p. 3.
[2] The subject of pitch and tuning is dealt with in Chapter VII.

voices and organ—are scored in C, while the other two—(3) flutes-violoncello and (4) oboes-bassoon—are in D, in the autograph score and printed parts. The inference from this strange dissimilarity is clear: the organ of the Mühlhausen Marienkirche, in which the cantata was performed on 4 February 1708, was tuned to high (Chorton) pitch. The young composer consequently put the low-pitched Cammerton flutes, oboes, and bassoon up to D, and transposed the violoncello also to the higher key to keep it uniform with its associated flutes in the second 'Coro'.[1]

Of no other instrument is Bach's characterization so clear and consistent as the Blockflöte. His comparatively infrequent employment of it indicates that he associated with it peculiar qualities to be reserved for particular uses. To him, as to Mersenne,[2] it expressed 'le charme et la douceur des voix', tender, plaintive, eloquent of the pious emotions of the soul, appropriate to voice the quiet agony of death, or mental sorrow, and by its purity to carry the soul's devotion to the throne of God. No other instrument identifies itself so closely with the simple piety of Bach. It voices his tenderness for his Saviour, his serene contemplation of death as the portal to bliss eternal. Only rarely, in cantatas No. 71 and No. 119, it intrudes into a score of pomp and circumstance. Elsewhere, as in No. 65, it is the vehicle of the mysticism so deep-rooted in Bach's nature.

Guided by this key to Bach's treatment of the Blockflöte, we approach the scores in which it occurs. As Table VIII discloses, he employed it chiefly in the cantatas, where we most readily apprehend his meaning. Cantata No. 13 is inspired by the Saviour's words, 'Mine hour is not yet come' (St. John ii. 4). Its two arias consequently are in a mood of sorrow, to which the flutes communicate their poignant note. In cantata No. 18, however, they seem to owe their presence less to congruity with the text than to the orchestral limitations of the Lenten season. Bach's stalwart Protestantism never failed to build an impregnable musical foundation when his topic, as here, is the 'Word of God'. To the solid structure of the opening Sinfonia and the soprano aria

The Word of God my treasure is

with its confidently moving continuo, the flutes make a contribution incongruous with their normal utterance. In the aria they weave an arabesque of almost purring contentment.[3]

---

[1] The violoncello and bassoon parts are not identical. Had they been so, another reason for the former's transposed part could be proposed.

[2] Bk. V, p. 237.

[3] Schweitzer, ii. 145, supposes that the flutes here represent waves, a figure incongruous with the text.

In cantata No. 25 the word 'Jesu' evokes from Bach a spasm of tenderness which the flutes interpret. In the same soft murmurous tones in which they sound the melody of the penitential hymn 'Ach Herr, mich armen Sünder', in the opening chorus, they echo the melodious petition of the soprano aria:

> Hearken to my halting praises,
> Jesu, with a gracious ear!

In a similar mood of prayerful approach they weave an embroidery of tender feeling round the soprano aria of cantata No. 39:

> Father, all I bring Thee
> Thou Thyself hast given me.

In cantata No. 46 (*Schauet doch und sehet*) the flutes express another mood. The chorus 'Behold and see if there be any sorrow like unto my sorrow' is a persisting wail of lamentation, in which they raise their tempered voices, one answering the other, as if in rivalry to express their grief. Their threnody continues in the following tenor recitative, 'Lament, lament God's city now in dust!' In contrast with these gloomy numbers is the alto aria:

> But Jesus still His faithful shieldeth,
> A present help in danger's hour.
> His sheep He loves, their love beseecheth,
> And folds them safe when storm-clouds pour.

Here, as always, the thought of Jesus as the Good Shepherd moves Bach to fashion a pastoral scene, to which the flutes contribute their decorous piping.

The practice of his generation, and his own strong inclination, always moved Bach to give nature's moods pictorial illustration. So, in cantata No. 81, which treats of Christ's stilling of the tempest, the flutes and strings in the opening chorus undulate in gentle wavelets on the lake's surface. But, significantly, the strings alone portray their furious motion in the tenor aria:

> The waters of Belial
> Their storm-crests are tossing
> And raging like hell!

Here the flutes are silent in a scene incongruous with their gentle nature. They are scored, in fact, only in the first chorus and do not reappear even in the concluding Choral.

In the next two[1] cantatas in the Table the flutes, as in No. 46, are the vehicle of lamentation. In No. 103 the unusual intrusion of the piccolo into the opening chorus undoubtedly indicates Bach's desire to emphasize the word 'heulen' (howl, yell). Soaring

---

[1] For cantatas Nos. 71 and 96 see *supra*, p. 66.

to its highest register it sounds a piercing cry. Again in No. 106,
a funeral anthem, the flutes assist its sombre mood. Associated
with two *viole da gamba*, in Schweitzer's[1] vivid words, 'their
veiled *timbre* belongs to the very essence of the music. We seem
to see an autumn landscape with blue mists floating across it.'
In cantata No. 122 the flutes have another meaning. They sound
only in the soprano recit., and with evident significance. The
text pictures the angelic host filling the sky with the incense of their
praise. Bach puts a song into their mouths, the Christmas hymn
'Das neugebor'ne Kindelein', and gives the melody to the flute
high above the stave; for the text speaks of the angelic singers
'in lofty choir'. A similar impression of sound from ethereal spaces
is conveyed by the flutes in cantata No. 127, in the soprano aria:

> In Jesu's arms my spirit resteth
> While earth-bound still my body lies.
> So, call me hence, sad bells of mourning!
> Death, sound thy summons! Fear I'm scorning!
> For Jesus beckons from the skies.

Here, in Bach's customary device, the pizzicato continuo tolls the
'sad bells of mourning', and the flutes' persistent quavers measure
the endless seconds of a timeless sphere. For their note is not
funereal; rather they express the soul's quiet contentment, at rest
in the Saviour's arms. As Pirro writes,[2] 'elles chuchotent, pour ne
point troubler ce grand sommeil, mais elles ne gémissent pas'.
Cantata No. 152[3] provides another example of Bach's disposition
to address the Saviour directly through the flûte douce, as here in
the soprano aria, where he is apostrophized as 'the Corner Stone':

> Rock, beyond all else my treasure,
> Aid me ever all my days
> Faith to show Thee without measure,
> Build on Thee my hope always,
> Soon in heaven to do Thy pleasure!

The continuo moves with the always confident pulse of Bach's
music when the thought of man's reliance on God is uppermost,
while the flute and viola d'amore, in happy mood, illustrate the
word 'Seligkeit'.
The thought of death ever excited ardent longing in Bach.
The flutes give it expression in cantata No. 161. In the opening
alto aria they stress the recurring word 'süss':

> Kindly [süsser] Death, come, quickly call me!
>   .   .   .   .   .   .
> Grant me, Lord, a gentle [süsse] passing!

[1] Vol. ii. 126.
[2] P. 228. 'They speak in whispers, unwilling to disturb this everlasting sleep;
but with no note of lamentation.'   [3] See *supra*, p. 66, for No. 142.

Again in the final chorus they illustrate the word:

> Heaven's joy, so calm [süsse] and blissful.

In the intervening alto recit.:

> Then, hasten, Death! O make no long delay!
> Come, toll thy knell and let me hence away!

we hear the tolling bells and the flutes' echo of them in the high
ether.

Bach's association of the flute with a pastoral scene was natural,
and has already been remarked in cantata No. 46. In No. 175 the
opening tenor recit. and following alto aria provide another
instance:

> (R.) 'He calleth his own sheep by name, and leadeth them out' (St.
> John x. 3).
> (A.) Come, lead me hence!
> My spirit yearns to walk in heaven's pasture.
> With eager eyes and longing sighs
> I wait Thee, Shepherd, Master.

Both movements are scored for continuo and three flutes, which
in the aria pipe a deliciously care-free measure as they lead the flock
to the green pastures of Paradise.

That Bach selected the flûte douce to voice his most sacred
emotion is particularly evident in cantata No. 180, one of five
scores in which the traverso appears as well. The latter is obbligato
in the tenor aria.

> Arouse thyself, the Bridegroom knocks!
> Throw open wide the gates before Him!

The music is animated, eager, joyous; yet its vivacity is physical
rather than emotional. But in the opening chorus, alto recit., and
soprano aria, where the gentler instrument is prescribed, Bach
prostrates himself before the Great Mystery:

> He, our God, so gracious minded,
> Hath for us a feast provided.
> He Who in the heavens reigneth
> Here to feed His children deigneth.

In cantata No. 182 (*Himmelskönig, sei willkommen*), Bach's only
extant anthem for Palm Sunday, the flute apparently owes its
presence to the conditions of the Lenten season. Normally Bach
would have put other colours on his canvas.

Besides the church cantatas, the flûte à bec is scored in the
Easter Oratorio, St. Matthew Passion, the secular *Was mir behagt*,
and three orchestral Concertos. Bach presents both varieties of

the instrument in the first two, and in each employs the flûte à bec in but one movement. To the tenor aria of the Oratorio:

> Death's a sleep! I fear no longer.
> 'Tis a slumber.
> Jesus risen hath made it so.

it lends its murmurous tone. But the joy of Easter is voiced by the traverso. In the *St. Matthew Passion*, too, its note is pathetic (tenor recit., No. 25):

> O grief! How throbs His woe-beladen heart!

In *Was mir behagt*, as in cantata No. 175, its piping is pastoral (aria of Pales, No. 9):

> Happy flocks in surety wander
> While the shepherd watch doth keep.

These examples completely reveal Bach's usage of the flûte à bec. That the traverso was of more general utility is evident from Tables VIII and IX. But the flûte à bec had his deeper regard. For in its clear tones he could utter the ponderings of his devout mind. But its delicate *timbre* put it at a disadvantage in the orchestral era that followed the death of Handel. The very qualities that commended it to Bach prejudiced its competition with the rougher and louder rival. So, it passed from the orchestra to the museum,[1] superseded, but not excelled, by its competitor.

The Transverse Flute

Germany's particular association with the transverse or orchestral flute is implicit in the fact that both France and England, throughout the eighteenth century, distinguished it from the other variety as 'the German flute' (*flûte d'Allemagne*; *flûte allemande*). The crosswise manner of holding it gave it the appellations *flauto traverso, traversa, flûte traversière, Traversflöte, Querflöte*. The same characteristic caused Sebastian Virdung,[2] writing in 1511, to name it *Zwerchpfeiff*. The tradition that it piped the Swiss to battle at Marignano in 1515 impelled Agricola a few years later (1528) to call it the *Schweizerpfeiff*. Bach generally adopted the Italian styles *flauto traverso, traversa*, but occasionally uses the French indication *traversière*.

---

[1] There has been, of late years, a revival of interest in the *Blockflöten*. Instrument-makers are again building them, and manuals of instruction are published, e.g. Robert Götz's *Schule des Blockflötenspiels* (Verlag P. J. Tonger: Cöln) and Waldemar Woehl's *Blockflötenschule*. The latter is published by the firm of Bärenreiter at Cassel, from whom can also be obtained a set of instruments. Those made by Mr. Arnold Dolmetsch are of particular excellence, and a full consort is to be heard at the Haslemere festivals.   [2] P. 14.

From Agricola's period onwards the transverse flute formed a family of three instruments,[1] (1) Discant, (2) Alto-Tenor, (3) Bass, at the respective pitches:

Praetorius,[2] ninety years later, puts them a fifth higher:

with a compass of two-and-a-half octaves in each case. He adds that the middle instrument was used as a discant, and so carries forward the tradition of the orchestral D flute from the age of Virdung and Agricola to that of Bach and Handel.

To this point the mechanism of the instrument was of the simplest. It formed a one-piece wooden tube, cylindrically bored, and pierced laterally with six finger-holes, sounding the chromatic scale over a compass of fifteen tones (two-and-a-half octaves). But, unlike the Blockflöte, it was improved in the seventeenth and early eighteenth centuries by various devices. Lully's introduction of it to the French Opera *circa* 1677 roughly dates the beginning of these changes, for which French makers are credited. They consisted, first, in the substitution of a conoidal for a cylindrical bore, its taper widening from the lower end towards the head of the instrument. At about the same time the one-piece tube was divided into three sections, respectively distinguished as the *tête*, *corps*, *pied*. Subsequently the *corps* itself was divided, so that inserted pieces of suitable length could adjust the instrument to the conflicting pitches then in vogue. These changes left the scale still controlled exclusively by the six lateral finger-holes. Towards the close of the seventeenth century, however, a metal key (*Klappe*; *clef*), pressed by the little finger of the right hand,[3] was added to the tail section (*pied*), enabling the player to sound and its octaves.

---

[1] Cf. Mahillon, i. 249 f.; *Encyc. Britannica*, 11th edn., x. 579 f.; Fitzgibbon, chap. 3.   [2] P. 22. See his Plate IX at p. 64.
[3] As may be seen in the picture of Lully and his flautists in the National Gallery, London, the key moved on an axle and was kept closed by a spring. Its mechanism was fitted into a wooden ring or rib encircling the tail section at the proper position. The picture is figured in Fitzgibbon.

· Thus, on the threshold of the eighteenth century,
flute in D sounded the scale in the fundamental oc
sively opening the finger-holes from the bottom
posing the key before opening the first:

By increasing the breath-pressure, and allowing it to impinge less
acutely on the outer edge of the embouchure, the upper octave

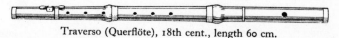

Traverso (Querflöte), 18th cent., length 60 cm.

was obtained. Semitones foreign to the scale—*d♯'*, *d♯''*, *d♯'''* ex-
cepted—were got by 'forking' or 'cross-fingering' (*doigté fourchu*;
Gabelgriffe). Thus, by closing the *e'* and *g'* and opening the *f♯'*
holes the note *f♮'* was obtained:

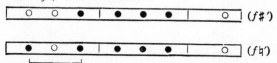

Similarly *bb'* was got by 'forking' the *a'* and *c♯''* holes:

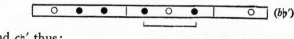

And *c♮'* thus:

But the notes obtained by 'forking' were impure and needed
manipulation for their satisfactory production. Flute makers consequently planned to extend the key system already in operation
for *d♯'*. During his stay in Paris in 1726, Johann Joachim Quantz,
subsequently flute-master of Frederick the Great, added a key
for *eb'*, flatter than the *d♯'* which so far served for it. Though
Germany approved the device, the innovation was elsewhere
ignored. Four years earlier (1722) two supplementary keys had

been added to the lengthened tail-joint for

Unlike the *d♯'* key, they sounded only their fundamental notes, adversely affected the tone of the instrument, and temporarily were abandoned.

Meanwhile a contrivance had been adopted to mitigate the inconvenience caused by the variety of pitches then in vogue, which necessitated the appropriate lengthening or shortening of the middle joint (*corps*). For the purpose a player needed to carry as many as seven pieces of varying length. This rough and ready adjustment, however, affected the relations of the other sections of the instrument, and therefore, in order to establish a just proportion, the tail-joint (*pied*) was now divided below the key, its two pieces being brought by a tenon-adjustment into accurate relationship with the middle-joint (*corps*). Instruments so constructed were known as *flûtes à registre*. Still more accurate tuning was aided by a device whose invention followed closely upon Bach's appointment to the Leipzig Cantorate. Quantz, about 1726, added a nut-screw regulating the cork-stopper in the upper joint (*tête*) of the instrument, on whose correct adjustment its accurate pitch in great measure depended.

The innovations described in the preceding paragraphs have been stated in reference to the discant or orchestral flute in *d'*. They were equally applicable to the other members of the family, which, when Quantz published his *Method of playing the transverse flute* in 1752, were four in number, pitched respectively, (1) a fourth below, (2) a third below, (3) a fourth above, and (4) an octave above the discant in *d'*. Nos. 1, 3, 4 were known respectively as the 'low fourth', 'little fourth', and 'octave' or 'piccolo'. No. 2, distinguished for its soft and mellow tone, was for that reason termed the *flûte d'amour*. Taking the ordinary discant or concert flute as a flute in C, these four instruments would be pitched as follows:

But, as the low C key was not in use, the lowest sounding notes on Nos. 1–3 were

Such was the equipment of the instrument as it reached Bach.

Excepting cantata No. 189, whose authenticity is challenged, there is no extant instance of his use of it until his prescription of 'due Traversieri' in the secular cantata *Durchlaucht'ster Leopold* at Cöthen in or about 1718. He employed it again in the fifth Brandenburg Concerto and other instrumental scores of that period.[1] But it was not until his appointment to the Leipzig Thomasschule in 1723 that the transverse flute regularly contributed to his concerted music. The compass chart in Table IX shows that, with the rarest exceptions, he preferred and used the discant in *d'*, introducing it most often into sharp keys, of which those of G and D major far outnumber the rest. Out of seventy-eight scores in which it is found, only fourteen have a flat signature.[2] A collation of his scores shows that at all periods his players—who in this case provided their instruments—were equipped with the *d#'* key. The note was not obtainable by 'forking', and its almost constant presence in his flute parts—whether as *d#'* or *eb'* or their octaves—supports the deduction. The key was in use before 1707, when Bach took office in the Blasiuskirche at Mühlhausen.

Whether Bach's players were also provided with the long keys extending the compass downward to *c'* and *c#'* is a point which repays investigation. They were added about 1722, and therefore were available when he went to Leipzig. On the other hand, they were generally condemned as blemishing the tone of the instrument, and on that account Bach might be expected to frown upon

them. In fact he seldom carries his flute parts below

The following are the rare exceptions to this restriction of compass. They not only settle his usage of the long keys, but also indicate definitely the members of the traverso family he preferred and employed.

1. Cantata No. 26. At bar 42 of the opening chorus the flute has this descending passage:

The *c'* is not repeated elsewhere, and, as the flute is in unison with the first oboe, it is not improbable that Bach momentarily

---

[1] See Table IX.
[2] Cantatas Nos. 55, 78, 101, 102, 114, 146, 164, 180, 189 (? authentic), *Ich bin in mir vergnügt*, the two *Passions*, Flute Sonata No. II, and the trio and canon in the *Musicalisches Opfer*.

overlooked its limitations of compass. It would be rash, in such conditions, to accept the single note as proof of a long key.

2. The second flute has a similar lapse in cantata No. 79 (1. Coro).

3. Cantata No. 45. At bar 79 of the opening chorus the second flute has this passage in unison with the second oboe:

The third bar, however, is a copyist's error. For elsewhere the c♯′ is avoided, and at bar 15 the same passage is correctly marked:

4. Cantata No. 164. In the soprano-bass duet the two flutes in unison touch c′ in the following bars:

Being in unison with the oboes and violins, their common part is printed on a single stave. But the repetition of the note puts the case in another category from that of No. 1, and a collation of the flute part at Berlin confirms the correctness of the Bachgesellschaft score. The player, however, may have used a B flute and transposed.

5. Cantata No. 192. In 'Verse 3' (chorus) the following passages occur:

As in the examples already given, the flutes share the stave with other instruments: the first is in unison with the first oboe and first violins, the second with the second oboe and second violins. In the original parts at Berlin there is no indication that they took the low notes at an upper octave, and we must therefore conclude that the second flute, at any rate, was the 'low fourth' in A.

6. The *Hohe Messe* in B minor. At bar 21 of the final movement the second flute plays

Here there is no room for doubt. The *c♯′* is definite in the autograph score. A long key can therefore be presumed to have been used if that note actually was played. But it must certainly be regarded as an oversight on Bach's part. For it is patent from the opening bars of the 'Kyrie' that the flute was not fitted with a long key. There the second flute is generally in unison with the second oboe. But on every occasion when the oboe touches *c♯′* the flute is provided with an alternative note within its normal register.

7. A similar intention can be inferred in *Angenehmes Wiederau*.

8. *St. Matthew Passion.* In the opening movement of the second Part (bar 69) the first flutes of both 'Cori' have the passage:

Here, again, the autograph score is definite: 'Trav. e Hautb. d'amour 1° concordant'. As in cantata No. 192 a 'low fourth' flute must have been used here, and in this movement only. Throughout the rest of the work the traverso in *d′*, with the *d♯′* key, was adequate.

9. *St. John Passion.* At bar 62 of the opening chorus the first flute plays:

The flute here is in unison with the first oboe, and the single *c′* can hardly establish the use of a long key. On the contrary, at bar 7 of a later chorus ('Sei gegrüsset'), where the second oboe descends to *c′*, Bach substitutes for the flute a note within its compass:

He does so again at bar 7 of the chorus 'Schreibe nicht'. The flutes here and throughout the *Passion* are the *d♯'*-keyed discant in *d'*. Alternatively, here, as in cantata No. 164, the player may have used a B flute.

10. *Vereinigte Zwietracht.* In the opening chorus the flutes are in unison respectively with the first and second *oboi d'amore*, and repeatedly sound the notes

They are therefore of the 'low fourth' variety. Elsewhere in the cantata Bach employs the normal discant in *d'*.

These conclusions emerge from the foregoing analysis:

1. Excepting four scores, Bach generally used the discant traverso in *d'*, but nowhere the high discant in *d''*.[1]

2. There is no satisfactory evidence that his instruments were fitted with a *c'* key, the general objection to which he must be held to have shared.

3. There is no convincing instance of his use of a *c♯'* key.

4. Other than the discant in *d'*, and perhaps a B flute, the only instrument of the traverso family for which he scored was the 'low fourth'. It is found only in cantata No. 192, the *St. Matthew Passion*, and *Vereinigte Zwietracht*. If, however, the authenticity of cantata No. 189 is conceded, the compass of its flute part (*bb'–d'''*) indicates the same instrument.

To an extent a modern composer of reputation would not tolerate, Bach's orchestras included amateurs. His flute players were generally drawn from the University Collegium Musicum, and there must have been periods when they were not forthcoming. For that reason, we may conclude, only forty-one of his Leipzig cantatas are scored for the traverso. They are scattered over the whole span of his Cantorship, but with intervals in their occurrence most apparent in its last active decade. We certainly should not be justified in measuring the ability of his amateur flute players by the parts he wrote for it. For there are many which

[1] The compass of the instrument in cantata No. 78 suggests the so-called 'military flute' in E flat. But the compass was easily obtained on the *d'* discant.

demand high executive skill. Moreover, contrary to Handel's general practice,[1] they most often cover the entire compass of the instrument. On that account we may suppose that, from time to time, Bach's professional oboists were also competent on the flute, though frequent instances of his employment of both instruments in the same score prove that he was not independent of amateur assistance. Still, it frequently happens that the oboist could, if required, play the obbligato parts in arias in which his own instrument was silent.

To the immaturity of his players we must attribute the fact that Bach's flute parts are so frequently written in unison with other supporting instruments. With comparative rarity he entrusts an aria solo obbligato to it, and the movements in which they occur belong chiefly to the last period of his fertility. When, as in cantata No. 102, he prescribes a violino piccolo, or, as in the *Easter Oratorio*, a violin, as an alternative to the traverso, we must not infer that he was indifferent as to which instrument was played, but that he was doubtful of the availability of a competent flautist.

Bach's treatment of the traverso has peculiar interest. His immediate predecessors, Knüpfer and Kuhnau, employed it occasionally and tentatively[2] during the supremacy of its rival. But, when Bach succeeded Kuhnau in 1723, the sovereignty of the Blockflöte was no longer conceded, and his scores reveal the fact. Mr. Fitzgibbon[3] advances the curious proposition that, 'living under Frederick the Great', Bach 'naturally paid considerable attention to the favourite instrument of that monarch'. As a Saxon subject, Bach owed no allegiance to Prussia, and his usage of the traverso goes back a quarter of a century before his famous visit to Quantz's pupil. Certainly Frederick's notorious preference may have accentuated the declining vogue of the Blockflöte. But, in matters affecting his art Bach was not swayed by the vagaries of fashion. In the traverso he recognized a useful orchestral voice, and his scores reveal his experimental usage of it.

We remark, in the first place, his disinclination to employ it in purely instrumental movements. There are many in the cantatas, sacred and secular. But the traverso is scored in only one of them (*Non sa che sia dolore*). The so-called 'pastoral' Sinfonia in Part II of the *Christmas Oratorio* is the only piece of sacred instrumental music to which he admitted the traverso, and there with obvious intention. Elsewhere he preferred the gentler Blockflöte. His secular instrumental scores declare the same preference. For, though the Flute Sonatas were written for the traverso, and also

[1] Fitzgibbon, p. 118.　　　[2] Cf. Schering, p. 151.　　　[3] P. 118.

the Trio in G for flute, violin, and bass, as well as the one in C minor offered to Frederick the Great, the instrument is found in his larger orchestral works only in the Brandenburg D major, the Clavier Concerto in A minor, and Ouverture in B minor. All of them have a characteristic in common with the Sinfonia of the *Christmas Oratorio* which explains Bach's preference of the traverso in them —in none are horns or trumpets prescribed. He was therefore not deterred from employing the coarser of the two flutes, whose tone, augmenting the brass, would have unbalanced his orchestral scheme. His concerted vocal music suggests a similar deduction. We should expect to find the traverso in choruses where his festival orchestra is employed, when trumpets and drums, or horns and drums, augment the normal body. In fact, it is more often absent than present. In the Leipzig cantatas it is omitted from twenty movements of this character.[1]

The cantatas and larger concerted vocal works exhibit Bach's employment of the traverso in every form then customary—chorus, aria, recitative, Choral. In the choruses, notwithstanding considerable variety of usage, one practically invariable rule is observed. So close seemed the instrument's affinity with the oboe, that in only two Leipzig flute cantatas—Nos. 173 and 184—are they not together. That these exceptions were due to abnormal conditions is evident from the fact that the two cantatas were performed on consecutive days, 14 and 15 May 1731. The rougher tone of the traverso clearly invited a closer association with the oboe than Bach was willing to sanction in the case of the Blockflöte. There is, in fact, only one instance of the latter being in unison with the oboe. It occurs in cantata No. 152, in the concluding soprano-bass duet. But the direction there is 'Gli Stromenti all'unisono' and includes other instruments than the two in question. It therefore does not challenge the general statement, that Bach nowhere links the Blockflöte with the coarse-toned oboe. On the other hand, it was his frequent practice with the traverso, whose tone was more congruous with the other instrument. Instances occur in cantatas Nos. 26, 45, 67, 78, 79, 110, 117, 191, 195, the *Hohe Messe*, *St. John Passion*, and *St. Matthew Passion*, but rarely in an aria.

In Bach's choruses the traverso serves one of two purposes, and occasionally a third. Either it adds an independent strand to the woven web of polyphony, or it merely strengthens the texture of one otherwise provided. Occasionally it is both independent and pictorial. It would be convenient to detect consistent develop-

[1] Nos. 19, 29, 41, 43, 50, 63, 69, 74, 80, 91, 120, 137, 143, 149, 171, 172, 190, 197, *Herr Gott, Beherrscher*, and *Christmas Oratorio*, Part VI.

ment in Bach's practice. In fact, examples of the three categories can be drawn from his earliest as from his latest Leipzig music. Excluding the suspect cantata No. 189, and the secular *Durchlaucht'ster Leopold*, composed at Cöthen, Bach's earliest use of the traverso in a concerted chorus is observed in the two major works whose performance distinguished his first year at Leipzig—the *St. John Passion* and the Latin *Magnificat*. In the former, performed on 26 March 1723, his use of the traverso is curious and was not repeated. It plays an independent part only in two soprano arias, the short chorus 'Wir haben keinen König', and the tenor arioso 'Mein Herz'. Elsewhere the two flutes either double the oboe parts, or (in unison) are concordant with the first violins or sopranos, or (in unison) play an octave above the violas or vocal tenors. There is no patent reason why Bach should have used the flutes in so many movements to sound the octave of the instrumental and vocal tenors. Either the reason was particular, or he disliked the effect: the experiment was not repeated.

The composition of the *Magnificat* must have been begun at no considerable interval after the performance of the *St. John Passion*. But it indicates a decided change in Bach's usage of the traverso. In the earlier work the instrument is an auxiliary, in the latter a principal. It contributes nothing original to the structure of the *Passion*. In the *Magnificat* it raises an individual voice, excepting the chorus 'Omnes generationes', where the accompaniment conforms to a fugal plan. Nor, excepting the alto-tenor duet 'Et misericordiam', where the flutes and violins are in unison, is it bracketed with another part. So, an instrument admitted on probation in March 1723 has the freedom of the orchestra in the following December.

But it must not be supposed that Bach thereafter consistently followed the method employed in the *Magnificat*. Certainly he did so in his other major church compositions—the *Trauer-Ode*, *St. Matthew Passion*, *Christmas Oratorio* (for the most part), and the latter part ('Credo' and 'Osanna') of the *Hohe Messe*. In all the Leipzig secular choruses, also, the traverso has an individual voice, excepting, to some extent, *Schleicht, spielende Wellen*. We can place in the same category cantatas Nos. 8, 9, 11, 107, 115, 123, 125, 173, 180, 184, 191 (in part), and 192. But they are matched by almost as many in which the instrument is for the most part auxiliary. Excepting the 'Qui tollis' and a few bars of the 'Cum sancto spiritu', the 'Kyrie' and 'Gloria' of the *Hohe Messe* are in this category. So are cantatas Nos. 45, 67, 78, 79, 110, 117, 191 (in part), and 195, already mentioned, to which we may add Nos. 101, 129, and 181. Among these only three obbligato solos are found (Nos. 45, 78, 79), and his treatment of the traverso in them generally supports the deduction already drawn—that it depended not infrequently on the competence of the players at his disposal.

In the arias Bach's experimental treatment of the traverso is apparent and in contrast with his usage of the Blockflöte in similar movements. The differing *timbre* of the two flutes explains the fact that he infrequently duplicates the traverso, but, excepting the two Weimar cantatas Nos. 152 and 182, never uses only one Blockflöte in an aria accompaniment. It is rare, again, for the Blockflöte to be supported by the continuo alone in movements of that nature: the only instances to the contrary are in cantatas Nos. 39, 119, 142, 175, 182, and *Was mir behagt*. On the other hand, the traverso is so treated in arias more frequently than any other combination, most often with an alto or tenor voice. These arias occur in cantatas Nos. 45, 55, 78, 79, 94, 96, 99, 102, 103, 113, 114, 123, 130, 164, 180, *Easter Oratorio, Phoebus und Pan*; *Ich bin in mir vergnügt*; *Schleicht, spielende Wellen*; *O holder Tag*; *Schweigt stille*; *Tönet, ihr Pauken*; and *Die Freude reget sich*. The presence of two *traversi* is unusual: they are found only in cantata No. 164 (which has already been discussed), the Mass in A, *Phoebus und Pan*, and *Tönet, ihr Pauken*, in which they have independent parts; and *Preise dein' Glücke*, where they are in unison, for the same reason, apparently, as in No. 164. In *Schleicht, spielende Wellen*, however, Bach's literalness compels him to use three flutes in one aria which sings of 'the choir of flutes' ('der Flöten Chor').[1] In cantatas Nos. 79 and 103 the traverso is alternative, in No. 79 to an oboe, in No. 103 to a violin. In the first Bach may have had the same player in mind for both instruments. In the second he proposed to fall back on his leader should a flautist not be available on the more or less distant date of performance.

In the traverso-continuo category must also be placed a few arias in which an organ accompaniment is definitely prescribed. The most familiar are the plaintive alto aria 'Buss und Reu' ('Grief for sin') in the St. *Matthew Passion*, and the tenor pastoral aria 'Frohe Hirten' ('Happy shepherds') in Part II of the *Christmas Oratorio*. Other instances are the soprano aria of cantata No. 100, the tenor aria (No. 6) of No. 107, the tenor aria of No. 110, the alto aria 'Esurientes' of the *Magnificat*, and the soprano aria 'Ich folge dir' in the St. *John Passion*. Excepting Nos. 107, 110, the *Passions*, and the *Magnificat*, these *obbligati* are for a single flute. In the soprano

---

[1] Notwithstanding his text, 'Schweigt, ihr Flöten', in the soprano aria in *O holder Tag*, however, Bach had to be content with one flute.

aria of the *Easter Oratorio* the continuo is augmented by a bassoon. As in the case of No. 103, the obbligato is alternatively for a traverso or violin, and for the same reason.

In general the traverso solo *obbligati* are such as Bach could not willingly have entrusted to an inexpert player. Nor are they merely decorative; on occasion they contribute to a pictorial design. In the tenor aria of No. 55:

> Have mercy, Lord!
> Look with pity on my crying,
> Let Thy heart regard my sighing,
> And for Jesu's sake, Who loved me,
> Turn Thy heavy anger from me!

the flute weaves an embroidery of lamentation reminiscent of the earlier 'Erbarme dich' ('Have mercy, Lord') of the *St. Matthew Passion*. In the alto aria of No. 94:

> O foolish world, O foolish world!
> Vain your power, pomp and gold!

the flute obbligato, flickering hither and thither, typifies the world's 'falscher Schein'. In the tenor aria of No. 99:

> Let nothing thee dismay, O fainting spirit!

Bach is at pains to paint the initial word 'Erschüttre'—shake, convulse, stagger—in agitated demisemiquavers and leaping intervals. A similar interpretation fits the flute obbligato to the tenor aria of No. 102:

> Affrighted, pause,
> O vain presumptuous spirit.

in which the traverso (or violino piccolo) discharges cascades of agitated notes. But this congruity between text and obbligato is not always observed. An instance occurs in cantata No. 130, where Bach adapts the words of the tenor aria:

> Thou of angel hosts the leader,
> Prince of God's heroic band!

to a tuneful gavotte introduced by the traverso:

No historical incident supports such treatment of St. Michael![1]
We must conclude that Bach was either indifferent to the incongruity or anxious to use and hear an attractive tune. Did he write it with one by François Couperin in his mind?

We frequently observe Bach's liking for a pizzicato or staccato continuo in arias in which a traverso is employed. The acoustic qualities of the Leipzig churches may account for a direction not otherwise explicable. Examples are found in cantatas Nos. 78, 102, 123, *Tönet, ihr Pauken*, and also in No. 107, the *St. Matthew Passion*, the *Magnificat*, and *Easter Oratorio*.

It cannot be altogether fortuitous that these traverso-continuo *obbligati* fall chiefly in the last years of Bach's fertility, that is, in the period 1735–44. It would appear that he could in those years rely on professional players whose executive skill exceeded that of the amateur *studiosi* on whom formerly he was dependent. The inference is buttressed by the significant fact that in that period two of his players, Johann Friedrich Kirchhof and Johann Christian Oschatz, were engaged as flautists by the Leipzig Concertgesellschaft. Both were skilled oboists, whose membership of the Kunstgeiger and Stadtpfeifer corporations dated respectively from 1737 and 1738. Their talents, however, must have been recognized and employed before their formal admission to that body.[2] With some confidence we may associate one or both of them with these traverso solos.

Next to its employment with the continuo only, Bach's most frequent usage of the traverso in the arias adds to it both strings and continuo. The examples are found in cantatas Nos. 8, 26, 30, 34, 115, 117, 129, 157, 173, *Ehre sei Gott*, Mass in A major, *St. Matthew Passion*, *Vereinigte Zwietracht*, *Preise dein' Glücke*, *Non sa che sia dolore*, *Durchlaucht'ster Leopold*, *Die Freude reget sich*, and *Mer hahn en neue Oberkeet*. Bach achieves in these examples a variety of combinations, sometimes obeying the prompting of his text, often impelled by an imperative inclination to experiment with his palette. Most frequently the flutes are set against a background of tone produced by the full orchestra of strings—violin, viola, and continuo. A familiar example is the soprano aria ('Blute nur') in the *St. Matthew Passion*, where the two flutes independently stress the poignant lamentation of the text. In a

---

[1] It has been suggested that for St. Michael, 'a parfit gentil knight', the courtly Gavotte was not inappropriate!   [2] *Supra*, p. 14.

similar setting, but in another mood, the traverso embroiders the
bass aria in cantata No. 8 with florid, care-free trills of melody
befitting the words:

> A truce to my sorrow, so noisily storming!
> My Jesus doth call me and who would not go?

Again, in the alto aria of No. 30 the flute lilts a glad greeting above
the strings:

> Come, ye sinners, wayworn, tearful!
> Come rejoicing, be not fearful!
> 'Tis your Saviour, hear His cry!

Here the first violins throughout are 'col sordino', now 'alcuni',
now 'tutti', tempered for the flute with which they are largely
concordant. The other parts are marked 'pizzicato', the organ
'staccato'. The alto aria of cantata No. 34 is similarly planned.
The two *traversi* are generally at the octave with the first and second
violins, which are muted, as also are the violas. The melody bears
evident relationship to that of the alto aria of No. 30 and exhales
the same ecstasy of spiritual happiness:

> Rejoice, ye souls, God's vessels chosen,
> Whom He His dwelling deigns to make.

The mood is present again in the alto aria of No. 117:

> So, all my mortal life along,
> O God, I'll sing Thy praises.
> All men shall hear the happy song
> My glad heart to Thee raises.

where a single traverso flutes to the accompaniment of the strings.
In the secular cantatas named above Bach invariably employs this
combination, in the soprano arias of *Non sa che sia dolore*:

> Away, then, with dismal repining!

and

> Go thy way and grieving, leave us!

in the dance-like soprano aria of *Mer hahn en neue Oberkeet*:

> Klein-Zschocher must be
> E'er blithe and bonny!

in the alto aria of *Die Freude reget sich*:

> The good things that God showers on thee,
> The praise that greeteth thee to-day,
> To us as e'en our own are dear

and in the two soprano arias of *Durchlaucht'ster Leopold*, in both
of which the two flutes in unison are in unison with the first
violins. The three instruments are similarly associated in the tenor

aria of cantata No. 173, save in the third bar from the end, where the violins descend below the compass of the traverso in *d′*.

Instead of setting the traverso against an accompaniment of string tone, Bach sometimes associates with it a particular instrument of that family in a duet over a continuo accompaniment. The examples occur in cantatas Nos. 26, 115, 129, 157, and *Ehre sei Gott*. In three of them a violin is paired with the traverso. The two instruments contribute to Bach's realistic picture of 'ein rauschend Wasser' in the tenor aria of No. 26:

> As swift in channels waters whirl,
> So quickly days and hours are flying.

In the soprano aria of No. 129 they perform a duet of formal character—the text invites no other—an ascription of praise to the Third Person of the Trinity. The violin part is marked 'Solo'. We cannot decide whether the omission of that direction from the flute part indicates Bach's desire for it to be played *tutti*. In the violin part the restriction is intelligible, for two or three players normally occupied the desks of both firsts and seconds. But Bach was precariously supplied with flautists. Here its absence from the flute part may imply no more than that the direction was superfluous. Yet there are six cases in which the instruction 'Solo' is attached to the traverso part: in cantatas Nos. 26, 96, 100, 102, 114, and 123. All belong to the period in which, as has already been suggested, Bach could rely on professional players. In these instances, therefore, the direction 'Solo' may instruct his *studiosi* to be silent. Still, we may not conclude that, when the direction is absent, more than one player was available.

In the bass aria of No. 157 the traverso is again paired with a violin. The movement breathes the yearning happiness which Bach always found in the contemplation of death:

> Ah yes! I hold to Jesus firmly
> While faring on my homeward way.
> For at the Lamb's high feast awaits me
> A glorious crown of purest ray.

The rhythmic continuo speaks the word 'feste' (firmly) in every bar, and above it, in one of Bach's characteristic 'joy' rhythms, the flute and violin voice the happy assurance of the text.

The remaining instances in this category—cantata No. 115 and *Ehre sei Gott*—substitute a violoncello for the violin as the traverso's associate. In the opening alto aria of the Christmas *Ehre sei Gott*, in which two flutes discourse, the violoncello has an independent and significant part. The words address the cradled Jesus:

Precious gift beyond compare,
Come forth from Thy cradle lowly,
Take my heart and make it holy,
Meet for Thee, a dwelling fair!

To the movement, a tender lullaby, the violoncello contributes a persistently rocking figure of patent meaning. In the soprano aria of No. 115 the traverso is paired with a violoncello piccolo over a staccato continuo. The movement bears one of Bach's infrequent markings, 'Molto Adagio':

Ever trustful raise your prayer
In the night's long vigil!

Flute and violoncello converse in a duet of intimate emotion, to which the latter instrument adds, in M. Pirro's words,[1] the 'verdeur suave d'une voix jeune'.

A curious device is used in the soprano arias of the Mass in A and *Preise dein' Glücke*, of which the Ascension Oratorio (cantata No. 11) affords a third example. Bach dispenses in all three with the normal continuo and substitutes the violins and violas in unison. In the aria of the Mass the two flutes discourse above the 'Violini

e Viola all'unisono', whose part, however, falls to and

whose staccato crotchets, rising in steady and recurring progressions, contribute a detail to a picture vivid in Bach's mind. The words are the 'Qui tollis' of the *Gloria in excelsis*, the Church's petition to Christ the Mediator 'seated at the right hand of God'. By withdrawing the normal continuo and building on a higher foundation Bach reaches up to the supreme altitude where 'the one, full, perfect and sufficient sacrifice, oblation and satisfaction for the sins of the whole world' is offered and renewed. That this is the meaning of the device is evident from the Ascension Oratorio aria.[2] But the interpretation is not applicable to the third example —the soprano aria 'Durch die von Eifer entflammeten Waffen' in *Preise dein' Glücke*. Here also the *traversi* are accompanied by the 'Violini e Violetta' in unison. But the mundane words merely offer fulsome adulation to Augustus III. The incongruity is explicable. The music is borrowed from the *Christmas Oratorio*, where the aria is set in F sharp minor for a bass voice. In the secular cantata a soprano sings it in B minor, to an accompaniment pitched a fourth higher. It was not practicable to transpose the normal continuo to the higher key, and therefore Bach substituted

[1] P. 223. 'The fragrance and freshness of a youthful voice.'
[2] See *infra*, p. 90.

the 'Violini e Violetta'. It is worth observing that all three examples of this device fall round the year 1734.

The remaining example in the traverso—strings—continuo category occurs in the alto aria of *Vereinigte Zwietracht*. Here the two *traversi* have independent parts above a freely moving continuo, between which and themselves the first and second violins and violas, in unison and 'piano sempre', execute a persistent rhythmic figure:

$$\frac{3}{4}\ \text{♩·}\ \ \overline{♫♩·}\ \overline{♩♩·}\ \overline{♩}\ |\ \overline{♩·}\ \overline{♩♩·}\ \overline{♩♩·}\ \overline{♩}\ |\ ♩$$

It is not melodic, but alters its pitch to accord with the other parts. Its significance is revealed in the text:

> Should not this august occasion
> Into marble form be hewn?

Bach's inveterate disposition to make a picture employs the rhythmic figure to suggest the sculptor's mallet and chisel!

Having regard to the close association of the two instruments in the concerted choruses, it is curious to remark the comparative infrequency of arias in which the traverso and oboe are brought together. They are so associated in only sixteen scores—cantatas Nos. 11, 55, 125, 145, 146, 151, 181, 189, in both of the *Passions*, *Christmas Oratorio* (Part II), *Trauer-Ode*, and in the secular cantatas: *Phoebus und Pan*, *Ich bin in mir vergnügt*, *Angenehmes Wiederau*, and *O holder Tag*. They cover the whole span of Bàch's Leipzig Cantorate, but occur comparatively infrequently in the regular cantatas of the normal ecclesiastical year. These facts point, as before, to the occasional lack of competent players, though at special seasons Bach was not similarly impeded; for instance, in the second Part of the *Christmas Oratorio* he could muster four oboists and two flute players, and in the *St. Matthew Passion* could employ, or at least score for, four flutes and as many oboes.

Bach shows marked preference for the oboe d'amore in the arias associated with a traverso, and the combination serves voices of all registers, especially the soprano. It assumes various forms, and exhibits his inexhaustible curiosity in experiment. In the soprano aria of No. 146:

> Now see my teardrops falling
> From eyes with weeping sore!

the plaintive flute obbligato is accompanied by two *oboi d'amore*[1]

---

[1] Cf. the soprano aria 'Zerfliesse, mein Herze', in the *St. John Passion*, where *oboi da caccia* are associated with the *traversi* in a similar text.

and continuo. In the soprano aria of the Christmas anthem
(No. 151), accompanied by strings and continuo, an oboe d'amore
is in unison with the first violin, whose soothing tones complete
the lullaby for the infant Jesus:

> Comfort sweet! Lord Jesus comes
> In our flesh to dwell among us.

The traverso here pours forth a flood of loving emotion which
the picture of the Manger at Bethlehem always evoked from Bach.
The work belongs evidently to the period (1735–40) in which
he could rely on a competent flautist. In the tenor aria of the
Trauer-Ode the traverso is scored with an oboe d'amore, violins,
two gambas, two lutes, and continuo. The *Ode* was composed for
the service held in the Paulinerkirche in memory of the Electress-
Queen, and Bach's choice of instruments was guided by his desire
to make the most decorous and restrained gesture of homage to
a personality deeply loved.[1] Here the traverso, standing out over
a sedate accompaniment, sheds the kindly glance an earlier movement had invited:

> Turn, Princess, turn an earthward glance
> From Salem's star-bespangled haven,
> To see our scalding tears fast falling
> Amid thy funeral circumstance!

Again, in the soprano aria of *Ich bin in mir vergnügt*:

> Heavenly gift, O sweet content!

the traverso is obbligato in an accompaniment of strings and
oboes, the latter in unison with the violins. The first violins and
first oboe not infrequently reinforce its theme, but the traverso
is the principal, and 'Himmlische Vergnügsamkeit' the evident
key to its song. In the soprano aria of Part II of the *St. Matthew
Passion* its obbligato exhales the very essence of hopeless despair:

> For love of me my Saviour's dying

and its poignancy is increased by the accompaniment of two *oboi
da caccia* without continuo.

The familiar alto aria that opens Part II of the *St. Matthew
Passion* exhibits the traverso in an unusually intimate association
with an oboe d'amore. The two are in unison in the expressive
obbligato which so graphically pictures Zion's eager and baffled
search for the Saviour. They are associated also in the bass aria
of *Phoebus und Pan*, where, against a background of muted strings,

---

[1] As the ceremony was a University function, however, Bach may have been
restricted to instruments available among the *studiosi*.

their melodious obbligato expresses the word 'Verlangen' in every bar:

> With fond *longing*, see, I kiss thy cheek so tender.

In the concluding soprano aria of *O holder Tag* the two instruments, largely in unison, deliciously supplement each other in a *vivace* movement very apt to the mood of this wedding cantata:

> Joy be yours, happy lovers!
> Happy lovers, joy to you!

In four arias the traverso shares the obbligato with another instrument in a quasi duet in which it generally has the upper part. In No. 11 (*Ascension Oratorio*; soprano aria) two flutes (in unison) are paired with the first oboe over a continuo provided only by the violins and viola in unison. The movement has already been referred to.[1] The high-pitched continuo was certainly suggested by the text, which pictures the Saviour, heavenward rising, bestowing a last look of love on his faithful below. The tender, melodious obbligato-duet seems to float on the upper air, as though it were indeed the 'Gnaden-Blicke' (loving glance) of which the text speaks:

> Jesu, Thy last glance, so loving,
> Can I still in fancy see.

In the opening tenor aria of No. 55 the traverso is paired with an oboe d'amore over a string accompaniment, from which the viola is omitted. Here the obbligato-duet is flagrantly incongruous with the words:

> Poor wretched man, a slave of sin,
> Before God's judgement-seat appearing,
> With dreadful awe and fearful trembling;
> Unjust, how can I justice win?

To a lilting gavotte, and not 'mit Furcht und Zittern' (with awe and trembling), the traverso and its partner conduct the sin-stricken soul on its fearful journey. In the alto aria of No. 125 the same instruments provide an obbligato over an irregular *basso ostinato* marked 'tutto ligato'; they express the wistful longing of the text:

> Toward Thee, my Saviour, am I gazing
> With eyes that see the coming gloom.

In another mood is the bass aria of No. 145. Generously scored for the Easter festival—tromba, traverso, two *oboi d'amore*, two violins (but again no violas), and continuo—the instruments are grouped in pairs, the two oboes together, the two violins together,

---

[1] *Supra*, p. 87.

and the traverso with the tromba, with which it asserts an equality, soaring above it in its highest compass. In the vigorous bass aria 'Mighty Lord and King supernal' in Part I of the *Christmas Oratorio* they are again in comradeship.

The other examples in this category show the traverso less prominent in the aria score. In the bass aria of No. 181 it merely adds its note to a recurring and significant theme which it shares with an oboe and the first violins. The text was suggested by the Gospel for Sexagesima:

> Shallow natures, flighty creatures,
> Rob the soil of seeds that fall.

Bach marks the movement 'Vivace', the continuo 'staccato', above which the flute, oboe, and first violin announce vigorously a theme repeatedly stated but never developed, to which the first line of the aria is set—'Leichtgesinnte Flattergeister'. Schweitzer's[1] interpretation is not extravagant: 'We instinctively see a swarm of crows descending upon a field with beating wings and wide-stretched feet', an etching made more vivid by the downward flights of the continuo. In the two tenor arias of the doubtfully authentic No. 189 the flute is merely the discant in a quartet (flute, oboe, violin, continuo) accompanying the voice. In the exquisite alto aria 'Slumber, my dear one' of the *Christmas Oratorio*, Part II, however, it has a part effective, though auxiliary. The score also includes strings, two *oboi d'amore*, two *oboi da caccia*, and continuo. Excepting a few bars in the second part of the aria, the *oboi d'amore* and first violin have the melody of the accompaniment in unison. The second violin, viola, and *oboi da caccia* fill in the harmony above the continuo. The flute doubles the voice part at the octave. The effect of this crooning lullaby is inexpressibly tender.

The duets in which the traverso is scored do not indicate new varieties of treatment. Sometimes it is paired with an oboe d'amore in a duet-obbligato over a continuo, as in cantatas No. 9 and No. 99; or with an oboe da caccia to similar accompaniment, as in No. 101. With an oboe, violin, and continuo it supports the voices in No. 157, or supplements the strings in the melodious minuet-duets of No. 173 and *Durchlaucht'ster Leopold*, and in No. 184. In No. 164 a paucity of dependable players must explain the overloaded obbligato of the soprano-bass duet, in which the flutes, oboes, and violins are in unison over a continuo. Again in the soprano-bass duet of No. 192 and the 'Et misericordia' of the *Magnificat* (alto-tenor) the traverso is in unison with an oboe and

[1] Vol. ii, p. 199.

violin, or with violins alone. Concisely, it is only independent and individual in the soprano-tenor duet of No. 191, the 'Domine Deus' (soprano-tenor) of the *Hohe Messe*, and the alto-tenor duet of *Aeolus*.

In his recitatives Bach's infrequent use of the traverso is adventurous, sometimes surprising. In a few cases a couple of flutes play over a continuo sustained or detached notes, such as elsewhere he writes for strings in similar movements: for instance, in the brief bass and alto recits. of the *Ascension Oratorio* (cantata No. 11); in the bass and alto recits. of Part III of the *Christmas Oratorio*; in the soprano-bass recit. (No. 10) of *Aeolus*; in the bass recit. (No. 8) of *Tönet, ihr Pauken*, in which two oboes also are employed; and in the bass recit. of the *Trauer-Ode*, which is similarly scored. A less normal example of this type is afforded in the bass recit. (No. 65) of the *St. Matthew Passion*. Here the two *traversi* and continuo sound short staccato notes to the sustained chords of the gamba.

Bach occasionally embellishes his recitatives with a flute duet over a continuo, and makes it interpretative of the text. (Those it thus embellishes are lyrical, never Biblical.) The most familiar example is the alto recit. (No. 9) 'Du liebster Heiland' of the *St. Matthew Passion*, in which the flutes' obbligato expresses the most poignant melancholy. Another example is in cantata No. 184. Its text being based on the Gospel of Christ the Good Shepherd, the opening tenor recit. apostrophizes the 'longed-for, joyous Light' vouchsafed to man 'through Christ our Lord and Shepherd'. Schweitzer[1] interprets the phrases uttered by the two flutes in thirds as 'the flute-call of the shepherd . . . sounded brokenly, as if [he] were walking on distant heights, and his melody floated down only in fragments'. One supposes them rather inspired by the word 'Freuden*licht*', and that, appropriately in this Whitsuntide anthem, they represent the Pentecostal tongues of flickering flame. A third example of similar usage is provided by the soprano recit. 'Ja, ja! Gott ist uns noch' in *Preise dein' Glücke*. 'Doth not the Baltic', the singer challenges, 'where Vistula her waters pours, own Augustus' sway?' The two flutes speak for the river—'der Weichsel Mund'—in detached and rippling wavelets of homage. In the soprano recit. of the wedding cantata *Dem Gerechten muss das Licht* (No. 195) the flute part again has pictorial significance. 'The nuptial knot is tied,' declares the singer. Thereon the flutes, over *oboi d'amore*, in a series of scales, ascending and descending, weave the word 'knüpfet', and almost boisterously 'tie' or 'bind'

[1] Vol. ii, p. 163.

the contract. No particular significance attaches to the smoothly
flowing duet-obbligato which the traverso and oboe d'amore contribute to the soprano recit. (No. 9) of *O holder Tag*.

In two cases the flutes take part in a recitative elaborately scored.
In the alto recit. of the *Trauer-Ode* their repeated high-pitched
semiquavers sound the harmonics of the tolling bells—'The bells'
repeated thrilling sound the anguish of all hearts recordeth, and
in our mourning souls vibrateth'. In the bass recit. (No. 2) of
Aeolus they augment the colossal clash of elements the angry
potentate commands.

Bach's earliest associations were with the flûte douce, and to the
end he used it to express his most intimate moods. But, from his
usage of it, he evidently admired the qualities of the traverso, and,
on the ground of general utility, even preferred it. As he himself
wrote in 1730,[1] 'The present *status musices* is quite different from
what it was'. The sweeter, less noisy flute was no longer fitted to
the uses the newer technique required it to fulfil. For, in the
eighteenth century, music enlarged its platform from the chamber
to the concert-room and opera-house. The gentle-toned instruments of an earlier age ceased to be heard, and the traverso came at
length into its kingdom. Leipzig, perhaps more than any other
community in that period, was soundly educated by Bach to
appraise its qualities.

[1] Terry, p. 203.

CHAPTER V

THE OBOES AND BASSOON

EXCEPTING the flutes, the wood-wind instruments of Bach's orchestra trace their ancestry to the 'Bombart' or 'Pommer' family, known to the French, writes Praetorius,[1] as the 'Houtbois', to the English as 'Hoboy', and their discants as 'Schalmei' (*anglice* Shawm). He names six members:

(1) Klein Schalmei,   (4) Tenor Pommer, or Basset,
(2) Discant Schalmei,   (5) Bass Pommer,
(3) Alt Pommer,   (6) Gross Doppel Quint-Pommer.[2]

They differed in size, from the smallest, some eighteen inches long, to the largest, a monster nearly ten feet in length. But uniformly they were blown through a double reed, and, pierced with six finger holes, sounded respectively as their lowest notes:

Keys permitted all but Nos. 1 and 2, lengthened, to extend their compass downwards, No. 6 (4 keys) to 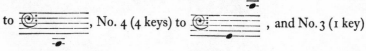, No. 5 (4 keys) to , No. 4 (4 keys) to , and No. 3 (1 key) to . In the course of the seventeenth century the names

'Pommer' and 'Schalmei' were superseded by the one the instrument has since retained. In France, where they were extensively used, Nos. 1–4 were distinguished as 'haulx bois' or 'hautbois', and their larger relatives (Nos. 5 and 6) as 'gros bois'. The distinction achieved general currency, and thus the 'hautbois' of France became the 'oboe' of Germany, the 'hautboy' or 'hoboy' of England, and the 'oboè' of Italy. In the same period, moreover, two of the hautbois (Nos. 1 and 4) fell into disuse, leaving the discant (No. 2) and alto (No. 3) to become the ordinary oboe and oboe

[1] Chap. X.
[2] Nos. 1–5 are illustrated on his Plate XI at p. 96; No. 6 on his Plate VI at p. 160.

d'amore of Bach's orchestra, retaining their traditional pitches of d' and a. The alto instrument also survived as the oboe da caccia, while the two 'gros bois' became the fagotto and contra-fagotto of modern usage.

The Oboe

In the form in which Bach used it, the oboe made its début at the production of Robert Cambert's *Pomone* in the Paris Salle du Jeu de Paume de la Bouteille on 19 March 1671. Sounding d' when its six finger-holes were closed, it was equipped[1] with two keys for c' and $d\sharp'$. Its tube being conical, from the reed downwards, the player could overblow the octave in a compass of fifteen notes (c'–d'''), and, excepting $d\sharp'$, whose small key was sometimes duplicated to suit right and left-handed players, could obtain the chromatic scale by fork-fingering and lipping the reed for the octave. The production of semitones was eased by the duplication of the lowest of the upper set of three finger-holes, two small ones side by side displacing the single larger one. By closing one of them $g\sharp'$ was obtained, by closing both, $g\natural'$. But the $g\sharp'$ thus produced was not in perfect intonation, and $a\sharp'$, got by fork-fingering, was as unsatisfactory. Hence, in 1727, four years after Bach's appointment to the Leipzig Thomasschule, Gerhard Hoffmann,[2] later Bürgermeister of Rastenberg, added keys for those two notes. Bach must have been acquainted with the innovation; for Hoffmann entered ducal service at Weimar a few months after he abandoned it, and left in 1728 on his appointment as 'Cämmerer' at Rastenberg, a town not far from Cöthen. Hoffmann's keys, however, were not approved by makers till after Bach's death: it is reasonably certain that his players were at no time provided with them.

Somewhat earlier than Hoffmann's innovation, the flautist Quantz is credited with the addition of a long key for $c\sharp'$. But contemporary opinion regarded it with little favour, and, since fork-fingering was impracticable in that position, players were restricted to the only method by which the note could be sounded. By partially depressing the $c\natural'$ key the d' hole was 'shaded' sufficiently to flatten it. Got by this method, however, the note was risky and impracticable save as a passing-note. Bach's scores abundantly disclose his disinclination to use it. It occurs in only thirty-four cantatas—Nos. 2, 17, 24, 25, 28, 29, 30, 31, 34, 35, 43, 44, 45, 50, 57, 68, 70, 86, 94, 104, 110, 113, 128, 129, 136, 148, 149, 152, 157, 169, 171,

---

[1] Certainly before 1688, when an English drawing of a 'French Hoboy' reveals them. Cf. *Encyc. Brit.* (11th edn.), xix. 951.
[2] Gerber, i. 654, gives a considerable account of Hoffmann.

174, 185, and 193. Most often the note is a rapid quaver or semi-quaver, generally occurs in the second oboe part, and only twice (cantatas Nos. 24 (Coro, No. 3), and 157 (Duetto, No. 1)) is a semibreve. In the larger concerted works it occurs with equal rarity—in Parts I and VI of the *Christmas Oratorio*, three move-ments of the *St. Matthew Passion*, two choruses of the *St. John Passion*, the 'Credo' and final chorus of the *Hohe Messe*, the *Magnificat*, the Masses in G major and G minor, four secular Cantatas (*Aeolus, Hercules*; *Tönet, ihr Pauken*; *Preise dein' Glücke*), and the first Ouverture in D. But this analysis does not fully reveal Bach's aversion. Unsatisfactory and difficult on the ordinary instru-ment, the note could be got with ease and accuracy as the *e'* and *d♯'* of the low A and B flat oboes. In twenty-three of the 34 cantatas[1] one or other of them was used. There remain only eleven in which Bach adventured the note on the ordinary oboe, never frequently, never emphatically, and sometimes, one supposes, absent-mindedly.

Oboe, 18th cent., length 57 cm.

Bach's usage of the oboe extended over nearly half a century, from the cantatas composed at Mühlhausen to those of his ripest maturity at Leipzig. Most frequently he gives the instrument its French name 'hautbois'. In his Mühlhausen scores, however, he prescribes '2 Obboe' (No. 71), and 'una Oboe' (No. 131). At Weimar and Cöthen he usually adopted the French form, and at Leipzig employed it with rare exceptions, as in cantata No.

95 ('Oboe ordinaria'), the *Hohe Messe* ('3 Oboi'), and *St. John Passion* ('2 Oboe'). Table X establishes his preferential use of the ordinary C oboe: the number of scores in which the compass falls below *c'* is small. In these exceptional cases he either used a B flat oboe, a whole tone below the ordinary instrument, of which specimens are extant, or an alto A oboe, of the same pitch and compass as the oboe d'amore, but with an open bell instead of the closed 'Liebesfuss' of that instrument. At Mühlhausen he seems to have used the C instrument exclusively, and at Weimar generally the oboe in B flat. At Cöthen and thenceforward his use of the C oboe is almost regular. He regarded *c'–d''''*—two octaves and a note—as its normal compass, agreeing therein with J. G. Walther (1732) and Diderot and d'Alembert (1751). In three cases, however,

[1] See Table X.

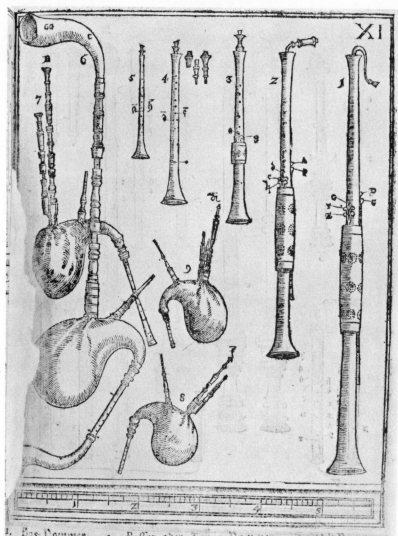

OBOES AND BASSOONS
(*Praetorius*)

he carries it actually to *e'''* (cantatas Nos. 43, 128, 192)! They are all dated *c.* 1735 and probably indicate the services of a particularly expert performer. With the other two instruments he was less exacting, though he carries the B flat oboe to *d'''* in the opening choruses of cantatas Nos. 10 and 35, and the A oboe to *c♯'''* in the first chorus of No. 17.

Normally Bach sets the oboe in the treble G clef. In cantata No. 132, however, written for the Weimar ducal chapel, he adopts an unusual device. The work is in A major, and the oboe part is thus written:

Using the second signature, the player put his oboe at high Cammerton in accord with the organ at Cornett-Ton, a minor third higher. Ordinary transpositions of the oboe part, for the same purpose, occur in cantatas Nos. 31 and 152, both of which were written for the Weimar chapel. At Leipzig, during the Cantorate of Bach's predecessor Kuhnau, the flutes and oboes were at low Cammerton pitch, a semitone below high Cammerton. In his early Leipzig cantata No. 194 Bach was similarly served;[1] otherwise his wood-wind instruments there were at high Cammerton.

Table X appears to indicate an abnormal compass in a number of scores in which the oboe part falls below the range even of the alto instrument. But the table records the extreme range of the instrument in the entire work, and not necessarily its compass in a particular movement. In cantata No. 21, for instance, the compass is given as *b♭–d'''*. But the player did not accomplish this upon one instrument exclusively; for the single movement in which his part soared to *d'''* he used the ordinary oboe, and for the rest the oboe in B flat. Bach, however, generally avoided a duplication of instruments. He was careful to write in keys which offered no complications. The three sharps' signature in cantatas Nos. 17, 86, 132, 136, 185, *Aeolus*, and *Preise dein' Glücke* is quite abnormal. A four sharps' signature appears only in cantata No. 45. Three flats are rare (cantatas Nos. 12, 47, 48, 102, 105, 140, 159, *Mein Herze schwimmt im Blut*, and the Mass in G minor).[2] As a general rule, Bach writes for the oboe in C, G, D, F, and B flat, the signature of two flats far outnumbering all others. Moreover, though not only on this account, he avoids changes of tonality in the course of the work, particularly those of a nature to complicate

[1] Cf. Spitta, ii. 324, 677. [2] Also in the last chorus of both *Passions*.

the task of his players. When they do occur, the modulation is of the simplest. Thus, in general, an initial flat signature indicated a B flat oboe for the entire work, and one in sharps invited the ordinary instrument in C. The players' preferences would guide their selection, but cases in which a single instrument would not suffice for the entire work are few in number, namely:

Work	Oboe in		
	C	B	A
Cantata No. 21	Movement No. 11	Movements Nos. 1–3, 6, 9	..
,, 94	,, 1	.. ..	Movement No. 3
,, 192	,, 1, 2	.. ..	,, 3
,, 193	Movement Nos. 1, 3, 7	.. ..	,, 5
Christmas Oratorio, Pt. I	Movement No. 1	.. ..	,, 7
Hohe Messe	Generally	.. ..	,, 13
Aeolus	Movements Nos. 1, 2, 15	.. ..	,, 3

From its introduction into the Opera orchestra, onwards to the period when it asserted an individuality of its own in the classical Symphony, the oboe, like the violin, was used in pairs, and generally as a ripieno instrument in unison with the violins. Bach observed both conventions. His fidelity to the latter explains the fact that in ten scores the oboe, and especially the second oboe, is invited to descend to *g*, the lowest note of the violin register:

Cantata	Movement	Instrument	Compass
No. 2	5. Aria	Ob. I, II	*g–d'''*; *g–d'''*
,, 16	1. Coro	,, II	*g–d''*
,, 29	1. Sinfonia	,, I, II	*g–c'''*; *g–a''*
,, 43	1. Coro	,, I, II	*g–e'''*; *g–d'''*
,, 44	6. Aria	,, II	*g–a''*
,, 70	8. Aria	,, I	*g–b''*
,, 76	1. Coro	,, II	*g–b''*
,, 105	1. Coro	,, II	*g–f''*
,, 169	1. Coro	,, II	*g♯–a''*
Ich bin in mir vergnügt	8. Aria	,, I, II	*g–d'''*; *g–b♭''*

These instances cover the whole period of Bach's activity. But his players were certainly never provided with an instrument capable of sounding *g*, except the taille, whose use here is not in question. The note's presence in these scores is due to the fact that always when it occurs the oboes are in unison with the violins. Writing out their respective parts, Bach, or his copyist, failed to remark that the strings were carrying the oboes out of their depth, till the work was rehearsed and the error was corrected verbally. Cantata No. 169, however, affords an instance of miscorrection. Bach lets the second oboe descend to *g♯* in a passage otherwise unisonous with the second violins. Remarking the oboe's inability, he inadvertently takes the second violins up to *e'*, leaving the oboe part uncorrected:

We might conclude that the Bachgesellschaft edition is in error, did not the original score and parts confirm its accuracy.

Though eighteenth-century custom favoured the use of the oboe in pairs, Praetorius[1] had remarked its agreeableness when three were employed ('drey und drey zusammen'). Bach, but infrequently, endorsed the opinion. His memorandum to the Leipzig Council in August 1730[2] complains that no player was available for the '3 Hautbois oder Taille'. And though the vacancy caused by Meyer's departure[3] was soon filled, Bach must often have been similarly handicapped; for more than two oboes are prescribed only in thirty-two cantata scores, the 'Sanctus' of the *Hohe Messe*, one secular cantata, and three orchestral pieces.[4] We might suppose that he deemed a trio or quartet of oboes inappropriate in any but festal scores but for the fact that over half the cantatas in which they appear are of a ferial character. Certainly the only one (No. 31) in which he employs four oboes is for a festal season, and three are in the scores of all those for Michaelmas. But, in general, the chief consideration that weighed with him was the availability of competent players. For his third oboe he uses, in place of the taille, an oboe da caccia in six cantatas (Nos. 6, 74, 87, 110, 128, 176), the two instruments being identical in pitch (*f–g''*). The taille, however, was a straight-tubed tenor with an open bell, while the oboe da caccia was curved, and, at a later period, had a closed bell similar to that of the cor anglais. Its employment in the six cantatas was evidently due to circumstances of the moment, for four of them (Nos. 74, 87, 128, 176) were performed consecutively (May 15, 19, 29, and June 5) in 1735.[5]

The association of oboes and taille accorded with Praetorius's

---

[1] P. 37. [2] Cf. Terry, p. 202. [3] *Supra*, p. 14. [4] See Table X.
[5] Abnormal low notes in cantatas Nos. 19, 31, 35, 56, 122, 186, are in association with the viola. A Basset oboe is hardly to be inferred there.

'ander [Art] zum Tenor und Alt'. His 'Art zum Bass' is less frequently illustrated in Bach's association of oboes and bassoon. The partnership of the latter exclusively with the ordinary oboe is found in only twelve scores.[1] They exhibit Bach's practice at Mühlhausen, Weimar, and Cöthen. In the later of his Leipzig periods he seems to have been less inclined to treat the oboe-bassoon combination as an integral and separate section of the orchestral body.

The oboe had served a military apprenticeship before its admission to churches and concert-rooms. Military bandsmen in Germany were known as 'Oboisten'; for instance, Bach's younger brother Johann Jakob, whom he designates by this title in the *Ursprung*.[2] In the English Guards the oboe displaced the fife early in the eighteenth century, and its participation in church music apparently dates from the same terminus. For, of Bach's immediate predecessors, only Kuhnau, the most recent, employed it.[3] It is therefore curious that Bach should have seldom put it to orchestral use. It is found in the first and second Brandenburg Concertos, the Violin Concerto (Sinfonia) in D major, and three *Ouvertures*. In the first Brandenburg Concerto a quartet of oboes and bassoon performs in jovial antiphony with the strings. In the second Brandenburg Concerto the single oboe is for the most part ripieno in the first movement, but in the *Andante* and *Allegro assai* plays on equal terms with the other obbligato instruments —flute, violin, and tromba. In the Concerto (or Sinfonia) in D major the two oboes link the strings and 'choir' of drums and trumpets, now supporting the violin concertante, now adding individual touches to the string accompaniment, now swelling the volume of the *tutti* passages. In the Ouverture in C they are treated in another manner. Associated with the bassoon, they form a body to which obbligato passages marked 'Trio' are frequently assigned in the opening movement. As a trio they are scored in the second Gavotte, second Bourrée, second Passepied, and (excepting the second Bourrée) always to the accompaniment of the strings. Otherwise the two oboes and bassoon double the first violin and continuo. In the more familiar Ouverture in D Bach's subservience to tradition is equally apparent. Except in the middle (fugal) section of the opening movement (in which the two oboes are in unison generally with the two violins), in the *tutti* passages, in those marked *piano* to which they make independent contribution, and in the second Gavotte, where also they unite with the two violins, the oboes throughout are in unison with the

[1] See Table X.   [2] Cf. Terry (3).   [3] Schering, p. 151.

first violin, whose melody they uphold against the voluble 'choir' of drums and trumpets. In the second Ouverture in D, as in the Sinfonia in D, Bach scores for a quartet of oboes and bassoon, and, as in the Sinfonia, gives it considerable individuality and independence, though, for a considerable part of every movement, the four instruments merely double the strings and continuo. But, beyond any other of the *Ouvertures*, Bach here frees himself from the restricting traditions which tied the oboe to the violin, making his quartet of *haut-* and *gros-bois* an equal partner of the 'choirs' of trumpets and strings above and below it. It is probable that the two Ouvertures in D are separated from the one in C by a considerable interval of years. The more modest score of the latter refers it to the Cöthen period. Dörffel associates the two in D with Bach's conductorship of his Leipzig Collegium Musicum. As probably they were written for the Dresden Hofcapelle, to which Bach was admitted as 'Compositeur' in 1736. (He had particularly offered his talents in orchestral music.[1]) Perhaps he may also have written for Dresden the Oboe Concerto attributed to him in Breitkopf's New Year Catalogue for 1764.[2] Since the work is there advertised as 'I', he would seem to have composed others. Handel expressed himself in that form in six still extant. Bach's Concertos have not survived.

No other wind instrument had such constant and varied usage by Bach as the oboe. It is absent from only sixty-two of the extant 198 church cantatas. Of those composed at Leipzig only forty-nine are without it. But as thirty-seven of the number are scored for oboe d'amore or oboe da caccia, the number of oboe-less Leipzig cantatas is actually twelve—Nos. 4, 51, 53, 54, 90, 143, 153, 165, 172, 173, 175, 184. Bach's Leipzig audience was consistently educated to regard the oboe as a natural participant in church music and to appreciate his use of it. It is found almost invariably in the choruses of the cantatas in which it is scored, sustains the *cantus* in their concluding Chorals, and generally accompanies at least one aria, but is rarely found in recitatives or duets. Bach, in fact, esteemed it chiefly as a ripieno instrument. This is particularly evident in his larger scores. Out of twenty-one movements in which it participates in the three Oratorios, only two are arias, and in only one of the two it is 'Solo'. In the two *Passions* it is freely used in the choruses and Chorals, but in only one aria and one recitative. In the *Hohe Messe* and *Magnificat* it is heard only in the choruses.

Bach's restricted usage is explained by the quality of the

---

[1] Cf. Terry, p. 216.　　　　　　　　　　[2] Spitta, iii. 143 n.

instrument, of which Mersenne[1] had written in the previous century: 'It is suited to large functions . . . because it makes a big noise and fine harmony. Indeed, excepting the trumpet, its tone is louder and more violent than that of any other instrument.' Its quality is revealed in the four scores in which Bach prescribes all three varieties of oboe. In cantata No. 80 it is used in the opening chorus and soprano-bass duet only to make prominent the obbligato Choral melody. In No. 110, excepting the opening and closing chorus, it is admitted only to the bass aria, where it strengthens the strings to support the trumpet obbligato. In No. 128 it is excluded from all but the opening chorus and concluding Choral. In No. 147, as in No. 110, it occurs only in those movements in which the tromba is scored, and for the same purpose. Cantata No. 95 affords another illustration. The music, inspired by the thought of death, is of the tenderest texture. Bach therefore prescribes the oboe d'amore. But, at the point where the melody 'Mit Fried' und Freud' ich fahr' dahin' is introduced into the opening chorus, he marks the oboe parts 'Oboe ordinaria'. It is the only instance of his substitution of one kind of oboe for another in the same movement, and its significance is clear.

The rude sonority of the instrument is exemplified also in a number of arias which Bach scores for three oboes and continuo. They are found in cantatas Nos. 20, 26, 41, 52, 68, 91, 101, 148, and *Was mir behagt*. Their text (exc. No. 148) indicates an assertive, militant, sometimes truculent, mood, which a trio of oboes was qualified to interpret. In No. 20 (bass aria, No. 5) it maintains God's righteousness, and in No. 26 (bass aria, No. 4) expresses contempt of the world's treasure. In No. 41 (soprano aria, No. 2) it hails the New Year. In No. 52 (soprano aria, No. 5) and No. 68 (bass aria, No. 4) it is again defiant. In No. 91 (tenor aria, No. 3) it salutes the majesty of the infant Jesus. In No. 101 (bass aria, No. 4) it utters the harsh sentence of Divine wrath, and in *Was mir behagt* offers to the lord of Weissenfels a ceremonious flourish.

One cannot in the same manner interpret the few arias in which the oboe part is marked 'Solo'. The most familiar is the soprano 'Flösst, mein Heiland' in Part IV of the *Christmas Oratorio*:

> Tell me, Saviour, I entreat Thee,
> Need my soul show dread to meet Thee?
> Must it one day reckoning pay?
> 'Nay,' Thou answ'rest gently, 'Nay!'

Here Bach uses the oboe to produce the answering echo with which text and music make such play. In the alto aria of No. 22,

[1] Vol. v, p. 303.

again, his phrasing of its obbligato clearly illustrates the words '*ziehe* mich nach dir':

> Lord Jesus, *draw* me near to Thee!

But generally the texts of the arias in which the oboe has a solo obbligato do not invite pictorial treatment, and to that circumstance the oboe generally owed its selection.[1] In brief, Bach's oboe was not the plaintive, nervous voice of the modern orchestra, but an adaptable ripienist, convenient for yoking with instruments of every *timbre*, and even as a competitor with the trumpets and horns not despicable.

The Oboe da Caccia

More deliberately than the ordinary oboe, the alto Pommer developed into the oboe da caccia of Bach's usage. Longer than its fellow, it assumed, some time in the eighteenth century, a curved form for the player's convenience in handling, an innovation attributed to the brothers Giovanni and Giuseppe Ferlendis, Italian oboists in service at Salzburg.[2] The attribution, if correct, would imply that Bach was only familiar with the instrument in its earlier form, for Giuseppe Ferlendis was not born till five years after his death. In fact, the attribution is problematical. Moreover, the innovation was not found satisfactory; for, since it was impracticable to bore a curved tube, the latter needed to be made in two pieces, of maple or boxwood, glued and bound with leather. But, as the inside of the tube remained rough, preventing good tone, makers speedily reverted to the vertical Pommer form. Meanwhile, the curved instrument's supposed resemblance to an English hunting-horn is alleged to have given it the name 'cor anglais' (*corno inglese*, English horn) it has since retained. There is no record of such an instrument in English usage, and, more probably, 'cor anglais' is a corruption of 'cor anglé', a term appropriate to the early bent specimen. Bach never gives it that designation, though it was so called by Gluck for the performance of his *Alceste* at Vienna on 26 December 1767. It was unknown, however, or at least not in use, when Gluck's opera was repeated in Paris on 23 January 1776; oboes consequently were used. But it was merely a difference of nomenclature: for the Paris substitute was the alto Pommer or 'haute-contre de hautbois'.

Whether curved or straight, the oboe da caccia at Bach's disposal was uniform in compass and mechanism. Its practicable register (with the 'C' key) was f–g'', though he never takes it above $f\sharp''$,

---

[1] The respective movements are indicated in Table X.
[2] *Encyc. Brit.* (11th edn.), xix. 952. Mahillon, i. 231, places them at Strasbourg.

and most often is satisfied with *d″* or *e″*.[1] He uses it generally to the lowest extremity of its (keyed) compass, and in the tenor aria of cantata No. 186 twice takes it down to *d*, each time on an emphatic note. But this was beyond its ability.[2] As with the ordinary oboe, Bach uses the simpler keys: sharp signatures are rare, those of two and three flats the most numerous. The chromatic scale was obtained as on the ordinary oboe, and the key system was similar. By means of 'C' and 'D♯' keys—the latter generally doubled, as on the other instrument—*f* and *g♯* were got. As or the ordinary oboe, too, the bottommost of the three top finger-holes—'G' (*c′*)—was generally duplicated; and, for the same reason, the topmost of the lower three—'F♯' (*b*)—was frequently doubled also. The note *f♯* was as difficult to get as its counterpart *c♯′* on the ordinary instrument. Bach avoids it: it occurs only five times (cantatas No. 65, coro; No. 80, duetto (twice); No. 176, coro; and No. 186, aria), either as a quaver, semiquaver, or demisemi-quaver. The bell, as yet, was open, the tone penetrating, mellower and more plaintive than the ordinary oboe's.

The instrument is scored exclusively in Bach's Leipzig music. For, though found in cantata No. 147, performed at Weimar on the Fourth Sunday in Advent (20 December) 1716, the movement in which it occurs (the alto recitative in Part II) is a Leipzig addition to Salomo Franck's original text. It is scored for two *oboi da caccia* and continuo, but the parts exist on paper bearing the watermark of the period 1723–7, while the relative pages of the score indicate the year more precisely as 1727. The cantata thus revised can be attributed to the Feast of the Visitation (2 July 1727).

So, the *St. John Passion* exhibits Bach's earliest usage of this instrument. The work was performed on 26 March 1723, some weeks before his formal induction into the Cantorship, and in the main was composed at Cöthen in circumstances of unsettlement and anxiety. It is strange that he should have introduced himself in a score containing an instrument which till then he does not appear to have used. Nor did he employ it frequently thereafter. It is scored in the *St. Matthew Passion*, the second Part of the *Christmas Oratorio*, in twenty-two church cantatas, but nowhere in his secular music, vocal or instrumental. In his sacred music he introduces it into every variety of movement, and in the arias associates it with all four voices. He uses it infrequently in choruses, in which he often sets one or two ordinary oboes above it. He treats it as non-transposing, puts it in the alto clef in the key of the movement, and leaves the performer to find his notes in the scale of the instru-

---

[1] See Table XI.   [2] The Basset oboe descended to *c*.

ment (f–f''). This satisfied an experienced player. Another might prefer his part to indicate C-scale fingering, leaving the instrument automatically to make the transposition. In that event—since f was equivalent to c'—the part needed to be written a fifth higher than the required notes, and so under a signature of one sharp more or one flat less than the key of the movement. In a single movement (the alto-tenor duet of cantata No. 80) Bach adopts the latter method. Evidently he desired to give the player the utmost assistance, for the oboe part there not only transposes down a fifth, but is also in the soprano G clef. It is the only exception to his normal practice.

The texts with which Bach associates the oboe da caccia reveal its qualities. Vibrant and somewhat metallic, it was appropriate to express grief and tragedy. Its notes breathe the quintessence of anguish in the *St. Matthew Passion*, in which it has no voice until the dark agony of Gethsemane is unfolded (No. 25). It speaks again (Nos. 57 and 58) when Christ stands condemned before Pilate, again at the supreme moment on Calvary (Nos. 69 and 70), and for the last time at the Tomb (No. 75). In the earlier *St. John Passion* its use is more restricted, but its voice is the same. Bach withholds it almost till the end, when the Victim hangs lifeless on the Cross (Nos. 62 and 63). The instrument can also express the emotion of adoration, as in the *Christmas Oratorio*. How tender and serene is the pastoral scene it helps to sketch in the opening Sinfonia of Part II! And what deep emotion underlies the alto's cradle-song (No. 10)!

> Slumber, my dear one, and take Thy repose!
> Soon Thou'lt awaken, new joy to earth bringing.
> Lulled on my breast
> Find comfort and rest
> While to Thee our hearts are singing.

It is significant, too, that the aria texts with which Bach associates it seem, with the rarest exceptions, to come direct from his own devout lips, expressing his unswerving faith and spiritual exaltation. For example, in cantata No. 1:

> With longing and rapture my spirit is yearning,
> With fervour is burning
> To taste here, a mortal, love's heavenly feast.

And in cantata No. 13 (with the addition of two flutes):

> Lord, my weeping, tears, and sighing
> Melt my heart with aching care.
> Ah, dear God, in pity spare!
> Save me, hopeless, doomed, and dying!

Or in cantata No. 16:

> O blessèd Jesu, Thou alone
> My heart's fond treasure art, mine own!

In cantata No. 74:

> Come, come, my heart is open to Thee,
> Thy dwelling-place, Lord, of it make!

And in cantata No. 87:

> Forgive, O Father, our offence!
> Have patience still, nor drive us hence,
> As for Thy grace we pray Thee.

Again, in cantata No. 177:

> I pray Thee, from my deepest heart,
> My foes be all forgiven!
> Lord, bid, this hour, my sins depart,
> And grant me rest in heaven!

In cantata No. 179:

> Sin afflicts me grievously,
> Poison rankles in my being.
> Help me, Jesus, God's dear Lamb,
> Lest in shame to death I come!

And, once more, in cantata No. 186:

> My Saviour worketh only
> In deeds of love and mercy.

Even in arias in which the instrument is set in a larger score it appears to owe its inclusion to the same characteristic in the text. For instance, in cantata No. 65:

> Take me, Saviour, for Thine own!
> See, my heart is laid before Thee!
> All I have is Thine alone,
> Every thought and deed adore Thee.

Again, in cantata No. 74:

> From hell's dreadful slavery
> There's naught can protect me
> But Jesu's dear care.
> His Anguish and Passion
> Have won me salvation:
> Hell's fury I dare!

In cantata No. 180:

> Sun of heaven, shine upon me,
> Thou Who all my being art!

And in cantata No. 183:

> Blessèd Spirit, Comfort rare,
> Guide me ever, lest I err
> And mar my wandering way!

The infrequent Chorals in which the instrument is scored have the same note of personal feeling. Its dark tone explains its use in cantata No. 6, whose Easter text is based on the evening walk to Emmaus, and in cantata No. 87, where its colour appropriately suggests the 'gloom' of which the alto aria (No. 3) sings. In cantata No. 46 Bach secures an appropriate pastoral atmosphere for the alto aria, in which the thought of Christ as the Good Shepherd is uppermost, by giving the accompaniment to two flutes and two *oboi da caccia*; the latter are in unison and serve as a continuo. They are used in the same manner, but with different purpose and effect, in the poignant soprano aria (No. 58) of the *St. Matthew Passion*:

> For love of man the Saviour dieth,
> Who knoweth naught of shame and sin.

In cantata No. 65 they seem intentionally to add a bizarre decoration to the Wise Men:

> Three kings from the east, as long foretold,
> Did come with myrrh and incense and gold.

But these are the instrument's abnormal tones. Bach used it primarily for a more intimate purpose, and among the instruments of his orchestra it can be linked with the Blockflöte as the object of his regard.

The Oboe d'Amore

The opinion may be hazarded that the oboe d'amore (*hautbois d'amour; Liebesoboe*) owed its construction to the vogue of the viola d'amore in the earlier half of the eighteenth century. The traditional association of the violin and oboe families invited it; for the ordinary viola was already matched with the alto 'A' oboe. It is at least noteworthy that the appearance of the oboe d'amore was coincident with the introduction of the viola d'amore to public notice. Attilio Ariosti was demonstrating the latter's qualities to London audiences while Bach was in service at Weimar, and published his *Lezioni per Viola d'amore* five years (1728) after Bach's migration to Leipzig. Between those dates the oboe d'amore also made its début. The name and locality of its inventor are unknown. Two examples of it were in the Prince's collection at Cöthen,[1] and Bach used it uninterruptedly from 1723 onwards, more consistently and adventurously than any of his contemporaries. After his death it fell into desuetude till Richard Strauss revived it for his *Sinfonia domestica* in 1904.

In appearance and mechanism the oboe d'amore was the counterpart of the ordinary instrument, excepting the bell, which, being pear-shaped, with a contracted outlet, produced the veiled tone that gave the instrument its name. In pitch it stood between the

---

[1] B.-J. 1905, p. 43.

ordinary oboe and oboe da caccia. It sounded the scale *b–b'* and
its octave, the chromatic intervals being assisted by duplicated
'F♯' and 'G' finger-holes. The addition of a 'C' key extended its
compass downwards and gave it an effective range of *a–b''*. Bach
actually takes it down to *g♯* or *g* in six scores—cantatas Nos. 80, 103,
104, 195, the *Christmas Oratorio* (Part I), and the *St. John Passion*.
Certainly, there was in use in that period an alto oboe d'amore
in G, having an open bell, and Mahillon[1] describes two instruments
in the Brussels collection which, though giving the scale *a–a'*, were
in the one case almost, and in the other fully, a tone below the
normal. Such an instrument would be convenient for use with a
high-pitched organ. In that case, however, the part would need
transposition, which it does not receive in any of the six scores.
The problem would be solved if we could suppose that the natural
scale of the oboe d'amore was *a–a'*, and that the 'C' key lowered it
to *g*. But that conjecture is refuted by the notation of cantatas
Nos. 75 and 76.[2] So, either these abnormal notes were an oversight,
or Bach must have prescribed them for an alto 'G' oboe. The former
alternative is the more probable. For the oboe is always in unison
with a violin, and in the alto aria (No. 4) of the *Christmas Oratorio*
(Part I), where *g* is sounded twice, receives a significant quaver
rest for the first, but is uncorrected for the second.

With few exceptions,[3] Bach uses the French designation, 'hautbois d'amour', but in cantata No. 157 names the 'Grand-Oboe', a
title English rather than French. He treats *b''* as the upper limit
of the instrument's compass, but occasionally takes it up to *c♯'''*—
as in cantatas Nos. 49, 145, *O holder Tag*, and *Phoebus und
Pan*, and even to *d'''*—as in cantatas Nos. 103, 120, 195, and the
St. Matthew Passion. But these abnormal notes are generally supported by the violin in unison. Only in the *St. Matthew Passion*
and *Phoebus und Pan* is this not the case. The instrument is scored
almost universally in sharp keys; those of D and A major are the
most frequent; E major is very rare. Only in cantata No. 55
the oboe is used in a flat key (G minor).

Bach's early scores indicate indecision as to the notation of the
instrument. The earliest in which it is found are the *St. John
Passion* and cantatas Nos. 75 and 76, all three of which were
composed at Cöthen in the months immediately preceding his
call to Leipzig. In the first the oboe simply doubles another part.
But in both cantatas, in which it is obbligato, Bach adopts a com-

---

[1] Vol. ii. 251. [2] *Infra*, p. 109.
[3] Cantata No. 30, '2 Oboi'; cantata No. 100, '1 Oboe d'Amore'; *St. John
Passion*, '2 Oboe'; *Hohe Messe*, '2 Oboi'; *O holder Tag*, '1 Oboe d'Amore'.

plicated notation, which reveals uncertainty as to the experience of his Leipzig players in handling the new instrument:

Bach here offers alternative clefs and alternative fingering. Since the instrument sounded a minor third below the ordinary oboe, the signatures A minor—C minor, E minor—G minor, were exchangeable. Thus the performer could either play the notes in the C clef in the scale of the movement, or treat them as transposing down a minor third in the G clef. The alternative notation had the practical advantage of assisting a player familiar only with the fingering of the ordinary instrument. This is the only instance of the kind. But in one of his latest scores (cantata No. 138) Bach uses the two G clefs in the same way (see p. 110) and for the same reason. In cantata No. 24 he uses the soprano C clef alone, and in three scores (cantatas Nos. 95, 145, and 157[1]) the French violin G clef on the first line; only in the last two the instrument is transposing. These instances, no doubt, are accounted for by

---

[1] In the parts, but not the score, of No. 157.

Coro.   Cantata No. 138.

particular circumstances. For it was his otherwise almost invariable rule to score the instrument in the ordinary G clef and key of the movement and treat it as non-transposing. To this there are few exceptions—cantatas Nos. 60, 69, 100, 136, 147, the *Magnificat*, and *Schleicht, spielende Wellen*, in which the part is scored in that clef a minor third above the notes as sounded.

Bach's earliest use of the oboe d'amore, as of the oboe da caccia, is discovered in the *St. John Passion*. To establish the statement it is necessary to disqualify the competing claims of two Weimar scores—cantatas Nos. 147 and 163—which, if allowed, would also indicate an earlier year for the instrument's invention than has so far been accepted. The earlier of the two, No. 163, was performed at Weimar on 24 November 1715. But the extant score and parts leave no doubt at all that in its existing state the work belongs to the Leipzig period, when Bach revised its instrumentation.[1] The second cantata, No. 147, has already been examined.[2] Produced at Weimar on 20 December 1716, it was revised at Leipzig eleven years later, and in its existing form was performed there on 2 July 1727. Bach's usage of the oboe d'amore, as of the oboe da caccia, was therefore restricted to his Leipzig period, so far, at least, as his extant music is an indicator.

It is a misfortune that Bach's oboe music is so seldom rendered by the instruments for which he wrote it. The modern oboe accurately replaces neither his ordinary instrument nor the oboe d'amore, for which it is generally made to deputize. The cor anglais, too, is not an entirely satisfactory substitute for the oboe da caccia. And, at the best, we hear only two contrasted oboe voices, whereas Bach coloured his scores with three. He nowhere brings them together in a single movement, but prescribes them all in four cantatas (Nos. 80, 110, 128, 147), in which his apprecia-

---

[1] Cf. Spitta, i. 640.   [2] *Supra*, p. 104.

tion of their contrasted voices is apparent. In these works, as elsewhere, his chief use of the oboe d'amore is as an obbligato instrument in arias. He seldom scores it in simple Chorals, preferring the coarser-toned ordinary oboe to lead the congregational voice. In those of the two *Passions*, in which they are numerous and congregational, the oboe d'amore has no part. In those of the cantatas in which it is found it owes its place to his preference—evident in all six Parts of the *Christmas Oratorio*—to end a work in the same colour-mood as that in which it opens. Only in cantatas Nos. 81 and 168 is this rule broken, and both are peculiar in not having an initial chorus. In choruses, too, the instrument is infrequently used: it is present only in those lightly scored, in which its peculiar *timbre* would not be smothered. The strings, flutes, and occasionally horns, are its associates in them. Only in four movements is it scored with trumpets or trombones, but without an individual voice. In cantatas Nos. 120 and 121 it merely doubles the violins. In No. 195 and *Vereinigte Zwietracht* it is in unison with the flutes.

In the arias, especially those in which it is 'Solo', the individuality of the instrument expresses itself. A collation of them does not permit us to associate it in Bach's mind with a particular mood or pictorial colour. We may suspect that his sensitiveness to verbal suggestion prescribed it in certain arias in which he scores it; for instance, in the bass aria (No. 5) of the *Christmas Oratorio* (Part V):

> Erleucht' auch meine *finstre* (dark) Sinnen.

Or in the soprano aria of No. 94:

> Es halt' es mit der *blinden* (blind) Welt.

Even in the soprano aria (No. 3) of the *Magnificat*:

> Quia respexit *humilitatem* (lowliness) ancillae suae.

But in general Bach used it for its own sake, and, perhaps, because it seemed more decorous in church than its noisier relations. Thus, in his arias, he associates it over a continuo with the flute (cantatas Nos. 9, 99, 125, 195), violoncello piccolo (cantata No. 49), viola da gamba (cantata No. 76), violins and viola in unison (cantatas Nos. 151 and 154), *oboi da caccia* (cantata No. 183 and *Christmas Oratorio*, Part II, No. 10). And often he puts it in unison with the violin (cantatas Nos. 3, 7, 49, 88, 103, 104, 151, 154, 170, *Christmas Oratorio*, Part I, No. 4, *O holder Tag*, and *Preise dein' Glücke*. Still more frequently its peculiarly sensitive *timbre* is sounded by one or two of its kind over a continuo. In an instrumental score Bach evidently regarded it as unsatisfactory. In such a context, with the single exception of the short Ritornello in *Vereinigte Zwietracht*, he uses it not at all in his secular music. Its most familiar employment in an instrumental movement is in the Sinfonia of the *Christmas Oratorio*. He employs it also in those of cantatas Nos. 49 and 76. All three are lightly scored, and the last is an arrangement (for oboe, viola da gamba, and continuo) of the E minor Sonata for two manuals and pedal. Clearly Bach recognized the deficiencies which after his death doomed the instrument to neglect. It perished indeed, with the Church Cantata, which it was admirably fitted to embellish, but whose vogue hardly survived the Master whose genius had exalted them both.

The Bassoon

The Bassoon (*Fagotto*, *Basson*, *Fagott*), as has already been stated, was a development of the Bass Pommer, which it superseded because of its more easy handling. Praetorius, in his eleventh chapter, mentions four varieties: the

1. Discant Fagott,
2. Fagott piccolo,
3. Chorist Fagott,
4. Doppel Fagott.

The compasses of Nos. 3 and 4, according to his 'Tabella Universalis',[1] corresponded in their lowest register with those of the Bass Pommer and Gross Bass Pommer, the former sounding ![music notation], the latter ![music notation]. The precise year and locality in which the Chorist Fagott assumed its modern shape and characteristics are not known. In its earlier form it was cut from a single block of wood. But, at some time before Bach's birth (1685), it took the form of two separate parallel tubes conically bored, having a continuous, but bent, air column. Thus, while the compass of the Bass Pommer was retained, the bending of the air column reduced its unwieldy length to a manageable four feet or so. As early as 1532 such an instrument had suggested the jocular name 'Fagott', which the Italians gave it. The French and English preferred the word 'bassoon' to indicate its function as the bass of the wood-wind. Sounded through a double reed, and pierced with eleven finger-holes, three of them controlled by

[1] P. 23. See his Plates VI and XI at pp. 96 and 160.

finger-keys,[1] it made its public début, with the oboe, at the performance of Robert Cambert's *Pomone* at Paris on 19 March 1671, fourteen years before Bach's birth. Its compass was from

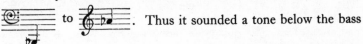 to . Thus it sounded a tone below the bass

Pommer, its lowest note *bb,,* being obtained by the action of a key. Two other keys gave the third and fifth above it, the keyed system

consequently controlling the notes .

Such was the instrument at Bach's disposal when, in 1708, he first introduced it into a score (cantata No. 71). Till the last decade of his career it underwent no important change, and then

acquired a fourth key sounding or .[2] Whether

the new key was at Bach's disposal cannot be determined with certainty. The note is absent from less than one-quarter of his scores—cantatas Nos. 63, 75, 147, 155, 160, the *Sanctus* in D, the Mass in F, and the two secular cantatas *Was mir behagt* and *Durchlaucht'ster Leopold*. More than half the number belong to his Weimar and Cöthen periods, and two others (cantatas Nos. 63 and 75) were not improbably composed before he was inducted into the Leipzig Cantorate. On the other hand, the note is found in over twice as many pre-Leipzig scores as those from which it is omitted (cantatas Nos. 18, 21, 31, 61, 70, 71, 131, 150, 162, 185, 186, the first Brandenburg Concerto, Ouverture in C, and *Mein Herze schwimmt*). The presence of the note in a score is therefore not a safe indicator of a finger-key. Greater significance attaches to the fact that Bach avoids signatures which made its use natural and frequent. A three sharps signature occurs only in cantatas Nos. 42, 185, and *Durchlaucht'ster Leopold*, and a three flats signature only in cantatas Nos. 12, 21, 159, and *Mein Herze schwimmt*. Moreover, his use of the note is always economical. In several scores it is not sounded more than once or twice, and with the utmost rarity is sustained for more than a beat or a fraction of a beat. Hence, even if the *g♯,* key was in use earlier than 1751, in which year Diderot and d'Alembert's *Encyclopédie* specifically mentions it, Bach's scores cannot safely be adduced in evidence.

[1] Cf. Heckel, p. 13.
[2] The key is on an English bassoon dated 1747, owned by Canon Galpin, and on another at Brussels (No. 997), dated 1730. Cf. *Encyc. Brit.* (11th edn.), xix. 952.

Table XIII reveals the fact that Bach rarely takes the bassoon to the limit of its lowest register. In only five scores—cantatas Nos. 31, 42, 69, 71, 155—he carries it below ♩. In the last four of the five he writes an occasional $b_{,,}$ or $bb_{,,}$. But in the first (No. 31) the part frequently descends to ♩, and the instrument used was not the 'Chorist' or ordinary bass bassoon, but the 'Doppel Fagott' described by Praetorius, with a compass descending to ♩. Bach appears to have had little liking for that instrument, whose faulty construction and rattling tone[1] caused its disuse until the late Dr. W. H. Stone revived it. Bach prescribed it also in one of the versions of the *St. John Passion*,[2] but otherwise neglected it.

Bach accepts ♩ as the normal limit of the bassoon's upper compass. Praetorius put it at ♩, and in a few scores —cantatas Nos. 97, 149, and 177—Bach touches that note. In the bass aria (continuo) of cantata No. 42 and the obbligato to the 'Quoniam' (No. 10) of the *Hohe Messe* the bassoon actually reaches ♩, a peak to which Haydn also took it in his 'Military' Symphony in G, sixty-one years later (1794). Bach's notation is practically invariable: with two exceptions he puts the bassoon in the bass clef and treats it as non-transposing. The exceptions are cantatas Nos. 131 and 150. The latter belongs to his Mühlhausen period, but, unlike cantata No. 71, does not appear to have been composed for the Mühlhausen churches. It is apparently a funeral anthem, whose simple score (two violins, bassoon, and continuo) indicates that the musical resources of its locality were slender. No. 131, scored for a violin, two violas, oboe, bassoon, and continuo, supports the same inference. In both the bassoon part transposes, sounding in No. 131 a tone, and in No. 150

---

[1] Cf. *Encyc. Brit.* (11th edn.), vii. 41.
[2] A 'Continuo pro Bassono grosso' part is mentioned.

a minor third, below the notes as written. The transposition adjusted the instrument's scale to an organ tuned respectively to Chorton (No. 131) and Cornett-Ton (No. 150). The infrequent use of it in his church music indicates that Bach did not employ the bassoon as a regular continuo instrument. At the same time, its most frequent function in his usage was as a ripienist to support the continuo, in other words, the violone and violoncello. Even so, the occasions on which the instrument was heard at Leipzig were relatively few. Of the thirty-six church cantatas in which it is scored nearly half were composed at Mühlhausen and Weimar. Of Mühlhausen's town musicians we have no information. Weimar's Capelle supported only a single 'Fagottist', and at Cöthen Bach could occasionally command the services of one. At Leipzig ability to play it was not one of the tests to which an aspiring 'Stadt Musicus' was subjected, and, as we learn from Bach himself,[1] the general apprentice of that body was entrusted with it. His experience cannot have been considerable, and his skill was certainly immature. It is not surprising, therefore, that Bach gave him infrequent opportunities, and that, of the scores in which it is obbligato, those of the Leipzig period—cantatas Nos. 42, 66, 143, 149, 177, 197, the *Easter Oratorio*, and *Hohe Messe*—are localized in two cycles of years, 1731-3, 1735-7. Evidently it was only in those restricted periods of his Cantorship that a player competent to undertake an independent obbligato was at his disposal.

It is observable also that Bach makes no use of the bassoon in the secular cantatas composed at Leipzig, and employs it hardly at all in his purely orchestral music. He scores it only in the first Brandenburg Concerto in F[2] and the Ouverture in C, both of which were composed at Cöthen. In both he treats it conventionally. While it reinforces the general continuo, it serves as a particular bass for the wood-wind—three oboes in the Concerto, two oboes in the Ouverture. In the former it belongs so intimately to that section of the orchestral body, that it is silent when only the strings are in action, leaving them to the support of the violone and violoncello. A similar purpose is apparent in the Trios which precede the final and general Menuetto. Each section of the orchestra advances in turn, performs a pirouette, as it were, and retires—first the oboes and bassoon, next the strings (Polacca), and finally the horns with oboes in unison. In the Ouverture, too, Bach's use of the instrument is conventional. In general, the oboes and first

---

[1] *Supra*, p. 9.
[2] The Sinfonia in F is the same music (omitting the Polacca and second *Allegro*), prepared, as is probable, for use in a church cantata.

violins are in unison; consequently, in these passages their continuos are consonant. But in the opening movement the strings are frequently silent while the oboes and bassoon perform an independent trio. In the second Bourrée also the latter play a similar part. Thus Bach's usage shows no originality in these early works. He treats the instrument as custom prescribed, denying it the individuality with which Handel endowed it in *Saul* (1738) some eighteen years later. There is evidence, however, of experimental development in the instrumental movements of the church cantatas in which the bassoon is scored. The Cöthen standard is apparent in those of the Weimar period—Nos. 12, 18, 21, 31, 150. The Sinfonia or Sonata which opens all of them generally exhibits the bassoon in strict unison with the continuo, or tied to the oboes when they are present. Though composed c. 1730, cantata No. 52 shows no advance; its Sinfonia is simply the first movement of the first Brandenburg Concerto in F. Similarly, the Sinfonia of cantata No. 174, a work composed in 1729, exhibits the older pattern; it is the first movement of the third Brandenburg Concerto, to the original continuo of which a bassoon is added to balance the three oboes which augment the original strings. But the Symphonies of cantata No. 42 and the *Easter Oratorio* reveal an advance on the original plan, and both fall within the cycle in which, as has already been suggested, circumstances allowed Bach to be adventurous. In the former the oboes and bassoon do not, as in the earlier scores, merely interpose an occasional trio. They function as a separate body throughout, independent of the strings, and make their own contribution to the thematic texture of the work. The bassoon consequently only seldom reinforces the continuo. In the *Easter Oratorio* it plays an individual part in florid passages distinguished as 'Solo'.

In concerted movements for voices and orchestra Bach's bassoon is usually a continuo instrument. Very infrequently it supports the vocal basses in the concluding Chorals, and the Mass in F affords the only example of its association with them in a general chorus. It is in the arias in which it is obbligato that Bach gives it an individual voice, showing himself as sensitive to its merits as his young contemporary, Haydn. To the duet (No. 4) of cantata No. 42 (1731) it contributes an obbligato in unison with a violoncello, a partnership customary in the Hamburg operas of the period,[1] with which Bach would be familiar. He had in fact employed the device some years before at Cöthen, in the bass aria of *Durchlaucht'ster Leopold*. It does not appear to have pleased him;

[1] Cf. Pirro, p. 237.

at least, these are the only examples of it in his scores. But the obbligato of cantata No. 42 is peculiar on other grounds. It was evidently written to accompany a melody *never actually sounded*, such as Gounod audaciously added to the C major Prelude (No. I) of the *Wohltemperirte Clavier*. The indication 'Choral' which heads the Aria affords the clue. The text is the first stanza of Joh. Michael Altenburg's hymn, and, since it was Bach's custom always to associate a hymn with its melody, we can feel reasonably sure that it was in his mind in the present case. The sympathetic relationship of the obbligato and continuo with the concealed melody is revealed in the bars associated with the first line of the hymn-stanza:

The violoncello-bassoon obbligato in *Durchlaucht'ster Leopold* does not call for particular notice. In cantata No. 66, though Bach's own hand has written 'Bassono oblig.', the instrument merely adds some exuberant ornamentation to the continuo. Its part is written under the oboes in the aria, and Bach styles it 'obbligato' in order to enforce the necessity of its association with them to complete the wood-wind 'choir'.

Cantata No. 143 reveals a definite characterization of the instrument. Composed for the Feast of the Circumcision, it has a festival score—three *corni da caccia*, drums, strings, and continuo. Bach, however, adds a bassoon, not to augment the normal continuo, but to sustain the corno-timpani body, under whose parts its own is written in the score, and with which it is consistently associated. The work is a jubilant setting of Psalm cxlvi, *Lobe den Herrn, meine Seele*, in which the bass aria in particular (with a free bassoon obbligato) affirms God's sovereign majesty—'Der Herr ist *König* ewiglich'. That Bach framed his score in order to offer the salute the word 'König' demanded is evident when we discover a similar combination of instruments in the bass aria 'Quoniam tu solus *Dominus*' of the *Hohe Messe*. In the latter case he employs two bassoons and a single horn. But, as in cantata No. 143, the combination produces the ceremonious atmosphere he thought appropriate. Clearly he endorsed Mattheson's[1] appreciation of the bassoon's 'stately' deportment. M. Pirro[2] interprets its obbligato to the alto-tenor duet in the Michaelmas cantata No. 149:

> Watch o'er me, ye heavenly guardians!
> The shades of night are near.

as a 'voile d'ombre' appropriate to the second line of the text. He is surely in error. The obbligato is by no means sombre in colour, and seems rather a courtly salute to the captains of the angelic band. In the trio (A.T.B.) of cantata No. 150 the obbligato again has pictorial significance. Its stolid rhythm is in contrast with the agitated continuo, an antithesis invited by the text:

> Cedars tall, their branches tossing,
> Rent by tempests fiercely blowing,
> Oft are levelled to the ground.
> Comfort take! For God has spoken.
> Have no fear of hell and Satan;
> On God's Word thy going found!

A more exaggerated pictorial design is assisted by the obbligato to the alto-tenor duet of cantata No. 155:

> Be of courage, hope on ever,
> Let thine own God's will obey!
> When 'tis meet He'll comfort give thee,
> Filling all thy heart with joy.

Here the bassoon wreathes an embroidery of almost delirious

---

[1] 'Der stoltze Basson', he calls it (p. 269).   [2] P. 237.

ecstasy and confident faith, expressed in a formula expressive of both emotions:

The instrument skips with agile fluency, in a manner to astonish the bassoon player quoted by M. Pirro,[1] who in 1708 protested that he had never been asked to play a demisemiquaver! Writing the above passage eight years later, Bach made heavier demands on his Weimar 'Fagottist', Bernhard Georg Ulrich. Indeed, in the literature of the instrument this obbligato is a landmark, alike in Bach's adventurous experimentalism and in the general recognition of its qualities as an orchestral voice.

To the Leipzig period in which Bach was served by an exceptionally competent performer belongs cantata No. 177, in the tenor aria of which the bassoon is paired with a violin concertante over a continuo. To that epoch, too, we refer the exquisitely tender bass aria of No. 197, a wedding cantata. The young couple would not be aware that it was borrowed from the incomplete Christmas cantata *Ehre sei Gott in der Höhe*, where, appropriately, it is a cradle song. In the wedding cantata it is scored for an oboe, two violins (muted), 'Fagotto obbligato', and continuo. The bassoon gives out a rhythmically rocking figure, without meaning in association with the wedding text, but of obvious import in its original context.

The conclusion of this survey is patent and need not be stressed. Bach's scores show increasing independence in handling the bassoon. Accepting at first the conventions of his period, he was not backward in estimating the qualities in it which invited more intimate treatment. Not even his great successors surpassed him in the boldness of his usage of it and the fertility of his experiments. Had he been born into a later generation we cannot doubt that he would have anticipated Mozart's Concerto for the instrument and Beethoven's symphonic treatment of it. But, as in other instances, it was his lot to employ the instrument in forms of expression which from the outset the modern orchestra discarded.

[1] P. 236.

CHAPTER VI
THE STRINGS

FOR his stringed instruments Bach drew from two sources closed to the modern composer. Necessity, or inclination, caused him occasionally, but not frequently, to employ instruments then obsolescent or of lesser vogue. Thus he supplemented the violin with the violino piccolo, the viola with the viola d'amore and violetta, the violoncello with the viola da gamba, the cembalo with the lute. In the second place, the imperfect technique of his players, inadequate to extract full orchestral value from certain instruments then in use, impelled him to invent new ones. Thus he experimented with the violoncello piccolo and Lautenclavi-cymbel, which have vanished, as the curios of earlier generations. To the instruments of these two categories this chapter is mainly devoted.

The Normal Strings

It may be stated broadly that the louder-voiced violin family began to oust the gentler viols when music sought a public platform in churches and concert-rooms. Their supersession was not completely accomplished in Bach's period, though their supremacy had been threatened since the early seventeenth century. Praetorius[1] devotes but thirteen lines to the 'Violin de Bracio', excusing himself from a fuller exposition on the ground that the subject was familiar ('jedermänniglichen bekandt ist'). Mersenne, eighteen years later, wrote ecstatically of 'le Violon . . . le Roy des instrumens',[2] of which Jacques Cordier, Queen Henrietta Maria's dancing-master, was already a famous exponent. In Italy, Giovanni Legrenzi was writing sonatas for it some twenty years before Bach was born. Tommaso Albinoni was eloquent in the same art in the same period, and Arcangelo Corelli published his first set of sonatas for two violins two years (1683) before Bach came into the world. In Germany the instrument was also in vogue. Johann Jakob Walther, formerly of the Dresden Capelle, published his *Scherzi di violino solo* in 1676, and twelve years later (1688) his *Hortulus chelicus, uni violino, duabus, tribus et quatuor subinde chordis simul sonantibus*. England was in no wise behind her contemporaries. William Young published his 'Sonatas' at Innsbruck in 1653. Orlando Gibbons, John Jenkins, William Lawes, and, later, Purcell were pioneers in the same field. These names are signifi-

[1] Chap. 22. [2] Bk. III. 177.

cant; they indicate the growing literature of the instrument when Bach was first attracted to it at Celle and Weimar. With the works of Legrenzi and Albinoni he was early familiar, and of those of Antonio Vivaldi, a younger pen, he made extensive use.

Praetorius names the following members of the violin family in his 'Tabella Universalis':[1]

1. Klein Discant-Geig:

2. Discant-Geig Violino: — present day violin

3. Tenor-Geig: — modern viola

passed out of use   (1)   (2)   modern cello

4. Bass-Geig de Braccio:

5. Gross Quint-Bass:

No. 1 is Bach's violino piccolo, tuned a tone higher. No. 2 is the present-day violin. No. 3 is the viola of Bach's scores and modern usage. No. 4 (2) is the violoncello as he employed it, tuned then as it is to-day. No. 4 (1), the true tenor of the family, has unfortunately, and somewhat unaccountably, passed out of general use. Tuned originally a fifth below the alto (No. 3), and with a length of string some twenty inches from nut to bridge, it filled a distinctive place in the gamut of the violin family. Mr. Hayes[2] justifiably deplores its loss, as having robbed both the chamber quartet and the larger orchestra of a distinctive voice. The two *viole da braccio* Bach uses in the sixth Brandenburg Concerto appear, from their compass, to have been the alto (No. 3) rather than the true tenor (No. 4). For his continuo bass he generally used the six-stringed violone, a late survivor of the ancient viols,

tuned thus ———— and having a fretted finger-board.[3] There is

no positive evidence that he employed the contrabass (No. 5). But the score of *Was mir behagt* prescribes a 'Violone grosso'.[4]

[1] P. 26. See his Plate XXI, at p. 124.   [2] P. 204.
[3] See Praetorius, Plate VI, at p. 160.   [4] Cf. *supra*, p. 20.

The violin family provided the nucleus of Bach's orchestra. And yet, as has been made clear in an earlier chapter,[1] its players were generally casual amateurs or elder *alumni* of the Thomasschule. From only nine church cantatas[2] and a single secular cantata[3] is the full quartet of strings absent.[4] All of them, except *Ehre sei Gott*, are of the pre-Leipzig period. There are relatively few of his concerted scores in which the violin does not also receive an obbligato or solo part. But the frequency with which he sets the violins in unison over the continuo also carries the suspicion that he often lacked a player of adequate ability as an obbligatist. Yet the inference is not invariably well founded. Bach, no doubt, had good reasons for assigning the obbligato of the alto aria in the *St. Matthew Passion*, 'Können Thränen meiner Wangen' (No. 61), to the whole body of violins in unison, whereas in two other movements a first violin is solo. In the *Hohe Messe*, again, the player to whom he entrusted the *obbligati* of the 'Laudamus te' and 'Benedictus' could, no doubt, have undertaken that of the 'Agnus Dei', had Bach desired. On the other hand, the obbligato of the 'Benedictus' is only by assumption given to the violin. Professor Tovey expresses 'grave suspicions of violin music that never goes below the compass of the flute', and fails to detect any unmistakable violin figure in it, observing that 'any of Bach's flute solos in minor keys will present constant resemblance to its turns of phrase'.

The weakness of Bach's violins in numbers and technique is indicated occasionally by his direction to the violas to unite with the violins in an obbligato.[5] A similar deficiency in the violas is in three cases[6] suggested by the unison of violins and violas in a part written in the alto C clef. But here again the deduction is qualified by the fact that the violin obbligato to the bass aria of cantata No. 178 is in the alto clef. In the bass aria of cantata No. 62 the violins and viola are directed to play 'sempre col Continuo': their part, in the score, stands actually in the bass clef!

A collation of Bach's violin *obbligati*[7] reveals his disinclination to use the instrument in its highest register. In this he obeyed the conventions of his period. Writing in 1756, the sixth year after

---

[1] *Supra*, p. 9.

[2] Nos. 18, 106, 118, 150, 152, 158, 160, 189, and *Ehre sei Gott* (incomplete).

[3] *Amore traditore.*   [4] The score of No. 118 puts it in a class apart.

[5] Cantatas Nos. 61, 80, 83, 85, 156, 166, 172, 174, and *Vereinigte Zwietracht.*

[6] Cantatas Nos. 24, 140, Mass in A.

[7] In cantatas Nos. 2, 13, 26, 29, 30, 32, 36, 39, 51, 57, 58, 60, 66, 74, 76, 83, 84, 86, 97, 101, 103, 108, 117, 120, 129, 132, 137, 139, 147, 148, 157, 158, 160, 171, 177, 182, 184, 197, the *Christmas Oratorio, Easter Oratorio, Hohe Messe*, Mass in F, Mass in A, *St. Matthew Passion, Weichet nur, betrübte Schatten, Ich bin in mir vergnügt, Aeolus, Schleicht, spielende Wellen, Was mir behagt.*

Bach's death, and the year of Wolfgang's birth, Leopold Mozart[1] states that there were in use two ways of holding the violin, 'sideways against the breast' ('an der Höhe der Brust seitwärts'), or under the chin and on the shoulder. In the former position only four notes above the open string would be within the easy compass of the player, since the left hand needed to maintain a firm unshifting grip. So held, the effective range of the instrument would be g–b''. Even expert professional players who adopted the other position apparently used its opportunities with conservative caution. The 'half-shift', or second position, is said, probably inaccurately, to have been the belated invention of Nicola Matteis, a London player at the period of Bach's birth; it advanced the compass of the violin to c'''. The ascription is contested, but the material point is that Bach learnt the instrument at Eisenach when its compass was thus restricted. In the *obbligati* already mentioned, and also in the Sonatas, he takes the instrument comparatively rarely beyond the 'little finger' note d'''. Only in eleven scores[2] it soars above e''', and the seventh position (to a''') is required only in the *Hohe Messe* and Violin Concerto (Sinfonia) in D major. But, if their compass is generally moderate, Bach's violin parts demand advanced technique; his double-stopping is frequently of the most intricate complexity, requiring from the executant powers of the highest order. If, as is probable, Bach wrote no violin music he could not play himself, we can judge his ability to have been exceptional. Probably he disliked the modern Italian inward-curving bow, and preferred the older arched bow, which facilitated the player's execution, since it permitted him to vary tension by the pressure of the thumb on the hairs.[3]

Bach's particular affection for the viola is stated by Forkel.[4] Of his orchestra it was a normal member, and from the scores of only six cantatas[5] is it omitted. His memorandum to the Leipzig Council in 1730[6] demanded four viola players for the proper accompaniment of church music. Since he drew them from amateur sources, he cannot regularly have had that number at his disposal. Indeed, he rarely scores more than one viola part. There are two in cantatas Nos. 4, 12, 31, 54, 61, 131, 172, 182, *Hercules*, and the sixth

[1] P. 53.
[2] To f''' in the Concerto I in A minor, Fugue in G minor, and Solo Sonata in G minor; to $f\sharp'''$ in the *Hohe Messe* ('Benedictus') and Cantata No. 171 (soprano aria); to g''' in *Aeolus* (soprano aria), Solo Sonata in C major, Partita in D minor, Cantatas Nos. 101 (tenor aria) and 158 (soprano-bass duet); and a''' in the *Hohe Messe* ('Laudamus te') and Sinfonia in D major for violin and orchestra (B.-G. XXI (1)).
[3] Cf. B.-J. 1904, p. 113; Hayes, pp. 202–4.   [4] P. 108.
[5] Nos. 118, 150, 158, 160, 189, and *Ehre sei Gott*.   [6] Terry, p. 201.

Brandenburg Concerto; three in cantata No. 174 and the third Brandenburg Concerto; and four in cantata No. 18 only. As an obbligato instrument he seldom employed it by itself: its part is 'solo' only in the tenor aria of cantata No. 5, where it gives the murmurous effect of deep waters.[1] Bach's inclination to put the violins and violas in unison has been referred to above, and to the examples given there may be added the alto aria of cantata No. 132, where the instrument is in unison with a 'solo' violin. Another curious example is in the alto aria of cantata No. 170, where the violas serve as the bass for an organ obbligato.

Bach's violoncello was normally a continuo instrument.[2] For obbligato purposes he preferred the violoncello piccolo, whose usage is explored in a later section of this chapter. Infrequently, however, he employed the ordinary violoncello in that manner. The instances occur in only seven scores and fall into two groups:

(a) Pre-Leipzig

Work.	Movement.	Date.	Occasion.	Compass.
Cantata No. 163	3. Aria (B.)	24 Nov. 1715	Trinity XXIII	$e,-g'$
Cantata No. 70	3. Aria (A.)	6 Dec. 1716	Advent II	$c,-a'$
Durchlaucht'ster Leopold	7. Aria (B.)	29 Nov. 1718?	Prince Leopold's birthday	$d\sharp,-f\sharp'$

(b) Leipzig

Cantata No. 42	4. Duet (S.T.)	1 Apr. 1731	Easter I	$b\sharp,,-g'$
Cantata No. 172	5. Duet (S.A.)	13 May 1731	Whit-Sunday	$c,-f'$
Cantata No. 56	2. Recit. (B.)	30 Sept. 1731	Trinity XIX	$d,-d\flat'$
Cantata No. 188	3. Aria (A.)	14 Oct. 1731	Trinity XXI	$c,-e'$

The *obbligati* call for little comment. They are generally *cantabile*, without chording or double stopping, and their compass in the higher register falls short of that of the violoncello piccolo by about a fifth, i.e. of a fifth string. Only in cantata No. 56 the violoncello reveals a pictorial design. 'Our journey through the world', the voice declaims, 'is as one fares at sea. Affliction, stress and woe, like billows our destruction threaten, and day by day to shipwreck beckon.' The obbligato's curving periods outline a heaving surface, too regular, however, to menace shipwreck. For Bach had in mind the stanza's concluding promise of safe harbourage in the heavenly haven-home. In cantata No. 188 the obbligato merely reinforces the organ continuo.[3]

[1] Bach appropriately repeated the subject in the opening chorus of cantata No. 7.

[2] C. P. E. Bach remarks (*Versuch*, Pt. II, p. 3): 'The most perfect accompaniment for a solo . . . is afforded by a keyed instrument along with a violoncello.'

[3] The incomplete cantata *Ehre sei Gott* contains the fragment of an aria having a violoncello obbligato.

2. Kleine Poschen / Geigen ein Octav höher. 3. Discant-Geig ein Quart höher.
4. Rechte Discant-Geig. 5. Tenor-Geig. 6 Bas-Geig de bracio. 7. Trumscheit.
8. Scheidtholtt.

VIOLINO PICCOLO AND OTHER STRINGS
(Praetorius)

The chief interest of the Table is in the third column, which indicates that, after an interval of fifteen years, Bach wrote a violoncello obbligato for his Easter cantata in 1731; that in the course of the following six months he employed the instrument three times for that purpose; and, after 14 October 1731, ceased altogether to use it in that way. He had, in fact, on the previous Sunday (7 October) performed his first obbligato for the violoncello piccolo, which thenceforward he used exclusively for the purpose.

The Violino Piccolo

It is evident that in 1731 Bach was in a highly experimental mood. The alleviation of his circumstances since the arrival of Johann Matthias Gesner as Rector in September 1730,[1] and some abatement of his pedagogic duties, may partially account for it. But, whatever the cause, we find him at that period decisively turning his back on obsolescent instruments—the viola d'amore, viola da gamba, and lute—which till then he had been willing to employ, and bringing forward others long neglected or of recent invention. The series of organ *obbligati* which decorate his church cantatas in that year[2] also seem to indicate an experimental mood which bore fruit in the trial of more than one new instrument.

Another indication of Bach's peculiar alertness at that period is furnished by his introduction of the violino piccolo into a cantata score. Leipzig heard it, apparently for the first time during his Cantorship, on the Tenth Sunday after Trinity (29 July) 1731, again on the Twenty-seventh Sunday after Trinity (25 November) 1731, and thereafter, for the last time, some nine years later.[3]

The violino piccolo, as has already been stated, was the Klein Discant-Geig, described by Praetorius as the smallest member of the violin family. Though of lesser size, it exhibited the parts and proportions of the ordinary violin, in which respect it differed

from the 'pochette' or 'kit'. Praetorius gives its tuning as ,

a fourth above the ordinary violin, an octave above the viola. This appears to be generally accepted.[4] Mr. E. J. Payne, however, in the second edition of 'Grove'[5] gives its stringing as 'a minor third higher than the ordinary violin, its highest string having the same pitch as the highest string of the Quinton'.

On the evidence of Bach's manuscripts Mr. Payne is correct.

---

[1] Cf. Terry, p. 207.　　　　[2] *Infra*, p. 171.　　　　[3] See Table XIV.
[4] For instance, in Hayes, p. 211; Grove (3rd edn.), v. 525; and Dolmetsch, p. 455.　　　　[5] Vol. iv, 813.

For in the first Brandenburg Concerto and in the soprano-bass duet of cantata No. 140, the two scores in which it has an independent part, it sounds a minor third higher than the written notes, evidently for the convenience of a player accustomed to the fingering of the ordinary violin; its bottom note consequently sounded ♮ though written ♮.[1] The compass column of Table XIV indicates that Bach did not use its upper register conspicuously beyond that of the ordinary violin, and the closer approximation of their tunings partially explains the fact.

Violino piccolo, 18th cent., extreme length 55 cm.

Bach's use of the violino piccolo was infrequent and intermittent. It is found in only four scores, and in but two of them has a distinctly independent part. In the opening chorus of cantata No. 96 it is in unison with the flauto piccolo, for a reason suggested in the section on that instrument.[2] In the tenor aria of cantata No. 102 it is prescribed as alternative to the traverso. But it is obbligato in the soprano-bass duet of cantata No. 140, one of Bach's most dramatic scores. The duet is a dialogue between Christ and the Soul:

Soul. When com'st Thou, my Lord?
Christ. Behold Me, thine own!
Soul. Come, Jesu!
Christ. I seek thee, for thee am I yearning.

Round these tender words the obbligato wreathes an embroidery of spiritual exaltation which such a text always inspired in Bach. In the Brandenburg Concerto No. I, in F, the violino piccolo is definitely obbligato only in the *Adagio* and following *Allegro*, and is silent in the two Trios and Polacca. It is improbable that Bach scored the Concerto to suit the equipment of the Cöthen Capelle, which did not possess a violino piccolo during his period of office. He had left it at least three years before it acquired an instrument, dated 1726, from Gottlieb Hoffmann.[3]

Bach's restricted usage of the violino piccolo indicates its

[1] In the opening chorus of cantata No. 140, in which it is col violino I, the part once touches *a*; an oversight.
[2] *Supra*, p. 66.   [3] B.-J. 1905, p. 38.

declining vogue: in fact, it hardly survived his own career. Writing in 1756,[1] Leopold Mozart gives the reason. 'Whereas', he remarks, 'concertos were once written for the instrument, nowadays it can be dispensed with, since parts that formerly required it can now be played in the higher positions on the ordinary violin' ('Man spielet alles auf der gewöhnlichen Violin in der Höhe').[2]

The Violetta

In 1724, again in 1727, and for the last time in 1734, Bach employed an instrument called by him 'Violetta'. It is neither prominent nor indispensable in the three scores in which it is prescribed. In cantata No. 16 it is alternative to an oboe da caccia in the obbligato accompanying the tenor aria. In cantata No. 157 it takes the part of, and is indistinguishable from, the viola in the string accompaniment to the tenor recitative, and in the concluding Choral is in unison with the vocal tenors. Along with the violins, it provides a quasi-bass foundation for the soprano aria in *Preise dein' Glücke*. That is the extent of Bach's employment of it.

What was the instrument thus designated? Its name, the alto clef associated with it, the situation of its part in the score of cantata No. 157, and the general character of the music allotted to it, all indicate a stringed instrument of viola range. In the eighteenth century 'violetta' could denote the ordinary viola (Bratsche).[3] But it cannot have that meaning in Bach's scores, since he prescribes them both together in cantata No. 16 and *Preise dein' Glücke*. The viola d'amore also was occasionally indicated by the name. But it, too, must be ruled out; Bach would hardly call the same instrument 'viola d'amore' on 26 March 1723 (*St. John Passion*) and 'violetta' on 1 January 1724 (cantata No. 16). Again, in the sixteenth and seventeenth centuries the treble viol was sometimes styled 'violetta'. But its tuning gave it approximately the compass of the violin, a fact which, along with the disuse of the smaller viols in Bach's period, puts it out of consideration in the present case. Canon Galpin has suggested tentatively[4] that Bach's 'violetta' was identical with the viola pomposa, whose invention is incorrectly attributed to him. But, since the viola pomposa was known to and used by his contemporaries under that name, he is not likely to have given it another. Nor do the diminutive 'violetta' and the adjective 'pomposa' seem appropriate to the same instrument. On the other hand, Herr Carl Engel draws attention to a Concerto by Joh.

[1] P. 2.
[2] But the tone-colour would differ.
[3] Mr. F. T. Arnold instances Porpora's MS. violoncello concerto with quartet accompaniment. Mr. Hayes (p. 182) gives others.
[4] *Music and Letters*, Oct. 1931.

Gottlieb Graun scored for 'Violino pomposo o Violetta concertata', or, as in a duplicate MS., for 'Violino o Viola Pomposa concertata'. The compass of the part for the instrument bearing the alternative names Violino pomposo and Viola pomposa is g–$c\sharp'''$, which indicates a violin tuning incongruous with Bach's violetta parts. At the same time, the Concerto proves that the violetta, of one kind, was interchangeable with the viola pomposa.[1]

The correct interpretation is perhaps afforded by Walther,[2] who describes the violetta as 'a medium violin' ('eine Geige zu Mittel-Partei'). He adds that the alto viola da gamba also bore the name. Either would fit Bach's violetta parts, whose character indicates that the unfamiliar instrument was employed as a convenience, not as an embellishment. In all three works in which it is employed it raises merely an alternative voice. Certainly its obbligato to the tenor aria of cantata No. 16 is written on a separate sheet inscribed 'Violetta'; but the oboe part also has it. Its inclusion in the score of cantata No. 157 was an afterthought: its part is on a separate sheet in the alto clef, but the score indicates only traverso, oboe, violin, and continuo. In *Preise dein' Glücke*, though the score prescribes 'Violini e Violetta' in the soprano aria, the ordinary viola part contains its notes, without any indication corresponding to that direction. Since Bach was able to prescribe it over the decade 1724–34, it was evidently permanently accessible, probably among the instruments of the two churches. It may have conveniently supplied one of Bach's amateurs whose 'Bratsche' was temporarily out of commission.

The Viola d'Amore

Having regard to the regularity of his routine, Bach's employment of certain stringed instruments then in declining vogue was infrequent and irregular. After scoring the violino piccolo in 1721 he made no further use of it till 1731, and allowed nearly as long an interval to elapse before he employed it again. Of the viola da gamba his use was as economical: at Leipzig he scored it every second year, and after 1729 not at all. The viola d'amore he used once at Weimar, apparently not at all at Cöthen, at Leipzig in 1723 for the *St. John Passion*, again in 1725 for *Aeolus*, once more for *Schwingt freudig euch empor* some five years later, and thereafter not at all. We cannot suppose these infrequent scores to have been the only ones Bach deemed appropriate to the instruments he so sparingly used. Rather, we must infer, they indicate the intermittent periods when competent players were available. For all of them he was

[1] *Zeitschrift f. Musikwissenschaft*, Oct. 1931, p. 58.   [2] P. 637.

dependent at Leipzig upon persons outside his professional body; the only stringed instruments in which candidates for admission to it were tested were the violin and 'der grosse Violon', by which the contrabass is probably indicated.[1]

The viola d'amore appears to have been originally a smaller form of the viola bastarda.[2] Though he does not mention the viola d'amore by name, Praetorius[3] speaks of the vibratory strings, which were its characteristic, as being a contemporary English invention.[4] The instrument so named, strung with wire, but without sympathetic strings, was a novelty in 1679, however, and also, as re-corded by Burney, nearly forty years later (1716).[5] Its vogue, more established in Germany than elsewhere, was advanced by Attilio Ariosti, who published his *Lezioni per Viola d'amore* in 1728, having introduced the instrument to a London audience sixteen years earlier. Vivaldi wrote a concerto for viola d'amore and lute towards the end of his life (*ob.* 1743). Bach's use of it falls between those two boundaries.

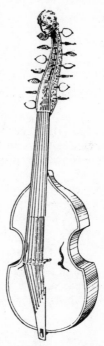

The viola d'amore exhibited the qualities both of the viols and violin. It was akin to the former in its possession of more than four strings, in its non-uniform tuning, in the structure of its body, and in the 'flame' type of its sound-holes. On the other hand, it was bowed and held like a violin, and its finger-board was not fretted. But, unlike both, it was fitted with sympathetic strings

Viola d'amore, 18th cent., extreme length 82 cm.

of fine brass or steel, which passed from the tail-piece through small holes drilled in the lower part of the bridge, and thence under the finger-board to pegs or wrest-pins in the peg-box, which the head of a blindfold Cupid usually surmounted. The sympathetic strings, responding to the vibration of the ordinary strings, produced an ethereal silvery ring which won it the sentimental name it bears. The suggestion that its name is a corruption of 'viol de Moor',

---

[1] Cf. *Archiv f. M.*, pp. 44, 45; Quantz, p. 219.
[2] The viola bastarda is figured in Praetorius's Plate XX at p. 132.
[3] p. 47.
[4] John Playford (1661) attributes it to Daniel Farrant.
[5] Cf. Dolmetsch, p. 452; Hayes, p. 215; Mahillon, i. 321; Grove, v. 515.

indicating an Eastern origin, seems fantastic. The Arab 'Kamanga rûmî', however, was fitted with similar sympathetic strings.[1]

The gut strings on the finger-board were uniform neither in number nor tuning. Extant examples at Eisenach, Brussels, Berlin, and elsewhere, suggest that six strings were most common, tuned as follows:

$(d-d'')$

A seven-stringed specimen (No. 36) in the Bach Museum at Eisenach carries the compass down a fourth:

$(a,-d'')$

Though the finger-board, relatively to the strings upon it, was not so long as the ordinary viola's, it is probable that upon instruments thus tuned the player could touch the octave of the top string,

. In two secular cantatas[2] Bach takes the instrument to

 and down to 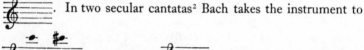. For both, it may be con-

cluded, a six-stringed instrument, tuned as above, was employed. Cantata No. 152, composed at Weimar, was served by an instrument tuned a tone higher than the seven-string viola at Eisenach:

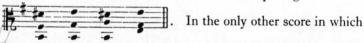

This is inferred from the chords of the opening Concerto:

. In the only other score in which

Bach employs the instrument—the *St. John Passion*—the movements in which it participates are in a flat key, and the compass extends $f-c'''$. This would be playable on a normally strung instrument, or upon one strung a tone higher than the seven-stringed specimen at Eisenach, raising the top string (*chanterelle*) to e'', a tuning that possibly required the player in that work to use the first position in only three bars in one movement.

[1] Cf. Mahillon, i. 188.   [2] See Table XVI.

The infrequent examples of his use of the viola d'amore inadequately buttress Dr. Curt Sach's assumption[1] of Bach's 'love' for the instrument, and Schweitzer's opinion,[2] that only in the *St. John Passion* need its loss be deplored, cannot be confidently contested. In cantata No. 152, the only church cantata in which it is scored, it sustains the tenor part in an instrumental quartet (flute, oboe, viola d'amore, viola da gamba) in the opening Concerto, is in unison with the other instruments in the soprano-bass duet, and is obbligato in the soprano aria, a lullaby over the infant Jesus of the utmost beauty and tenderness, to which the 'tender and languishing' quality Mattheson found in the instrument is peculiarly appropriate.[3] In *Aeolus* again it is scored along with a viola da gamba in the tenor aria, where its part is in the soprano G clef. Bach evidently desired to suggest the languorous atmosphere of the 'frische Schatten' invoked by Zephyrus:

> Shady hollows, ye're my pleasure!
> Can I see you droop and wither?
> Come, reject the cruel smart!
> Stir your leaves to life, dear branches!
> Throw sad glances
> On my sorrow-laden heart!

The soprano aria of the secular cantata *Schwingt freudig* (viola d'amore and continuo) was used by Bach on at least four occasions, for three of which he retained the original line of the text:

> Auch mit gedämpften schwachen Stimmen
> (With notes all hushed and distant sounding).

The score of one of the three is lost, but in it, as in the other two, no doubt, he painted literally the word 'gedämpften'. In cantata No. 36 he gives the obbligato to a *muted* violin, and in the secular cantata similarly entitled employs a viola d'amore in the treble clef. His purpose is obvious when it is observed that in the secular cantata *Die Freude reget sich*, in which he used the movement a fourth time, he changed the words and substituted the traverso for the viola d'amore.

Of the two movements in the *St. John Passion* in which the viola d'amore is prescribed, only the tenor aria (No. 32) was not in the original version performed in 1723. The bass arioso that precedes it also was added for a later occasion.[4] In both Bach employs two *viole d'amore* and puts their parts in the treble clef. The two movements follow the narrative of the scourging of Jesus, and the

---

[1] Sachs (3), p. 11.   [2] Vol. ii. 431.
[3] 'Die verliebte Viola d'Amore . . . führet den lieben Nahmen mit der That und will viel *languissantes* und *tendres* ausdrücken' (p. 282).   [4] *Infra*, p. 143.

instrument contributes its plaintive tone to the poignant situation. In the tenor aria, accompanying the rhythmic figure of scourging, its melodic lines seem to sketch the rainbow of forgiveness of which the text speaks:[1]

> God's rainbow light of grace is glowing,
> To show thee pardoned in His sight.

The silvery violas increase the ethereal beauty of both movements so charged with emotion.

The term 'obsolescent' applied to the viola d'amore needs qualification, perhaps withdrawal: it survived Bach's usage of it and is still occasionally scored by composers. Carl Stamitz (1746–1801), one of the famous Mannheim orchestra, was a noted performer on it. Meyerbeer introduced it into *Les Huguenots* (1836). Karl Zoeller (1840–89), bandmaster of the Second English Life-guards, was the author of an authoritative treatise on it. Louis van Waefelghem (1840–1908), also well known in London, devoted himself to its study and revival. Richard Strauss employed it in his *Sinfonia domestica* (1904), and Paul Hindemith wrote a concerto for it in 1928. In America Charles Martin Loeffler used it in his symphonic poem *The Death of Tintagiles* (1897).

The Viola da Gamba

The ancient family of the consort viols, or *viole da gamba*,[2] had five members: the

1. High discant (Pardessus de viole),
2. Discant (Dessus de viole),
3. Alto (Haute-contre),
4. Tenor (Taille), and
5. Bass.

Of these No. 5 was the viola da gamba *par excellence*. Until the period of Bach's birth (1685), it was a six-stringed instrument, tuned, after the manner of the lute, in fourths, with a midway interval of a third:

Marin Marais and Sainte-Colombe are stated to have added a seventh string  and to have increased the sonority of the

---

[1] Cf. Schweitzer, ii. 181.　　　　[2] See Praetorius, Plate XX, at p. 132.

2. 3. Violn de Gamba. 4. Viol Baſtarda. 5. Italianiſche Lyra de bracio.

VIOLA DA GAMBA, VIOLA BASTARDA, AND LYRA DA BRACCIO
(*Praetorius*)

three lower ones of the six by strengthening their texture.[1] Thus equipped, the instrument, though about the size of the violoncello, exceeded it in compass. Its top string was tuned a fourth higher, and, owing to its greater length and more delicate texture, was more extended in its upper register. It lacked the volume of the violoncello, but its tone was more delicate, its chords richer and more varied, and its fretted finger-board more assistant to the player's accuracy. France preferred the seven-stringed tuning. England and Germany were more conservative in their liking for the

six-stringed variety, tuning down the lowest string to ░░░░ ,

however, when the key of the composition required the change. Bach's scoring demands a seven-stringed gamba only in the *St. Matthew Passion* and the Gamba Sonata in D. Elsewhere he was content with the six-stringed instrument at its normal tuning, though in cantata No. 76, the *St. John Passion*, and *Aeolus*, he

takes down the lowest string to ░░░░ .

The classic period of the viola da gamba was in the seventeenth and early eighteenth centuries, when it attracted players whose technique excelled that of the performers on the violin: in England, Alphonso Ferrabosco (*ob.* 1628), John Cooper (*ob.* 1627), Tobias Hume (*ob.* 1645), William Brade (*ob.* 1630), John Jenkins (*ob.* 1678), and especially Christopher Simpson (*ob.* 1669); in France, Marin Marais (1656–1728), Antoine Forqueray (1671–1745) and his son, Jean Rousseau (fl. 1678–87), Louis de Caix d'Hervelois (*ob.* 1760); in Germany, August Kühnel (b. 1645), Johann Schenk, and Ernst Christian Hesse (*ob.*1762). Excepting de Caix d'Hervelois and Hesse, all were of an earlier generation than Bach, who handled the instrument in a period in which its vogue was no longer general.

The viola da gamba was the last of its family to disappear. Early in the seventeenth century the discant viol was challenged by the violin, and *c.* 1650 the alto-tenor had to meet the competition of the viola. But the viola da gamba maintained its monopoly. It was everywhere the popular instrument of accompaniment, the foundation of instrumental *ensemble*. It held the violoncello at bay, relegating its rival to the continuo, as Bach generally used it. So it lived to decorate music more lofty than ever before had used it. But, from the advent of Haydn, Mozart, Beethoven, and the string quartet, it associated unequally with the violins and viola, and at

---

[1] Cf. Hayes, p. 8.

length gave place to the violoncello. Bach's son's friend and London partner, Carl Friedrich Abel, was the last of its *virtuosi*. Gerber wrote truly in his revised *Lexicon* that Abel's instrument passed in 1787 with Abel himself into the oblivion of the grave.

Viewing the circumstances set forth in the preceding paragraph,

Viola da gamba,
seven strings, 1725;
extreme length 121 cm.

Bach's infrequent use of the viola da gamba is not surprising. At Weimar he found it useful in two cantatas, Nos. 106 and 152. At Leipzig he introduced it into five scores, sparingly in the two *Passions* and *Aeolus*, more lavishly in the *Trauer-Ode* and cantata No. 76. After 1729, apparently, he made no use of it, a significant fact in view of his subsequent employment of the violoncello piccolo. Of chamber music for the instrument he wrote little, and exclusively at Cöthen, where Prince Leopold was a player of it, and Christian Ferdinand Abel, the father of the above-named Carl Friedrich, was a member of the Capelle. The three Sonatas for cembalo and viola da gamba, in G ma., D ma., and G mi., may well have been written for the former; the cembalo, as providing two out of the three obbligato parts, dominates; and the gamba has comparatively little opportunity to display its technique; indeed, the first Sonata is an adaptation of one for two *traversi* and continuo, in which the viola da gamba receives the part of the second traverso. Forkel[1] observes that 'they are admirably written and pleasant to listen to, even to-day (1802)'. But their interest is in the music rather than their instrumental technique. In the sixth Brandenburg Concerto the two *viole da gamba* generally complete the harmonic accompaniment.

In his concerted music, also, Bach's viola da gamba parts do not generally permit the instrument to display its traditional technique. In cantata No. 76, excepting the Sinfonia and alto aria of Part II —where it forms a trio with an oboe d'amore and bass—it strengthens the continuo. In cantata No. 106 ('Actus tragicus'), as in the *Trauer-Ode*, the two *viole da gamba* contribute an elegiac colour to the funeral music. In cantata No. 152, where the instru-

[1] p. 130.

ment is confined to the opening concerto, it is again closely
associated with the continuo. In the tenor aria of *Aeolus* it plays
a second to the viola d'amore over a bass. But in the two *Passions*
it stresses the emotion the unfolding drama evoked from Bach's
pondering soul. What depth of feeling is expressed in its solo obbligato to the alto aria 'Es ist vollbracht' ('It is finished') of the *St. John*
Passion! In the bass aria, 'Komm, süsses Kreuz', of the *St. Mat-*
thew Passion Bach writes his only typical viola da gamba part.
It yields a colour the violoncello cannot impart, is eloquent over
a compass that instrument could not equal, and reaches to depths
it could not plumb.[1] How Bach met the exceptional orchestral
demand the *St. Matthew Passion* made on his slender and irregular
resources is a matter for wonder. That he had the services of a
finished viola da gamba player is evident, for the obbligato needs
one. Is it improbable that Christian Ferdinand Abel from Cöthen
was a guest for the occasion?

The Violoncello Piccolo

Bach certainly regretted the absence of an instrument of bass
quality adequate for solo *obbligati*. The violoncellist had not
developed the necessary technique. The viola da gamba was
deficient in tone on the public platform it had exchanged for the
intimate atmosphere of its classic period. As far as we know, Bach
never introduced it into a score after his composition of the
St. Matthew Passion in 1729. Two years later, at Easter 1731, he
for the first time used the violoncello at Leipzig as an obbligato instrument. He repeated the experiment thrice in the course of the
following six months, and for the last time on 14 October 1731,[2]
having on the previous Sunday (7 October 1731) made his first
trial of a new instrument, invariably called 'violoncello piccolo'
in his scores. Four years elapsed before he used it again, in 1735,
on four occasions between 24 April and 31 May. In 1736 he scored
it twice, and that his interest in it was prolonged to a later date is
evident in cantatas Nos. 115 and 180.

It is not without significance that the inventory of instruments
belonging to the Cöthen Capelle discloses a five-stringed violoncello piccolo by J. C. Hoffmann, of Leipzig, bearing the date 1731,
the year in which Bach first employed it. That it was the product
of their joint planning and experiment can be supposed. But,
as Dr. Kinsky[3] observes, Bach's association with the instrument is

[1] In an alternative version of the tenor recitative (No. 40), 'Mein Jesus
schweigt' (B.-G. iv. 290), a viola da gamba supplements the two oboes of the
original score. The addition is of doubtful authority.
[2] Nos. 42, 172, 56, 188.   [3] *Zeitschrift f. Musik.*, March 1931, pp. 325 f.

mentioned by no writer during his lifetime. Moreover, its identi-
fication and quality are confused by nearly contemporary writers,
who, as is probable, miscall it 'viola pomposa'. Johann Nikolaus
Forkel, the earliest to give particulars of it, so names it in his
Musicalisches Almanach für Deutschland (1782). Johann Adam
Hiller mentions it in his *Lebensbeschreibungen berühmter Musikgelehrten* (1784), and Gerber records precisely in the 'Instrumenten-
Register' at the end of his second volume (1792): 'Viola pomposa:
Erfand Joh. Seb. Bach zu Leipzig, ums Jahr 1724.' Bach, he states
in a short biography, was led to experiment with it owing to 'the
stiff manner in which the violoncello was played at that period'.
He remarks that it rendered 'very high and rapid passages' easier
of performance; that it was somewhat longer than a viola, was tuned
like the violoncello, but with a fifth string a fifth higher; and that
in use it was laid on the arm ('an den Arm gesetzt wurde'). Forkel,
who gives the same particulars, adds that it was fitted with a strap
or ribbon ('mit einem Bande befestigt') for the easier holding of
it 'vor der Brust und auf dem Arme'.

Thus—the deduction is material—Bach's so-called 'viola
pomposa' was designed to make good the deficiencies of a *bass*
instrument, particularly in rapid and high-pitched passages. To
that end it had the violoncello stringing, with an additional fifth
string sounding *e′* :

Is there corroborative evidence of an instrument so named and
strung? We learn from Hiller[1] that, shortly before Lent 1738, the
violin virtuoso Franz Benda visited Dresden at the invitation of
Concertmeister Pisendel, and on one occasion was accompanied
by him on a 'viola pomposa'. He does not describe it as a new
instrument, neither does he associate Bach with it. Nor, in fact,
does Bach himself use the term 'viola pomposa' in his scores.
Moreover, a 'viola pomposa' was in contemporary use elsewhere
than Dresden. Mr. F. T. Arnold[2] has brought to light a 'Sonata
à solo per la Pomposa col Basso' by C. G. Lidarti, written apparently about 1760. Canon Galpin[3] has revealed two duets for viola
pomposa (or violin) and flute by G. P. Telemann, published at
Hamburg in 1728. It would be easy, of course, for an instrument
invented by Bach about 1724 to make its way to Hamburg by

[1] p. 45.   [2] *Zeitschrift f. Musik.*, Dec. 1930.
[3] *Music and Letters*, Oct. 1931, p. 354 and *Zeitschrift f. Musik*, Oct. 1931.

1728, and to Pisa or Vienna about 1760. But Canon Galpin has recently argued that the viola pomposa used by Lidarti and Telemann and, no doubt, Pisendel, was another instrument altogether, not of bass, but of viola quality, probably tuned *d*, *g*, *d'*, *g'*, *c''*, and therefore in compass distinct from the violoncello-strung viola described by Forkel and Gerber, whose lowest strings carried down the compass of the instrument two whole fifths below that of the authentic pomposa. The latter, indeed, with a compass extending from *d* to *c'''*, was almost mezzo-soprano in pitch, and by Telemann, at least, was grouped with the violin. That Forkel, and Gerber, who copied his statement, associated its name with Bach's instrument must be attributed to misinformation: after all, Bach's scores were not accessible to them.

Viola pomposa,
c. 1750,
extreme length 75 cm.

Of the Telemann-Pisendel-Lidarti pomposa at least five examples are extant. The Bach Museum at Eisenach exhibits one (No. 56), made 'Mitte 18. Jahr.', with the following dimensions: total length about 30 inches (75 cm.), length of body about 18 inches (45·5 cm.), upper breadth about 8¼ inches (21·5 cm.), lower breadth about 10¼ inches (26 cm.), and the depth of ribs about 3 inches (8 cm.).

Another example is in the Brussels collection (Allemagne, 1445). It was made by Hoffmann himself. Its dimensions accord closely with those of the Eisenach specimen: total length 31½ inches (80 cm.), maximum width about 10½ inches (27 cm.), depth of ribs about 3 inches (75 mm.). Two examples, also by Hoffmann, are in the Heyer Collection at Leipzig. One is dated '1732': total length about 30½ inches, body length about 18 inches, and depth of ribs about 3½ inches.[1] The other is dated '1741'. Dr. Kinsky[2] instances another example, also by Hoffmann, dated 1732, and at present in the possession of Herr Albin Wilfer, violin-maker, Leipzig, who claims that it can bear the *c,*, *g,*, *d*, *a*, *e'* tuning alleged by Gerber and Forkel.

Thus, as Canon Galpin concludes, the authentic viola pomposa varied in total length from about 29½ inches to 31½ inches, with a

¹ Figured in *Grove*, v. 524.   ² *Zeitschrift f. Musik.*, Dec. 1931, p. 178.

vibrating length of string from nut to bridge of 16¾ to 17¾ inches, and a rib-depth of 3 inches to 3½ inches. It was, in fact, a large-sized viola, midway between the ordinary viola and the violoncello piccolo. Conceivably, it might have been played 'on the arm', certainly not under the chin, and could not effectually have borne the stringing Forkel and Gerber attribute to Bach's 'invention'.

The rejection of the Telemann-Lidarti pomposa as the instrument attributed to Bach by Forkel and Gerber establishes the violoncello piccolo as the one to which they confusedly refer. It was some 10 inches longer than the smaller instrument, some 7 inches longer from nut to bridge, and about 1 inch thicker in rib-depth.[1] Manifestly such an instrument could only have been played between the knees. Equally certainly, its lower strings can have had little sonority. It is, therefore, not surprising that in the nine movements Bach wrote for the violoncello piccolo the lowest string

is needed in only four (cantatas Nos. 41, 68, 115, 175). In no case is it employed for sustained notes or passages. In the florid obbligato of cantata No. 41 this string is touched for only thirteen notes, all but three of which are detached quavers or semiquavers, the bow merely flicked. In the still more lengthy obbligato of cantata No. 68 only sixteen notes are written for it, all of which are short and detached except the final minim. In cantata No. 115 fifteen notes only are sounded on it, all of them unstressed. In cantata No. 175 the string is touched lightly for no more than three notes in a movement of 130 bars.

Of the fourth string

Bach's use is hardly less economical. In cantata No. 85 it sounds less than thirty notes in a movement of 61 bars, and none of them are sustained. In cantata No. 180 the string is touched for four semiquavers only, in rapid arpeggios. In cantata No. 183, in an obbligato of similar character, it sounds eighteen notes, short and detached, in a movement of 46 bars. For sustained legato playing the fourth string is not used at all. As an obbligato instrument, consequently, Bach's use of the violoncello piccolo was

---

[1] An example is in the Kunsthistorisches Museum, Vienna.

almost restricted to its three upper strings, the topmost of which

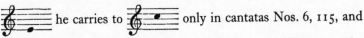 he carries to only in cantatas Nos. 6, 115, and

183; for the violoncello piccolo player was as diffident as the violinist in adventuring upon the highest register.

Bach employs a notation for the instrument neither uniform nor invariably simple. Its part falls within the compass of a single

(From left to right) Viola, extreme length *c.* 66 cm.; Violoncello piccolo, extreme length 99–105 cm.; Viola pomposa, extreme length 75–80 cm.

clef only in five scores (cantatas Nos. 6, 49, 85, 180, and 183). He uses the alto C clef in Nos. 6 and 180, the treble G clef in Nos. 49 and 85, and the tenor C clef in No. 183. Otherwise its part is written under the bass F and treble G clefs, as in No. 41; or in the bass F and alto C clef, as in No. 115; or in the bass F and tenor C clef, as in Nos. 68 and 175. These present no peculiarities. But others, written in whole or part in the treble G clef, exhibit a feature unusual, and at first sight confusing. For example, the following passages occur in No. 41:

Evidently the treble notes are intended to sound an octave below their written position, and the reason for the apparent complexity is revealed when we discover the obbligato, in Bach's autograph, written in a first violin part. For the four upper strings of the violoncello piccolo were tuned to the same intervals as those of the violin, but an octave lower. Consequently, the fingering being so similar, it can be concluded that in cantatas Nos. 41, 49, 85, where the violoncello piccolo part is wholly or partly in the treble G clef, it was played by a violinist rather than a violoncellist, a supposition supported by the duplicate copy for the instrument already noticed. Otherwise, it seems probable, the part was entrusted to a viola player, who would be equally at home on the four lower strings, and for the same reason. Both players, however, would be more inconvenienced than a violoncellist by the 'à gamba' position.

As we should infer from the reasons for its invention, the chief characteristic exhibited by the violoncello piccolo in Bach's scores is agility in its upper and middle compass. Otherwise it displays no qualities which can have invited him to employ it; it has no consistent characterization in his usage, and is associated with arias of diverse sentiment—with a picture of the Good Shepherd (Nos. 85 and 175), an evening scene (No. 6), a eucharistic hymn (No. 180), prayer (No. 115), a eulogy of peace (No. 41), a challenge to death (No. 183). Or it simply expresses care-free gaiety, as in No. 49, or light-hearted joy, as in the soprano aria, 'My heart ever faithful', of No. 68. Generally Bach associates it with a soprano voice, but with a bass not at all. Its lack of tone probably explains his disinclination to associate another obbligato instrument with it—in six of its nine movements the continuo alone supports it, and in the others a traverso or an oboe (with violin) are its partners.

Excepting the Sonatas for the viola da gamba, Bach wrote no music with clavier accompaniment for any instrument of violoncello quality. The six Suites for violoncello solo composed at Cöthen are the only chamber music for the instrument, a fact which may indicate the high talents of Christian Bernhard Linigke, a former member of the Berlin Hofcapelle, whom Prince Leopold secured as violoncellist during Bach's period of office as Capell-meister. Both Schweitzer[1] and Spitta[2] suppose that the sixth Suite was written for viola pomposa—that is, for Bach's violon-cello piccolo. Their assumption is based on the fact that the original MS. has the heading:

Suitte 6ᵐᵉ a cing acordes

The tuning is that of the five-stringed violoncello piccolo. A good deal of use is made of the top string, but otherwise there is little to distinguish the Suite from the other five. Nor is there evidence, or indeed in the circumstances, likelihood, that the instrument existed at the period (*c.* 1720) when the Suite was composed. The Cöthen specimen of Hoffmann's handiwork was dated 1731. But the Prince also owned two ordinary violoncellos by Hoffmann, dated 1715 and 1720 respectively, and also one by Jakob Steiner,[3] one or more of which may have been five-stringed.[4] On the other hand, the possibility cannot be excluded that the sixth Suite was a Leipzig addition to the other five. Bach's original autograph of the set is lost. But a copy is extant in the hand of his wife, Anna Magdalena, the title-page of which indicates that it was written at Leipzig:

Pars 2
Violoncello Solo senza Basso
composée par Sr. J. S. Bach. Maitre
de la Chapelle et Directeur de la Musique a Leipsic.
ecrite par Madame Bachen. Son Epouse.

The paper bears the watermark 'MA', which Spitta[5] shows Bach to have been using about 1730, when the problem of the violon-cello piccolo was engaging him. The sixth Suite probably was written for it at that period.[6]

The Lute

The lute (*Laute, luth, liuto*), the favourite instrument of the sixteenth and seventeenth centuries, declined in vogue in the earlier half of the eighteenth, and passed from use in the half-century following Bach's death (1750). For domestic music it was superseded by the clavichord and guitar, and on the public

---

[1] Vol. i. 393.   [2] Vol. ii. 100.   [3] B.-J. 1905, p. 38.
[4] Five-stringed violoncellos are rare.   [5] Vol. ii, p. 690.
[6] Canon Galpin remarks that a five-stringed violoncello existed with a vibrating string an inch or so less than the ordinary violoncello. He conjectures that the sixth Suite was written for this instrument.

platform was excluded from the new orchestra: its latest appearance
in such company is said to have been at the production of Handel's
opera *Deidamia* in 1740. Bach therefore employed it almost at
the moment of its disappearance.

Yet, at Leipzig more than elsewhere, its tradition was cherished,
its disuse regretted.[1] Cultural relations with Silesia, Poland, and
Bohemia had always been close, and those countries produced the
best lute players. From Breslau came Johann Kropfgans (b. 1668)
and his son of the same name, who visited Bach in 1739. Silvius
Leopold Weiss (1686–1750), for whom, it is probable, Bach composed or arranged lute music, was another Bohemian. Adam
Falkenhagen was teaching the lute in Leipzig shortly before Bach
came to the city, and Johann Caspar Gleditsch (d. 1747), his principal oboist, composed for the instrument. Of Bach's own pupils
two were distinguished lute players—Rudolph Straube, an *alumnus*
of the Thomasschule 1733–40, who published two lute sonatas in
1746,[2] and eventually settled in London, a contemporary there of
Johann Christian Bach; and Johann Ludwig Krebs, an older
alumnus (1726–35), for whom his master had particular affection;
the Berlin Staatsbibliothek owns the autograph of two lute concertos by him.[3] Kuhnau, Bach's immediate predecessor, set great
store by the instrument: his request to be supplied with a bass lute
has been mentioned elsewhere.[4] A print of St. Thomas's organ-
loft during his Cantorship shows a lutenist among the players.[5]
Moreover, in Johann Christian Hoffmann Leipzig boasted a lute-
maker of European reputation.[6] It is therefore not surprising
that among the instruments that crowded Bach's lodging in the
Thomasschule were three of lute character, and that his lute
music must be referred to the Leipzig period.

A D minor 'eleven course' lute was tuned thus, all but the top
two strings being duplicated, in octaves or unison:

Such a compass was not always adequate: the lute part in the

Trauer-Ode, for instance, touches ⟨music⟩, and in two scores[7]

---

[1] Cf. Schering, pp. 413–23.
[2] The British Museum has a copy of the work.   [3] B.-J. 1931, p. 77 note.
[4] *Supra*, p. 19.   [5] See the frontispiece in Terry (4).
[6] Baron, chap. vii, particularly praises Hoffmann's lutes for their proportions
and tone.   [7] See Table XIX.

descends to 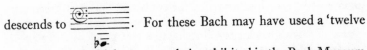. For these Bach may have used a 'twelve course' lute, of which an example is exhibited in the Bach Museum at Eisenach, tuned thus:

Excepting the top two 'melody strings', the catgut and silver-spun strings are duplicated. All are carried to a pegboard set at right angles to the finger-board, which is fretted to measure the semitones, eight or more frets to each pair of strings. The low $ab_{,,}$ would be got by the normal method of adjusting the octave strings to the tonality of the movement.

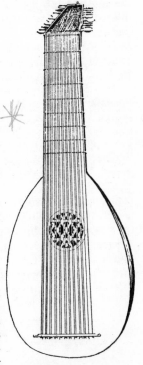

As has been already observed, Bach's practical interest in the lute was first dis- played at Leipzig, where he employed it in two concerted vocal works and a few instrumental compositions. The fact that both vocal works are associated with the year 1727 indicates that a lute player was then at his disposal. The earlier of them, a revised version of the *St. John Passion*, was performed in St. Thomas's on Good Friday (April 11) in that year. Bach wrote for it the bass arioso (No. 31) 'Betrachte, meine Seele', whose score indicates an accompaniment by two *viole d'amore*, lute, organ, and continuo. The lute part is missing, and an alternative one, marked 'Organo ò Cembalo (obbligato)' in Bach's autograph, was used at some other per- formance when a lute player was not available. He was not under that disability in October 1727 when he produced the

Lute, 17th cent., extreme length 105 cm.

Trauer-Ode in St. Paul's, the University Church. The occasion was of official significance and Bach was not restricted to the sources from which his players were normally drawn. The work, accordingly, is scored for two lutes, which, excepting the remarkable alto recitative (No. 4), where they echo the 'bebendes Getön' of the funeral bells, merely strengthen the continuo. This accorded with the practice of Court orchestras in that period;[1] Bach's exceptional conformity with it suggests that members of the Dresden Capelle assisted him at this ceremonial performance. There are no other extant examples of his employment of the lute in circumstances which invited his predecessor's frequent use of it. His neglect therefore cannot have been exclusively due to the lack of competent players. For strengthening his continuo, one supposes, he preferred instruments of more masculine tone.

In his instrumental music, also, evidences of Bach's interest in the lute are infrequent. 'III. Partite à Liuto Solo' by him were offered for sale in manuscript by Breitkopf in 1761.[2] They have disappeared. Others are extant, however, which were written for the instrument or adapted to it. In particular, the Suites in E major, E minor, and C minor, printed as clavier music in the Bachgesellschaft edition. The E major Suite:[3]

is also extant as the third Partita for violin,[4] in which the solo part is set an octave higher. The autograph does not indicate the instrument for which the work was composed. But Herr Hans Neemann, instructed by long and practical acquaintance with lute music, finds the Prelude unplayable on the normally strung instrument in D minor, and suggests that the work was composed neither for lute, clavier, nor violin, but for the harp![5]

The Suite in E minor:[6]

is among the manuscripts of Bach's pupil, Johann Ludwig Krebs, inscribed: 'Praeludio con la Svite da Gio: Bast: Bach aufs Lauten

[1] B.-J. 1931, p. 76.   [2] Spitta, iii. 166.   [3] B.-G. xlii. 16.
[4] *Ibid.* xxvii (1), 48.   [5] B.-J. 1931, p. 85.   [6] B.-G. xlv (1), 149.

Werck.' Its association with a 'Lauten Werck' is interesting. Among the instruments owned by Bach and valued in the inventory of his belongings were:[1]

1 Lauten Werck	.	.	.	.	30 Reichsthaler
1 „ „	.	.	.	.	30 „
1 Laute	.	.	.	.	21 „

Clearly Bach's 'Lauten Werck' was not the ordinary lute (Laute), and its greater costliness supports the conclusion that it was the lute-harpsichord or 'Lautenclavicymbel' built to his specification by the organ-builder Zacharias Hildebrand. Adlung[2] describes it as being shorter than the clavier, with two unisons of gut strings and an octave register of brass wire. The combination of tone, smothered by a cloth damper, produced sounds so like those of an ordinary lute that even a professional lutenist could not distinguish them. According to Adlung, Hildebrand made an instrument of this kind for Bach in or about 1740. But a more precise date can be suggested. In July 1739 Friedemann Bach came home from Dresden for a month's holiday, bringing with him the master-lutenists, Silvius Leopold Weiss and Johann Kropfgans.[3] A particular purpose must have invited the concurrent arrival of these *virtuosi*, and they produced 'something extra good in the way of music', reported Johann Elias Bach, then resident in the Cantor's house. Probably Bach's 'Lauten Werck' had been recently constructed, and Weiss and his colleague were invited to test its quality.[4] The Suite in E minor may have been composed for the occasion.

[1] Terry (Germ. edn.), p. 329.
[2] *Musica mechanica organoedi* (1768), ii. 139: 'Der Verfasser dieser Anmerkungen erinnert sich, ungefähr im Jahre 1740 in Leipzig ein von dem Hrn. Johann Sebastian Bach angegebenes, und vom Hrn. Zacharias Hildebrand ausgearbeitetes Lautenclavicymbel gesehen und gehöret zu haben, welches zwar eine kürzere Mensur als die ordentlichen Clavicymbel hatte, in allem übrigen aber wie ein ander Clavicymbel beschaffen war. Es hatte zwey Chore Darmseyten, und ein sogenanntes Octävchen von messingenen Seyten. Es ist wahr, in seiner eigentlichen Einrichtung klang es, (wenn nämlich nur ein Zug gezogen war,) mehr der Theorbe, als der Laute ähnlich. Aber, wenn der sogennante, und auch hier § 561 angeführte Lautenzug, (der eben so wie auf den beyden Clavicymbeln war,) mit dem Cornetzuge gezogen wurde, so konnte man auch bey nahe Lautenisten von Profession damit betrügen. Herr Friderici hat auch dergleichen gemacht, doch mit einiger Veränderung' (vol. ii. 139).
[3] Terry, p. 247.
[4] Dr. Curt Sachs, *Real-Lexikon der Musikinstrumente (s.v.* Lauten-Clavier), describes a similar instrument made by Joh. Christoph Fleischer of Hamburg in 1718. Adlung (*op. cit.* ii. 135) also mentions one made by Joh. Nikolaus Bach (1669–1753) of Jena. Herr Neemann is not convinced that 'Lauten Werck' and 'Lautenclavicymbel' are exchangeable terms, and judges the E mi. Suite to be normal lute music.

The Suite (*Fantasia, Sarabande, Giga*) in C minor:[1]

exists in the Leipzig Stadtbibliothek as a 'Partita al Liuto. Composta dal Sigre Bach', a MS. in the collection of Carl Ferdinand Becker, sometime organist of St. Nicholas's Church. Internal evidence indicates that the Suite, adapted subsequently for the clavier, was originally composed for the lute.[2]

In the same collection of 'Pieces pour le lut par Sre J. S. Bach' is the MS. of a Suite in G minor, the autograph of which, preserved in the Fétis Library at Brussels, bears the title: 'Suite pour la Luth à Monsieur Schouster par J. S. Bach.' Mons. Schuster was probably a member of the Dresden Capelle so named, who functioned as Chamber musician and bass singer, and was the father of Joseph Schuster, subsequently Capellmeister there. If so, the autograph can be associated with Bach's middle Leipzig period. The Suite, however, is not an original composition for the lute, but an arrangement, by Bach himself, of the violoncello 'Suite discordable' in C minor.

In addition to these elaborate works, a few short pieces are claimed for the lute. The third of the 'Zwölf kleine Praeludien', in C minor:[3]

is a simple two-part exercise. A copy of it by Johann Peter Kellner, a pupil of Bach's contemporary, Johann Schmidt, bears the inscription 'Praelude in C mol pour la Lute di Johann Sebastian Bach'. Dörffel[4] questions the ascription 'pour la Lute'. Herr Neemann finds the piece eminently 'lautenmässig'.[5]

---

[1] B.-G. xlv (1), 156.
[2] Cf. Dörffel's note in B.-G. xxvii (1), p. xviii, and B.-J. 1931, p. 79.
[3] B.-G. xxxvi. 119.   [4] B.-G. xlv (1), p. li.   [5] B.-J. 1931, p. 83.

No doubt exists in the case of the Prelude in E flat:[1]

Bach's autograph[2] indicates it as a 'Prélude pour la Luth ò Cembal'. It includes three movements—*Prelude, Fugue, Allegro.*

Finally in this enumeration must be recorded a 'Fuga del Signore Bach', the MS. of which in lute tablature is in the Leipzig Stadtbibliothek. Its authenticity is attested by the fact that it appears elsewhere as the fugue of the Violin Sonata in G minor[3] and of the Organ Prelude and Fugue in D minor.[4]

All three versions are so appropriate to their respective instruments that it is impossible to declare positively for which of them the music was originally designed.

But sufficient evidence has been adduced to establish Bach's intimate acquaintance with the technique of the lute, both as composer and player, though, so far as the material affords a clue, his interest in the instrument was confined to his Leipzig period, and to a restricted portion of it. In those years—the seventeen-thirties—the construction of the lute-harpsichord (Lautenclavicymbel) engaged him, and Spitta[5] supposes that the lute partitas were written for it. Pirro[6] expresses the same opinion. Herr Neemann[7] scouts the proposition. But the circumstances support the conjecture.[8]

[1] B.-G. xlv (1), 141.
[2] Formerly in the possession of Mr. Henry Huth, the autograph is now in the collection of Dr. Karl. Frh. von Vietinghoff-Scheel, Kaiserin-Augusta Strasse 75–76, Berlin, N.W.
[3] B.-G. xxvii (1), p. 4.   [4] B.-G. xv. 149.   [5] Sp. iii. 167.
[6] German edition, p. 178. The statement does not appear in the original French edition.   [7] B.-J. 1931, p. 87.
[8] Bach's lute music (ed. E. D. Bruger) is published by Zwissler, Wolfenbüttel (1925). See also Wilhelm Tappert's *Seb. Bachs Kompositionen für die Laute* (Berlin, 1901).

CHAPTER VII

THE CONTINUO

THE preceding chapters have reviewed the instruments of Bach's orchestra which appear in his scores under their individual names. There remain for consideration others which function anonymously, in a part generally distinguished by him as 'Continuo', and once (cantata No. 112) as 'Basso per Fundamento'. Considering its general currency after Viadana's *Cento concerti* (1602) brought it into use, early in the seventeenth century,[1] Bach's avoidance of the complete term 'Basso continuo' is noticeable. But, like it, his 'Continuo' provided a continuous or 'thorough' bass accompaniment supporting the musical structure. Whether it was unfigured, or figured with numerals indicating the composer's intended harmonies, was irrelevant to its function as the unbroken foundation of the vocal or instrumental parts above it. In Bach's usage, accordingly, the word 'Continuo' denotes two distinct orchestral voices: (1) the unfigured part for the bass instruments, strings and wind, supporting the keyboard bass ('Basso per l'Organo', 'Basso per il Cembalo'); and (2) the figured part, from which the organist or cembalist supplied the harmonic accompaniment the numerals indicated.

Thus the continuo was essentially 'the accompaniment', to which keyed, string, and wind instruments made their contribution in accordance with certain recognized conventions. The clearest and most definite exposition of the practice of Bach's generation is afforded by his son Carl Philipp Emanuel,[2] who introduces the second Part of *The correct art of clavier-playing*, which deals particularly with the art of accompaniment, with the following paragraphs:

'1. The keyed instruments most generally used for accompanying are the organ, harpsichord, fortepiano, and clavichord.

'3. For church-music, with its fugues, powerful choruses, and syncopations, the organ is indispensable.[3] It enhances the effect and keeps everything together. ("Sie befördert die Pracht und erhält die Ordnung.")

'4. But, for arias and recitatives sung in church, the harpsichord must be employed, particularly when the middle [instrumental] parts are of such simplicity as to leave the voice practically free and independent

---

[1] Arnold, p. 6.
[2] Bach, Pt. II, p. 1.
[3] A 'Bindung' was more than a syncopation. It implied a discord. Cf. Arnold, p. 127.

("alle Freyheit zum Verändern lassen"). Without it, as we are able to judge much too frequently, how bald the music sounds! . . .

'7. So, no piece is satisfactorily rendered except to the accompaniment of a keyed instrument. Even in music on the largest scale ("bey den stärksten Musiken"), in opera, even at open-air performances, where we might suppose a harpsichord unable to make itself heard, one misses it if it is absent. Listening from above, its every note comes through distinctly. I speak from experience, and any one can make the test.

'8. In their solos some people are content to be accompanied only by a viola, or even a violin, unsupported by a keyed instrument. If they do so for lack of competent harpsichord players they may be excused. But a performance of that kind is necessarily quite unbalanced ("sonst aber gehen bey dieser Art von Ausführung viele Ungleichheiten vor"). If there is a good bass part, the solo becomes a duet; if it is bad, how thin the piece sounds, lacking the harmony! . . . And how bare is the chording sometimes found in the instrumental part without a foundation-bass to support it! The beauties the harmony brings out are quite lost, especially in pieces of an expressive character ("bey affectuösen Stücken").

'9. The most complete and unexceptionable accompaniment to a solo is provided by a keyed instrument associated with a violoncello.'

If Carl Philipp Emanuel's prescriptions represented his own custom at Hamburg, they are no less appropriate to his father's circumstances at Leipzig. There, on every Sunday morning outside Lent and Advent, and also on certain saints' days and public festivals, Bach's office required him to compose or provide an anthem (cantata) for chorus, *soli*, and orchestra, of from twenty to thirty minutes' duration. Their scheme was uniform—an elaborate opening chorus, a couple of arias, as many recitatives, and a concluding Choral. Exceptionally the cantata was prolonged into a second Part, performed after the sermon. Sometimes, too, the arias and recitatives exceeded the normal number, or Bach inserted another of his 'starke Chöre', or an extra Choral, or an instrumental movement to serve as an introduction. But the ingredients remained constant—choruses, arias, recitatives, and Chorals. The singers, soloists and ripienists alike, were the *alumni* of the Thomasschule. The orchestra was formed by the Stadtpfeifer, Kunstgeiger, and amateurs drawn from the School and the University. The performances were given on alternate Sundays in the western gallery of the two principal churches, St. Thomas's and St. Nicholas's. Both were equipped with organs and maintained their own organist. Bach's peculiar duty was to conduct the performance. Whether he also took part in the accompaniments at the organ or harpsichord is a point for later discussion. Here it need be remarked only that, at least for a large proportion of the arias and recitatives, the accompaniment of a keyed instrument was imperatively required. An analysis of no more than those of the first twenty cantatas suffices to establish the statement:

	ARIAS.			RECITATIVES.		
CANTATA.	Fully scored.	Continuo only.	Continuo & obbligati.	Fully scored.	Continuo only.	Continuo & obbligati.
No. 1	1	..	1	..	2	..
,, 2	1	..	1	1	1	..
,, 3	..	1	1	..	2	..
,, 4	1	2	1	..	..	..
,, 5	1	..	1	..	2	1
,, 6	1	..	2	..	1	..
,, 7	1	1	1	1	1	..
,, 8	1	..	1	1	1	..
,, 9	..	..	2	..	3	..
,, 10	1	1	1	1	1	..
,, 11	..	..	2	..	4	2
,, 12	..	..	3	1	..	..
,, 13	2	..	1	..	2	..
,, 14	1	..	1	..	1	..
,, 15	1	..	5	..	2	..
,, 16	..	..	1	..	2	..
,, 17	1	..	1	..	3	..
,, 18	..	..	1	..	1	..
,, 19	1	..	1	1	2	..
,, 20	4	1	..	..	3	..
TOTAL	18	6	28	6	34	3

The Table reveals that, out of 95 movements, only 24—little more than one-quarter—are sufficiently scored to make a filling-in accompaniment by a keyed instrument, organ or harpsichord, dispensable. Of 52 arias only 18 are in a condition of completeness, of 43 recitatives no more than 6. How shall we explain this? Certainly the practice of Bach's period favoured figured basses in lieu of fully written-out accompaniments: they saved time and labour, particularly when instruments of another order shared the accompaniment with the harpsichord. But the explanation does not meet the fact that Bach allowed his players to sit inactive during so large a part of the performance in which they were engaged. Nor does the music itself afford a clue to his meagre treatment of one aria and elaborate decoration of another. The probable solution is that he shrank from overtaxing his ripieno players. It will be observed in the Table that arias accompanied by the continuo with obbligato instruments are the most numerous. They employed the professional players, who, relatively to the less expert amateurs, did not need similar consideration. The latter, we can suppose, would be sufficiently occupied in mastering their parts in the concerted movements. We can imagine, too, that even Bach's unflagging vigour could be daunted by the unbroken

monthly calls upon his genius. But, whatever the explanation of his
practice, it is as certain that a keyed instrument was essential for
the accompaniment of his arias and recitatives, as that the organ
was a regular member of his church orchestra.

It is evident, therefore, that Bach shared his son's views regarding the accompaniment of church music. But, as has already been
remarked, his continuo instruments function for the most part
anonymously. They are rarely prescribed by name in his scores,
and for their identity and service we need to turn to his orchestral
parts.

Having in view their recurring performances, it was Bach's
habit to file the parts of his church cantatas in a wrapper on which
he recorded its contents: e.g. cantata No. 78:

Dominica 14 post Trinit.
Jesu der du meine Seele.
â 4 Voci, 1 Traversa, 2 Hautbois, 2 Violini, Viola, e Continuo di Sig.
J. S. Bach.

The top line indicates the Sunday to which the cantata was
appropriate; the second records its title; the third shows its instrumentation, information assisting the Cantor-composer, looking
ahead, to select his anthem for a future occasion. The wrapper
normally contained a single part for each instrument engaged, but
duplicates were occasionally provided for the violins and, necessarily, for the continuo. The Table on p. 152, based on the
editorial notes in Jahrgang XXIV and XXVI of the Bachgesellschaft edition, gives representative examples.

We observe that a single copy sufficed for each of the four
parts (S.A.T.B.) of Bach's choir, a circumstance which is at
variance with the picture representing the organ-gallery of St.
Thomas's Church,[1] which displays the singers in separate quartets.
We notice also that the soloists were not provided with separate
parts: in fact, they were members of the chorus body. It is
evident, too, that a single desk for each part usually accommodated Bach's first and second violins and violas, and that in
numbers the instrumentalists almost equalled his singers. We
must conclude also that, if one of the two continuo parts was the
organist's, a single part usually accommodated Bach's continuo
basses. With the single exception of No. 119,[2] however, the instruments so employed are not specifically named in any of the twenty
cantatas included in the Table. They are rarely indicated on the

---

[1] *Supra,* p. 11.
[2] In the score the opening chorus is annotated: 'Violoncelli, Bassoni è Violoni
all'unisono col'Organo.'

CANTATA.	Voices.	Violin I, II.	Viola.	Flutes.	Oboes.	Horns.	Tromba or Cornetto.	Trombones or Timpani.	Continuo.	Total Parts.	Total Players.
No. 111	4	4	1	:	2	2	:	:	2	13	15
,, 112	4	4	1	:	2	2	:	:	3	16	17
,, 113	:	:	:	:	:	:	:	:	:	:	:
,, 114	4	2	1	1	2	1	:	:	2	13	13
,, 115	:	:	:	:	:	:	:	:	:	:	:
,, 116	4	2	1	:	2	1	:	:	2	12	12
,, 117	:	:	:	:	:	:	:	:	:	:	:
,, 118	:	:	:	:	:	:	:	:	:	:	:
,, 119	:	:	:	:	:	:	:	:	:	:	:
,, 120	:	:	:	:	:	:	:	:	:	:	:
,, 121	4	2	1	:	1	:	1	:	2	14	14
,, 122	4	2	1	:	3	:	:	3	2	12	12
,, 123	4	2	1	2	2	:	:	:	2	13	13
,, 124	4	2	1	:	1	1	:	:	3	11	11
,, 125	4	2	1	1	1	1	:	:	3	13	12
,, 126	4	2	1	:	2	1	1	:	3	12	12
,, 127	4	2	1	2	2	:	:	:	2	13	13
,, 128	4	2	1	:	3	2	:	:	2	14	14
,, 129	4	2	1	1	2	:	3	1	3	17	16
,, 130	:	:	:	:	:	:	:	:	:	:	:

The parts of Nos. 113, 115, 117–20, and 130 are not extant. In calculating the number of players, it is assumed that each violin and viola part served two, and, of the continuo parts, that one was the organist's, and that the other, or others, accommodated two players.

wrapper, on the continuo parts themselves, or in the score, the bottom line of which Bach generally simply labels 'Continuo'. For this indefiniteness a practical reason can be advanced. In an earlier chapter it has been shown that, before admission, a Stadt-pfeifer was tested in his competence on the violone.[1] That one or more played it when their principal instrument was not in use may be supposed. But we have Bach's statement that he depended on a more precarious source. In his report to the Leipzig Council in August 1730[2] he complained: 'Owing to the lack of more expert *subjecta*, I have had to take my viola, violoncello, and violone players from the *alumni* of the School.' These juvenile amateurs are not likely to have given him regular or expert assistance. And for the bassoon, the normal continuo wind-instrument, he was as in-adequately served. He depended for it, as we read in his report to the Council, on the inexperienced assistant-apprentice of the Stadtpfeifer body. To the precarious service of his continuo instruments, accordingly, his omission to particularize them must in part be attributed. Normally two players were at his service, who shared the single part he wrote for them. But, composing his score some weeks ahead of the performance, he could not foresee which instruments—violoncello, violone, bassoon—would be at his disposal, and therefore refrained from specifying them in particular. On such parts as are marked the violoncello and bassoon are most frequently indicated. The violone is definitely mentioned in less than twenty scores. In two cases (cantatas Nos. 76 and 152) a viola da gamba is specified, and in two others (Nos. 64 and 135) Bach was constrained to employ a trombone. That a contrabass was occasionally at his disposal is suggested by the apparent exis-tence of a part in the *St. John Passion* and *Was mir behagt*.

Bach normally prepared two continuo parts, an unfigured one for the string (violone and violoncello) or wind (bassoon) basses, a figured one for the organ. But in relatively few instances[3] the number of extant parts is greater, owing, probably, either to the replacement of lost copies subsequently recovered, or to a revision

---

[1] For an instance of this test see *supra*, p. 18. Agostino Agazzari, writing in 1607, prefers the violone to 'proceed gravely, sustaining with its mellow resonance the harmony of the other parts, keeping as much as possible to the thick strings, and often touching the octave below the bass', i.e. playing an octave lower than the notes written. Quoted in Arnold, p. 72.

[2] Terry, p. 203.

[3] Cantatas Nos. 5, 6, 13, 21, 24, 28, 30, 31, 33, 36, 40, 42, 43, 47, 48, 51, 55, 57, 58, 62, 63, 67, 70, 71, 81, 82, 93, 94, 96, 97, 98, 100, 108, 109, 112, 125, 129, 133, 134, 136, 172, 178, 182, 185, 187, 192, 194, 195, *Herr Gott, Beherrscher, Christmas Oratorio, St. Matthew Passion, St. John Passion, Sanctus* in C, *Sanctus* in G, *Hohe Messe* ('Sanctus'). See Table XX.

of the parts for a repeated performance. Moreover, a strengthened continuo would be required on festal occasions. Thus all six Parts of the *Christmas Oratorio* except the fourth have duplicate unfigured continuo parts. So have both *Passions*, the 'Sanctus' of the *Hohe Messe*, and about one-quarter of the cantatas.[1] Occasionally[2] we find the unfigured parts, two or more, in different keys, one in that of the movement, the other a tone lower. A figured organ part is lacking in all the cantatas specified except Nos. 5, 63, 185, and 194, and in all but Nos. 63 and 185 the score is wholly or partially unfigured. Since Bach occasionally completed his scores on the very eve of performance,[3] and as the figured continuo was the last part he prepared, the transposed unfigured copy in the sixteen instances mentioned in note 2 below may be an uncompleted organ part. In such circumstances, it is probable that Bach himself was at the organ.

In the irksome and continuous labour of preparing the orchestral parts Bach was assisted by his wife, sons, and pupils. Of a large number of cantatas the parts no longer survive. But such as are extant show that he usually made, or closely revised, the figured continuo himself. The figuring, in particular, is generally wholly or partly in his autograph. After collating the parts with the score, and adding infrequent dynamic markings, his practice was to indicate on the organ part the harmonic accompaniment he desired. That the process marked the final stage of his work is evident in the figured continuo parts of cantatas Nos. 124 and 126. Following the last bar of the latter he writes 'Fine S[oli] D[eo] G[loria]', to indicate the completion of his labour. In the case of No. 124, the unfigured continuo part concludes with 'Fine' in his autograph, but the figured part again is marked 'Fine S D G'. In general, it must be observed, dynamic expression, ornament, and figuring are found on Bach's parts rather than his scores. He rarely figured the latter;[4] cantata No. 186 is an unusual instance to the contrary.[5] In the Bachgesellschaft edition the figuring has generally been added from the organ part. An unfigured score indicates that that important manuscript is lost, or that it was not available to the editor.[6]

Bach's particular concern with the organ part was due to another cause. The circumstances under which church music was per-

[1] See Table XX.

[2] Cantatas Nos. 5, 25, 28, 48, 52, 55, 56, 63, 64, 85, 88, 116, 183, 184, 185, 194.

[3] e.g. *Tönet, ihr Pauken*, the *Trauer-Ode*, and cantata No. 174. The last, for Whit-Monday 1729, was finished on the previous day.

[4] Cf. B.-G. ii, p. iii.   [5] *Ibid.*, xxxvii, p. xxix.   [6] See Table XX.

formed at Weimar and Leipzig compelled him to transpose it at
an interval determined by the organ pitch in use. Seeing that in
the score the organ part is normally written in the key of the
movement, the preparation of a transposed part required more skill
than the simple task of copying. In most cases Bach reserved it
for himself. During his career he was served by organs tuned to
two pitches—Cornett-Ton and Chorton. The former stood a
minor third, the latter a major tone above the high chamber pitch
(hoher Cammerton) in general use for concerted music. To accom-
modate the organ to the latter it was necessary to transpose its part
down a minor third or whole tone, according as the instrument
was at Cornett-Ton or Chorton. At Weimar the former was in
use.[1] This is evident in the scores of several cantatas composed for
the ducal chapel. For instance: No. 31 is in C major, but the oboes
and bassoon are in E flat.[2] In No. 132 the continuo and strings
are in A major, but the oboe obbligato is in C. In No. 150 the
strings and continuo are in B minor, the bassoon in D minor.
In No. 152 the continuo and viola da gamba are in E minor, the
flute, oboe, and viola d'amore in G minor.[3] In the alto-tenor duet
of No. 155 the bassoon obbligato is in C minor in the original
score, but the voices and continuo are in A minor. A trumpet part
exists for the first and last movements of No. 185. The score is in
F sharp minor, but the trumpet is in G minor. As trumpet pitch
was a tone higher than Cammerton, the G minor part indicates,
like the other examples, that the organ was at Cornett-Ton.

The following is the specification of the 2-manual Weimar
organ as it existed in Bach's period of office:[4]

Upper Manual (Great Organ)

1.	Principal	8′	5.	Quintatön	4′
2.	Quintatön	16′	6.	Octave	4′
3.	Gemshorn	8′	7.	Mixtur, 6 ranks	
4.	Gedackt	8′	8.	Cymbel, 3 ranks	

Lower Manual (Choir Organ)

1.	Principal	8′	5.	Kleingedackt	4′
2.	Viola da gamba	8′	6.	Octave	4′
3.	Gedackt	8′	7.	Waldflöte	2′
4.	Trompete	8′	8.	Sesquialtera, 4 ranks	

[1] Cf. Spitta, i. 381.
[2] The existence of a fully figured organ part in B flat shows that this work was
also performed at Leipzig.
[3] They are printed in E minor in the B.-G. score.
[4] The specification is given by Gottfried Albin Wette, *Historische Nachrichten
von . . . Weimar* (1737), p. 174. See also Pirro (2), p. 84; Adlung, i. 282.

Pedal Organ

1. Gross-Untersatz	32'	5. Principal-Bass	8'
2. Sub-Bass	16'	6. Trompete-Bass	8'
3. Posaun-Bass	16'	7. Cornett-Bass	4'
4. Violon-Bass	16'		

Unlike the Weimar organ, those of the Leipzig churches, St. Thomas's and St. Nicholas's, in which Bach functioned as Cantor, and in which his cantatas, *Passions*, and oratorios were performed, were tuned to Chorton. Observing that Bach's figured continuo is generally duplicated,[1] one part standing in the key of the work, the other a tone lower, Moritz Hauptmann concluded[2] that the organs of those churches were at different pitches, St. Thomas's at Chorton, St. Nicholas's at Cammerton. He supposed the transposed part to have been prepared for St. Thomas's, and the other to have served St. Nicholas's, an error probably due to the fact that the organ of the latter church, with which he was familiar, stood at Cammerton. But it was not the instrument Bach used; it dated only from 1793, when it was erected at a cost of 7,000 thalers. Bach's organ was a veteran nearly a century old when he was born—it dated from 1597-8. Praetorius[3] gives its disposition at that period (1618), when it had twelve stops on the Great, four on the Brustwerk, ten on the Choir, and three on the Pedals. More than half of them (sixteen) were still in use in Bach's period.[4] Considerable repairs upon it were carried out by the Merseburg organ-builder, Zacharias Thayssner, in 1693, thirty years before Bach's arrival in Leipzig. It was again renovated in 1724-5, when 600 thalers were expended on it, and so remained throughout his Cantorate. In 1750-1 it again needed repair, and a generation later was replaced by a Cammerton organ, which was in use when the early volumes of the Bachgesellschaft edition were in course of publication, and survived until 1862.[5] Chorton being the normal organ pitch at Leipzig, the conversion of St. Nicholas's instrument to Cammerton during its renovation in 1724-5 would have been recorded had it been made. Moreover, it would have been foolishly unpractical to alter its pitch from that of St. Thomas's, seeing that both churches were platforms for the same music. It must, therefore, be concluded that the pitch of both organs was at Chorton, and that the transposed organ parts served them both.

---

[1] See Table XX. [2] B.-G. i, Preface. [3] P. 179.
[4] They are marked with an asterisk in the Table on p. 157.
[5] Cf. Schering, p. 110; Spitta, ii. 286, 676.

The 3-manual organ in St. Nicholas's in Bach's time was thus equipped:[1]

Oberwerk (Great Organ)

*1. Principal	8'		*8. Grobgedackt	8'
2. Sesquialtera	1⅗'		*9. Quintatön	16'
*3. Mixtur, 6 ranks			*10. Nasat	3'
*4. Super Octave	2'		11. Waldflöte	2'
*5. Quinte	3'		12. Fagott	16'
*6. Octave	4'		13. Trompete	8'
*7. Gemshorn	8'			

Brustwerk[2]

1. Schalmei	4'		5. Octave	2'
*2. Principal	4'		6. Sesquialtera	1½'
3. Mixtur, 3 ranks			7. Quintatön	8'
4. Quinte	3'			

Rückpositiv (Choir Organ)

*1. Principal	4'		*6. Quintatön	4'
*2. Gedackt	8'		7. Octave	2'
3. Viola da gamba	4'		8. Sesquialtera	1½'
4. Gemshorn	4'		9. Mixtur, 4 ranks	
5. Quinte	3'		*10. Bombard	8'

Pedal Organ

1. Cornett-Bass	2'		4. Octave-Bass	4'
*2. Schalmei-Bass	4'		5. Gedackter Sub-Bass	16'
3. Trompete-Bass	8'		*6. Posaun-Bass	16'

A smaller organ, which stood beside the larger one in St. Nicholas's west gallery, was broken up in 1693; its materials assisted the repair of the larger instrument.[3] It was not replaced.

St. Thomas's principal organ was of greater antiquity than the instrument in St. Nicholas's. After serving the Marienkirche at Eiche, not far distant, it was set up in St. Thomas's in 1525 and led the congregation in 1539, when Luther preached in the church. Its disposition at that period probably did not differ from that recorded by Praetorius[4] in 1618. It then had twenty-five stops—nine on the Great, two on the Brustwerk, twelve on the Choir, and two on the Pedals. Seventeen survived the many renovations of the organ, and were still in position in Bach's time.[5] In 1721, shortly before his appointment, the organ was thoroughly

---

[1] Schering, p. 111; Spitta, ii. 286. For the significance of the asterisks see *supra*, p. 156, note.
[2] The Brustwerk was not enclosed in a shuttered swell-case in Bach's time.
[3] Schering, p. 111.   [4] P. 180.
[5] They are distinguished by an asterisk in the Table on p. 159.

overhauled, yet needed attention in 1730 and renovation in 1747, when its condition rendered it almost useless.

A problem presents itself here. Bach's employment of the organ as a solo instrument in 1731[1] suggested to Rust[2] that St. Thomas's Rückpositiv had recently been made independent of the main organ by the provision of a separate keyboard coupled to the old action. The contrivance would enable the instrument to be used simultaneously on the two keyboards, one providing the accompaniment, its normal function, the other performing an obbligato part, rarely entrusted to it. Accepting Rust's hypothesis. Spitta[3] found supporting evidence in the accounts of St. Thomas's for 1730–1, which record the payment of fifty thalers to the organ-builder Johann Scheibe 'for the repair of the organ' ('vor die beschehene Reparatur an der Orgel'). With less than his customary care, Spitta supposed that the 'reparation' involved the building of a separate keyboard for the Rückpositiv, and found confirmation of his conjecture in the judgement of an organ-builder of his acquaintance, who assured him that fifty thalers would have sufficed in 1730 to carry out the work. Bach's relation to the performance of his church music would be clearer to us if Spitta's hypothesis could be accepted. In fact, it is untenable: in a letter dated 27 February 1730[4] Scheibe precisely specifies the work for which he was paid—the removal of dust and dirt from the pipes, their re-tuning, and the strengthening of the sixteen-foot Posaun-Bass on the Pedal organ. The Rückpositiv, no doubt, benefited by Scheibe's tedious labour ('eine langweilige und mühsame Arbeit'), but it was not the special object of his attention; still less did it receive a new and independent keyboard. Hence, throughout Bach's period of office the Rückpositiv was playable only on the lowest of the three manuals at the main console, and could not be simultaneously sounded by a second player. The Rückpositiv in St. Nicholas's was similarly conditioned.[5]

Apart from its alleged additional keyboard, the precise situation of the Rückpositiv bears on the conditions under which Bach performed his cantatas. Adlung[6] declares that it was no longer customary to set up the Rückpositiv in a separate case behind the organist, but rather to enclose its pipes with those of the Oberwerk, Brustwerk, and Pedal Organ, in the main frame. It was, however, still customary, he continues, to apply the term Rückpositiv to the lowest manual. The Leipzig organs were erected at a period when the Rückpositiv occupied the detached and rear position indicated

[1] *Infra*, p. 171.	[2] B.-G. xxii, p. xvi.	[3] Spitta, ii. 675.
[4] B.-J. 1908, p. 52.	[5] Spitta, ii. 676.	[6] Vol. i, p. 20.

by its name, a situation in which it assisted the performance of the double-choir motet. No authentic picture of St. Thomas's organ gallery in Bach's period survives, but Rust states that its Rück-positiv was an 'imposing' structure, projecting like an oriel window over the front of the choir-gallery ('das Erker-ähnlich über die Brüstung des Chores in die Kirche hineinragte'). The late Professor Bernhard Fr. Richter, himself the son of one of Bach's successors in the Cantorship, states with equal definiteness, that in both of the principal churches, St. Thomas's and St. Nicholas's alike, their Rückpositiv occupied this prominent and detached position.[1] In St. Nicholas's, Bach and his performers were probably less inconvenienced by the obstruction.[2] But in St. Thomas's, its bulky and decorated frame must have intervened, a deadening curtain, between him and his audience.

The specification of St. Thomas's organ, after its enlargement in 1721, was as follows:[3]

Oberwerk (Great Organ)

*1. Principal	16′	*6. Super Octave	2′
*2. Principal	8′	7. Spiel-Pfeife	8′
3. Quintatön	16′	8. Sesquialtera, doubled	
*4. Octave	4′	9. Mixtur, *6, 8, 10 ranks	
*5. Quinte	3′		

Brustwerk

1. Grobgedackt	8′	6. Cymbel, 2 ranks	
2. Principal	4′	7. Sesquialtera	
3. Nachthorn	4′	*8. Regal	8′
4. Nasat	3′	*9. Geigenregal (Violin	4′
5. Gemshorn	2′	Regal)	

Rückpositiv (Choir Organ)

*1. Principal	8′	8. Mixtur, 4 ranks	
*2. Quintatön	8′	9. Sesquialtera	
*3. Lieblich Gedackt	8′	*10. Spitzflöte	4′
4. Klein Gedackt	4′	11. Schallflöte	1′
*5. Traversa (Querflöte)	4′	12. Krummhorn	16′
*6. Violine	2′	*13. Trompete	8′
7. Rauschquinte, doubled			

Pedal Organ

1. Sub-Bass (of metal)	16′	*4. Schalmei-Bass	4′
*2. Posaun-Bass	16′	5. Cornett-Bass	3′
3. Trompete-Bass	8′		

---

[1] B.-J. 1908, p. 49.
[2] See the illustration of its organ-gallery in Terry (Germ. edn., No. 43).
[3] Cf. Schering, p. 108; Spitta, ii. 282; Pirro (2), p. 87. For the explanation of the asterisks see *supra*, p. 157.

St. Thomas's owned a smaller, and even older, organ. Built
in 1489, it remained in its original position in the western gallery
after the larger instrument was introduced there in 1525. The two
stood in close juxtaposition till 1639, when the smaller was trans-
ferred to a chamber on the opposite (eastern) wall of the nave. Here
it remained for just a century, used at high festivals and on exceptional occasions, but otherwise neglected. It was in a state of
semi-dilapidation in 1727, when Zacharias Hildebrand was com-
missioned to recondition it. Thirteen years later (1740) it was
dismantled, and such of its parts as were serviceable were put into
the new organ of the Johanniskirche. Bach's use of it must have
been restricted to the years 1728–40; indeed, we might suppose
that Hildebrand's renovation was undertaken at his request, in
anticipation of the production of the *St. Matthew Passion* in 1729.
But Johann Christoph Rost[1] makes no mention of it in that year,
though in his unpublished note-book he particularly records that
the *Passion* music was sung at St. Thomas's in 1736 (when the
St. Matthew Passion was certainly repeated) 'with both organs'.
The smaller was a 3-manual instrument with twenty-one stops:[2]

Oberwerk (Great Organ)

1. Principal	8′	5. Rauschquinte	3′ and 2′
2. Gedackt	8′	6. Mixtur, 4, 5, 6, 8, 10 ranks	
3. Quintatön	8′	7. Cymbel, 2 ranks	
4. Octave	4′		

Brustwerk

1. Trichter-Regal	8′[3]	3. Spitzflöte	2′
2. Sifflöte	1′		

Rückpositiv (Choir Organ)

1. Principal	4′	5. Octave	2′
2. Lieblich Gedackt	8′	6. Sesquialtera, doubled	
3. Hohlflöte	4′	7. Dulcian	8′
4. Nasat	3′	8. Trompete	8′

Pedal Organ

1. Sub-Bass (wood)	16′	3. Trompete-Bass	8′
2. Fagott-Bass	16′		

As Cantor, Bach's duties associated him only with the two principal churches ('Hauptkirchen'), St. Thomas's and St. Nicholas's.
But on at least two occasions he directed his own music in St.

[1] Cf. Terry (4), p. ix.   [2] Cf. Schering, p. 109; Spitta, ii. 284.
[3] 'a sort of *Vox humana*' (Pirro (2), p. 87). Cf. Adlung, i. 150.

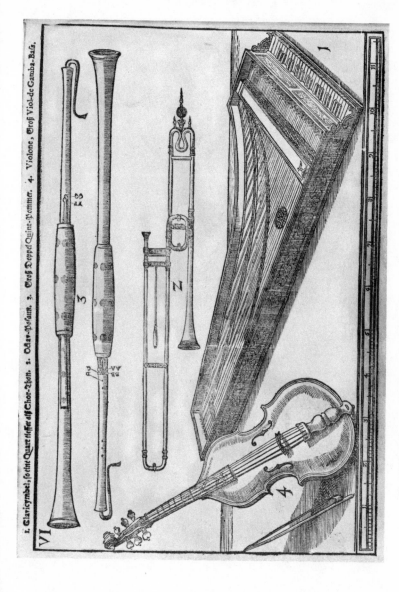

CLAVICEMBALO, OCTAVE TROMBONE, DOUBLE QUINT BASSOON, VIOLONE

(Praetorius)

Paul's, the University church. Thirteen years before his appointment, the Faculty of Theology had instituted Sunday services in
it (1710), and after much delay an organ was erected in the west
gallery. Bach knew it from the moment of its completion. At the
University's request he came over from Cöthen in 1717 to inspect
and report on it.[1] Ten years later, in 1727, his *Trauer-Ode* was
performed in the church, and at another memorial service, in
1729, his motet *Der Geist hilft unsrer Schwachheit auf* was sung.
Spitta[2] supposes that an instrument so superior to those of St.
Thomas's and St. Nicholas's—it was, in fact, one of the finest in
Germany[3]—was generally used by Bach for the exhibition of his
powers as an organist. But the jealousy with which he was regarded
by the University's official musicians makes it doubtful whether
St. Paul's organ-gallery was open to him, except at the academic
laureations in which the Cantor of St. Thomas's had an established
right to take part. Its specification was as follows:[4]

Hauptwerk (Great Organ)

1. Gross Principal	16′	8. Quinte	3′
2. Gross Quintatön	16′	9. Quint-Nasat	3′
3. Klein Principal	8′	10. *Octavina*	2′
4. Schalmei	8′	11. Waldflöte	2′
5. *Flûte allemande*	8′	12. Grosse Mixtur, 5 and 6 ranks	
6. Gemshorn	8′	13. *Cornetti*, 3 ranks	
7. Octave	4′	14. Zink, 2 ranks	

Brustwerk

1. Principal	8′	7. Nasat	3′
2. Viola da gamba	?	8. *Sedecima*	1′
3. Grobgedackt	8′	9. Schweizer Pfeife	1′
4. Octave	4′	10. Largo	?
5. Rohrflöte	4′	11. Mixtur, 3 ranks	
6. Octave	2′	12. Cymbel, 2 ranks	

Unter-Clavier (Choir Organ)

1. Lieblich Gedackt	8′	7. Viola	2′
2. Quintatön	8′	8. *Vigesima nona*	1½′
3. *Flûte douce*	4′	9. Weitpfeife	1′
4. *Quinta decima*	4′	10. Mixtur, 3 ranks	
5. *Decima nona*	3′	11. Cymbel, 2 ranks	
6. Hohlflöte	2′	12. Sertin(?)	8′

Pedal Organ

1. Gross Principal	16′	3. Octave	8′
2. Gross Quintatön	16′	4. Octave	4′

[1] Cf. Terry, p. 124.   [2] Vol. ii. 287.   [3] Schering, p. 319
[4] Spitta, ii. 287.

5. Quinte	3'	11. Gross Principal	16'
6. Mixtur, 5 and 6 ranks		12. Sub-Bass	16'
7. Grosser Quinten-Bass	6'	13. Posaune	16'
8. Jubal	8'	14. Trompete	8'
9. Nachthorn	4'	15. Hohlflöte	1'
10. Octave	2'	16. Mixtur, 4 ranks	

For these Leipzig organs (St. Paul's exceptionally) Bach prepared his figured continuo parts, transposing the bass down a tone in order to adapt their Chorton to the Cammerton of the other instruments and voices. The purpose they served, and Bach's general supervision of them, make the transposed usually more reliable than the untransposed continuo parts, and from the surviving cantatas of his Leipzig period they are rarely absent. From those whose parts are extant a figured organ part is lacking in only twenty-five: Nos. 11, 12, 17, 25,* 28,* 32, 34, 35, 45, 48,* 49, 52,* 55,* 56,* 64,* 69, 79, 85,* 88,* 103, 116,* 156, 169, 183,* 184.* Their loss is regrettable, but not surprising. But Table XX reveals that, for nearly half of them (marked with an asterisk), transposed, but unfigured, organ parts were prepared, in addition to the ordinary Cammerton continuo. In almost every case they are marked and revised by Bach; indeed, two of the three sheets of the unfigured transposed continuo part of No. 116 are in his autograph. Its incorrect deviations from the score, no less than the script itself, indicate that the task was undertaken in haste and left incomplete, a circumstance which invites a deduction applicable to all the cantatas in this category. We must suppose that Bach, in these comparatively rare cases, lacking leisure or inclination to revise and figure the parts, adopted the alternative of taking the organ himself and playing from his score or an unfigured continuo. That this was not his normal practice is self-evident: he would have figured the score rather than a separate and bare bass part had the accompaniment been regularly in his own hands. In fact, as has been shown, his score is rarely figured and a figured organ part is seldom missing.

Another problem is stated by the existence of non-transposed parts figured in whole or part. The supposition that they were prepared for St. Nicholas's lower-pitched organ has been considered and rejected.[1] If further disproof is needed, the rarity of these figured Cammerton parts provides it. Only twenty-seven survive over the whole range of Bach's Leipzig career—cantatas Nos. 3, 4, 6, 7, 10, 33, 38, 40, 42, 44, 46, 67, 81, 93, 96, 102, 109, 114, 136, 147, 166, 169, 176, 195, *Christmas Oratorio* Part IV, *Hohe Messe*

[1] *Supra*, p. 156.

('Missa'), and the *Sanctus* in G. Seeing that St. Nicholas's shared equally with St. Thomas's the privilege of hearing Bach's music, indeed enjoyed superior opportunities as the senior church, it is inconceivable that so few figured Cammerton basses should be found, if their purpose was as Moritz Hauptmann supposed.

Spitta[1] advances another untenable explanation. He concludes that when a figured Cammerton and a figured Chorton bass are found together, the latter was used in church, and the former at rehearsals elsewhere. If so, we should find at least as many of one part as of the other, for they were equally indispensable. But the suggestion can be challenged on other grounds. Rehearsals were held in the School-building, in the practice-room on the second floor, whose windows looked out on the Pleisse and its clattering mill.[2] But no harpsichord was available there, nor did the School possess one during Bach's period of office.[3] Pupils practised on his private instruments in his own apartments.[4] The School's only effective keyed instruments during the years 1723–50 were two Positiv organs.[5] One of them, acquired in the year of Bach's birth (1685), stood in the room on the first floor allotted to the Second Class. It was tuned to Chorton—so it cannot have required a Cammerton continuo part—and was only replaced by one at Cammerton pitch in 1756. A second Positiv, which Kuhnau induced the Council to purchase in 1720, stood, presumably, in the practice-room. It had two Gedackt stops of 8' and 4', a Principal of 2', and required four lads for its transportation when it accompanied the choir to private houses. Its pitch is not stated, but is not likely to have differed from its fellow. As it was in use until 1771, it is obvious that the figured transposed continuo parts served as well for rehearsals with the School Positiv as for performances with the church organ.

What, then, was the purpose of the figured untransposed basses? There is no question that they were written for a keyed instrument, and, since their pitch was not adapted to the church organs, they must have been prepared for a harpsichord. That they were not required for the general School-rehearsals has been demonstrated. There remain, therefore, two alternatives: either they served for private and individual practices in Bach's own apartments, or for the harpsichord which stood in the choir-galleries of both churches. In the former case we should expect them to be more numerous, for Bach must regularly have rehearsed his singers, and especially his soloists, under those conditions. Indeed, Johann Christian

---

[1] Vol. ii. 656. [2] Cf. Terry, p. 166. [3] *Supra*, p. 19.
[4] Schering, p. 63. [5] See Praetorius, Plate IV, at p. 18.

Kittel, one of his best pupils, recalled that, when his master 'performed' church-music, one of the most capable students accompanied 'auf dem Fluegel' ('on the harpsichord'), and that if he did his task badly he would find Bach's hands and fingers displacing his own on the keyboard, 'adorning the accompaniment with masses of harmony more impressive even than the unsuspected proximity of his strict preceptor'.[1] Kittel distinctly writes 'performed' ('wenn Seb. Bach eine Kirchenmusik auffuehrte'), but he was nearly eighty when he published the statement, and it is obvious that such incidents as he records occurred at general rehearsals in the gallery of one or other of the churches, and not at a public performance. A harpsichord was installed in both, and for what purpose if not for use? Yet, in a lengthy note,[2] Spitta concludes positively against Bach's employment of it. He instances the *Trauer-Ode* as the 'one single instance known to us' to the contrary, and insists that Bach was as much opposed to the harpsichord's regular use in church ('von einem ständigen Cembalo bei der Kirchenmusik') as to theatrical music there. Spitta, however, misstates the premisses on which he founds his positive conclusion. The *Trauer-Ode* is *not* the only instance of Bach's use of a harpsichord in church. In 1724 he was ready to deprive St. Nicholas's of its turn to hear the Good Friday Passion music, because, for one reason, its harpsichord was not serviceable.[3] A figured harpsichord (*cembalo*) part exists for cantata No. 8. Originally the accompaniment of the alto aria in No. 27 was for oboe da caccia 'e cembalo obligato'.[4] Among the parts of No. 109 is one definitely 'Continuo pro Cembalo' (Coro II) and figured. In No. 154 the tenor aria, in which the united violins and viola displace the continuo, is accompanied by a figured cembalo. In the *St. Matthew Passion* both organ parts and a 'Continuo pro Cembalo' are in Bach's autograph and figured. In his preface to the Bachgesellschaft edition[5] Julius Rietz remarks that the *secco* recitatives of the *Passion* were probably accompanied by the continuo basses and the cembalo,[6] an instrument, he adds, which Bach had always in readiness ('immer bei der Hand hatte'). Again, at one of the performances of the *St. John Passion* Bach substituted a harpsichord for the lute in the bass arioso 'Betrachte, meine Seele' (No. 31). These instances, though not numerous, suffice to indicate that Bach's attitude towards the harpsichord was not antagonistic, as

---

[1] Kittel, p. 10. Cf. Arnold, p. 34.
[2] Vol. ii, p. 655. The problem of Bach's use of the cembalo is also discussed in Schweitzer, ii. 447; B.-J. 1904, p. 64; B.-J. 1906, p. 11; B.-J. 1908, p. 64.
[3] Terry, p. 179.　　　[4] Spitta, ii. 451 n.　　　[5] B.-G. iv, p. xxii.
[6] The organ parts do not confirm this opinion.

Spitta supposes. It is therefore a feasible proposition that the figured Cammerton basses are other examples of its usage. In only a few cases the parts are not completely figured, and it is clear that they had a function distinct from and independent of the organ continuo. That they were used simultaneously is an improbable explanation, though both instruments may have been used when both chorus and orchestra were simultaneously in action. That the parts were employed alternatively is a more reasonable explanation, if we remember that Bach's cantatas received repeated performances, and that his organs, as has been shown, were not seldom undergoing repair. In such circumstances, to fall back on the church's harpsichord was natural, though the effect could not be completely satisfactory. The supposition, at least, is not contradicted by circumstances, as are the views of Hauptmann and Spitta. In regard to the parts partially figured there is less room for doubt; it is a fair inference that the cembalo was only active in those movements for which figured harmonies were provided. Instances have already been given, and another is found in cantata No. 114, where the transposed organ part is figured throughout, while the Cammerton continuo is marked only for the opening chorus and alto aria.

Of the Leipzig cantatas, three—Nos. 23, 97, 194—possess abnormal continuo parts, two of which indicate the participation of an organ at Cornett-Ton. In Leipzig, as at Weimar, that pitch was formerly in use. Writing to Mattheson on 8 December 1717,[1] Kuhnau, Bach's predecessor in the Cantorship, remarks: 'From the first moment of my appointment as director of church music here[2] I abolished Cornett-Ton, and substituted Cammerton, a tone or minor third, whichever you please, below it, though the consequent necessity of transposing the continuo parts is not always agreeable.' The change is explicable; for Kuhnau's period of office saw the decisive establishment of the new style cantata as the musical 'Hauptstück' of public worship, superseding the old style motet, with which the Stadtpfeifer had been traditionally associated. Cornett-Ton being the normal pitch to which that body conformed,[3] and as the organs were tuned to it, the necessity for a transposed continuo did not arise. Balancing the interests of music against his own convenience, Kuhnau decided for the former. The complications of transposition which he had consequently

---

[1] The letter is printed in Mattheson's *Critica musica* (1725), ii. 235. Cf. Schering, p. 244.

[2] Kuhnau became Cantor in 1701, having been organist of St. Thomas's since 1684.

[3] Riemann, ii. 856, defines it as 'die Stimmung der Stadtpfeifer'.

to face are illustrated by a note appended to the score of his Whit-Sunday cantata *Daran erkennen wir, dass wir in ihm verbleiben*: '1. This piece is set in B flat Chorton [C Cammerton] for viols,[1] voices, and thorough bass. 2. The trumpets [normally in D] are written in C natural; so they must be crooked a tone down to Cammerton. In like manner the drums must be tuned a tone lower to that pitch. The oboes and bassoons being in Cammerton, their parts must be written out a tone higher than those of the viols. In this way all will be consonant.'[2]

So, Cammerton was the performing pitch at Leipzig for nearly a quarter of a century before Bach succeeded Kuhnau. It is there-fore, at first sight, strange to detect an apparent indication of Cornett-Ton in Cantata No. 23, composed in 1723 and almost certainly performed in 1724. The explanation, however, is not far to seek. Bach wrote the music at Cöthen, intending to perform it as his trial piece ('Probestück') for the Leipzig Cantorship.[3] Excepting the figured continuo, the parts are in his autograph, as also is the score, written with particular care. The figured con-tinuo is neither in his script nor adapted to the conditions for which the cantata was composed: it is transposed a minor third down to A minor. The absence of a figured Chorton bass may be explained by Bach's desire to take the organ himself at the cantata's first performance. But the figured continuo in A minor must indicate a performance outside Leipzig, in a church whose organ was tuned to the older Cornett-Ton. Probably it was given under the direction of the writer of the transposed part. For, occasionally, Bach permitted others to use his scores, though with unwillingness always. A request for the loan of one received the following reply from his secretary-cousin, Johann Elias Bach, in 1741:[4] 'My cousin regrets he cannot send it; he has lent the parts to the bass singer Büchner, who has not returned them. As to the score, he won't allow it out of his hands; he has lost several through lending them to other people.'

Cantata No. 97 belongs to the year 1734. The score is in B flat and the normal continuo parts, both Cammerton and Chorton, are extant. In addition, there survives an incompletely figured organ part in G, written with extreme care by Bach himself, and interest-ing apart from its tonality. In his original scheme Bach marked the organ part 'tacet' in three movements—the tenor recitative (No. 3) and aria (No. 4), and the soprano-bass duet (No. 7)—and left them unfigured. For a later performance he figured the tenor recitative

---

[1] i.e. all the strings.   [2] Cf. Spitta, ii. 677.
[3] Cf. Rust's remarks in B.-G. v (1), p. ix, and Spitta, ii. 679.
[4] Terry, p. 249.

and aria, leaving the organ silent in the soprano-bass duet as before. Finally he re-wrote the whole part in G, and partially figured the duet. The fact that he left unfigured the last forty bars of it suggests that he took the organ himself on the occasion, and the tonality of the part indicates its use at a performance elsewhere than in Leipzig, perhaps in Weimar, with whose court he was on cordial terms since the death of the martinet Duke Wilhelm Ernst in 1728. Certainly, at some time subsequent to that event, he visited Weimar for a performance of *Was mir behagt* in the reigning duke's honour. It is not improbable that the score and parts of cantata No. 97 accompanied him for a Sunday service in the ducal chapel.

Cantata No. 194 was composed for the opening of a new organ at Störmthal on 2 November 1723. The work is in B flat, for strings, oboes, bassoons, and continuo. Among the parts are four for the continuo, two in B flat unfigured, another in A flat unfigured. There is also extant the fragment of a figured continuo in G. On the analogy of other similarly transposed organ parts, we should suppose the one in G to have been prepared for Störm-thal's presumably Cornett-Ton organ, and the other parts for use at Leipzig on a repetition of the cantata. The reverse is the case. The Continuo in G is marked 'sub Communione' at the beginning of the second Part, indicating its use during that portion of the Leipzig office; while the score and all other parts are inscribed 'post Con-cionem' ('after the address') at that point.[1] The explanation is found in the fact that all the B flat instrumental parts are marked 'tief Cammerton' ('low chamber pitch'), from which we learn that the oboes at Bach's disposal at Leipzig at the beginning of his career there were at that pitch, their B flat sounding A Cammerton. This necessitated tuning down the strings by a similar interval, and the transposition of the part for St. Nicholas's[2] Chorton organ down to G, which, at its high tuning, was the equivalent of A Cammerton.

So many of Bach's cantata scores having passed under his editorial eye, Rust[3] gave his emphatic opinion that, invariably in that period, 'Church music scored for an orchestra was accom-panied by the organ'. Bach's pupil, Kirnberger,[4] was no less positive to the same effect than Bach's son in a passage quoted on an earlier page.[5] We might therefore expect Bach's manuscript to yield abundant confirmation. In fact, in less than forty cantata

[1] B.-G. xxix, p. xx.
[2] As the senior church, St. Nicholas's presumably heard the cantata on Trinity Sunday, when it was repeated at Leipzig. If so, Hauptmann's opinion regarding its pitch (*supra*, p. 156) is conclusively inaccurate.
[3] B.-G. ix, p. xvi.   [4] Cf. Spitta, ii. 659.   [5] *Supra*, p. 148.

scores the organ is linked by name with the continuo.[1] In so few was Bach at pains to prefix 'Organo è' to the 'Continuo' which distinguished his bottom stave. Nor do his continuo parts add more than a few instances.[2] The reason is patent: the convention alleged by C. P. E. Bach and Kirnberger was so much Bach's normal habit that he deemed it superfluous invariably to specify the organ by name as a member of the continuo.

The organ (transposed) continuo parts rarely indicate Bach's intentions; he would convey them by word of mouth at rehearsals, or in private. Still, there is patent evidence that the organ accompaniment was discontinued in particular movements, or sections of movements. Certain numbers, for instance, were obviously planned to be independent of the organ, since they lack an actual bass: e.g. in the soprano aria 'Jesu, deine Gnaden-Blicke', of No. 11, the violins and viola in unison displace the normal continuo. Two *oboi da caccia* are similarly used in the alto aria 'Doch Jesus will' of No. 46. The violas provide the foundation in the soprano aria 'Wie zittern und wanken' of No. 105. In the alto aria 'Jesu, lass dich finden', of No. 154, the violins and viola are in unison at the octave of a figured cembalo bass. Evidently Bach desired to add clearness and distinctness to the latter. A similar intention is observed in the bass aria 'Streite, siege, starker Held!' of No. 62. Other movements lacking an actual bass are: the alto aria 'Wie jammern mich', of No. 170, in which the organ 'a 2 Clav.' is obbligato above the violins and viola in unison; the soprano aria 'Aus Liebe will mein Heiland sterben', of the St. *Matthew Passion*, which has an oboe da caccia foundation; the soprano aria 'Qui tollis peccata', of the Mass in A, in which the violins and viola in unison function as in No. 170; and the soprano aria 'Durch die von Eifer', of *Preise dein' Glücke*, where the violins and violetta play a similar part.[3]

Bach's scores and parts afford other indications of the organ's occasional inactivity. The second movement (tenor aria) of cantata No. 26 is pointedly unfigured, the only movement of the cantata so treated. In No. 94 the bass, alto, and soprano arias, marked 'tacet', stand unfigured in the organ part. In No. 95 the tenor aria is both unfigured and marked 'senza l'organo'. The original organ part of No. 97 is frequently labelled 'tacet' after the opening chorus. Similar directions exclude the organ from verses 2, 3, 5 of cantata

[1] Nos. 21, 26, 29, 30, 33, 36, 41, 42, 50, 52, 57, 61, 63, 64, 67, 71, 78, 80, 82, 94, 97, 100, 107, 110, 139, 161, 196, and the six parts of the *Christmas Oratorio*.

[2] e.g. Nos. 8, 13, 23, 111, 124, 125, 129, 162, 174, 177, 187.

[3] Cantata No. 118 is wholly without a continuo.

No. 100, and from verses 2, 3, 4 of No. 177. In No. 125, though
the organ part was figured by Bach himself, the alto aria is without
figures, and in No. 139 the organ is silent between the opening
chorus and final Choral.

It is incontestable, therefore, that some other instrument than
the main organ, and some other manuscript than the transposed
organ part, provided the accompaniment in the above instances.
That Bach himself undertook the task is a natural inference, and the
absence of supplementary figured parts indicates that he used his
score. In cases where the organ part is wholly unfigured he must
have played the main organ and placed his first prefect to beat time
in the choruses. But the instances before us are in another category,
since they indicate the substitution of another keyed instrument,
specifically the harpsichord, in movements which, on the ground of
their difficulty, or of his liking for them, or of his want of confidence
in the singer or organist, he preferred to accompany himself.

That Bach himself should have accompanied particular movements is not improbable, though each church had its own organist
—St. Nicholas's, Johann Gottlieb Görner (till 1730) and Bach's
pupil Johann Schneider; St. Thomas's, Christian Gräbner (till
1729) and Johann Gottlieb Görner.[1] Of the three men, Schneider
alone seems to have had Bach's full confidence, while Görner, his
associate throughout his Cantorship, was a player of moderate
ability and unbounded self-esteem. But even if their technique
had been extraordinary, Bach could not expect from them a completely accurate interpretation of his music. For, unlike the
modern organist, they could neither study their score beforehand,
nor play from one at the performance. Only a bare bass part
faced them above the manuals, figured in a script not always easily
deciphered. And, however legible, it left much to the skill and
imagination of the player, as is known to all who have endeavoured
to build up an accompaniment from Bach's figured indications.
Certainly, he rarely lays the exclusive burden of accompaniment on
the continuo, a responsibility which required the player at the keyboard to invent melodic interludes before and between the vocal
passages. It is further evident, in the Table on page 150, that his
continuo is 'solo' chiefly in recitatives. But even in those arias—
and they are the most numerous—in which a further exposition of
his scheme is revealed in fully written-out instrumental *obbligati*,
the responsibility of the player of the keyed instrument remained
onerous. That Bach on occasion instructed performers of his
figured basses has an interesting proof. The bass aria 'Empfind'

[1] Terry, pp. 156, 159.

ich Höllenangst und Pein', of cantata No. 3, stands in his score with no other accompaniment than an unfigured continuo. There is extant, however, in his autograph,[1] a fully written-out accompaniment of the first fifteen bars over the bass, interesting in itself, and particularly when placed alongside the effort of a modern editor. Here are the first half-dozen bars of Bach's autograph:

And here are the first four bars in the Breitkopf edition!

When we contemplate the enormous gap that generally separated Bach's conception from his accompanist's pedestrian performance,

[1] The autograph is facsimiled in Liepmannsohn's auction catalogue, 21 and 22 Nov. 1930.

we must picture him constantly exasperated by, or despondently acquiescent in, the imperfect accompaniments to which he was forced to listen. Michel de Saint-Lambert, in his *Nouveau traité de l'accompagnement du clavecin*, published in Bach's lifetime, is illuminating:

'When the *tempo* is so rapid that the accompanist cannot conveniently play all the notes, it will suffice if he play and accompany only the first notes of each bar, leaving to the [string] basses the task of playing them all, which they can do much more easily, having no accompaniment to attend to in addition. Very rapid *tempi* are not suited to the accompanying instruments. If very quick passages are encountered, even in a slow movement, the accompanist may leave them to the other [continuo] instruments. Or, if he plays them himself, he may so modify them as to play only the principal notes, i.e. the notes which fall on the strong beats of the bar.'[1]

We must attribute Bach's abnormal use of a solo organ in 1731 to exceptional circumstances. Only two examples occur before that year, only two after it. Cantata No. 47, which contains the earliest, was composed at Cöthen in 1720. Its soprano aria 'Wer ein wahrer Christ will heissen' is scored for continuo (figured) and 'Organo obligato'. The obbligato is simple, a solo such as might be allotted to a flute or oboe. In the second of the pre-1731 examples, No. 73, one of the earliest Leipzig cantatas, the 'Organo obligato', restricted to the opening chorus, merely deputizes for a 'Corno' generally sounding the Choral melody. We infer that Bach's horn player failed him, that he consequently prepared an organ part, placed on its lower stave the normal figured bass, and on the upper the horn part (Rückpositiv), with brief phrases for the Brustpositiv, on which, while his right hand was engaged with the Rückpositiv, the organist supplied the harmony with his left hand.

These simple devices are the only examples of Bach's use of a solo organ prior to 1731, when we come upon eight cantatas in which the organ is again obbligato. The following, in chronological order, are their titles:

No.	Title.	Occasion.	Date, 1731.
172	*Erschallet, ihr Lieder*	Whit-Sunday	May 13
170	*Vergnügte Ruh'*	Trinity VI	July 1
35	*Geist und Seele wird verwirret*	Trinity XII	Aug. 12
29	*Wir danken dir, Gott*	Council Election	,, 27
27	*Wer weiss, wie nahe*	Trinity XVI	Sept. 9
169	*Gott soll allein*	Trinity XVIII	,, 23
49	*Ich geh' und suche*	Trinity XX	Oct. 7
188	*Ich habe meine Zuversicht*	Trinity XXI	,, 14

[1] Quoted in Pirro (2), p. 80. Cf. Arnold, p. 196.

Rust's supposition, that Bach's obbligato use of the organ in 1731 was made possible by the recent addition of a separate keyboard to St. Thomas's Rückpositiv, has been shown to be groundless.[1] Another suggestion came, in 1887, from Franz Wüllner,[2] who hazarded the opinion that the second keyboard was provided by the School Positiv.[3] Professor B. Fr. Richter found confirmatory evidence in the School records,[4] which reveal its removal to St. Thomas's during the enlargement of the School buildings, an operation which compelled occupants and contents to find lodging elsewhere. This evacuation took place in the spring of 1731, and the reconstruction was not completed till the summer of 1732.[5] Thus, on the testimony of the School records, the School Positiv was available in the very period to which Bach's obbligato organ parts belong. Professor Richter computes that six, if not all, of the eight cantatas in which they occur were performed in St. Nicholas's, whereas the Positiv appears to have been housed in St. Thomas's. He is of opinion, too, that Bach wrote the obbligato organ parts as a compliment to, and for the use of, his pupil, Johann Schneider, organist of that church. In the latter conjecture Richter is probably incorrect; more practical reasons can be advanced for the production of these unique cantatas at this particular juncture.[6] And, as to the location of the Positiv, having once been loosed from its moorings in the School, it could be navigated as easily from one church to the other as from the School to St. Thomas's. The material point is that, when these eight cantatas were composed, Bach had at his disposal a keyed instrument not normally a member of his orchestra, which permitted him, if he desired, to employ the permanent organ of the church for other than its accustomed function.

The earliest of the 'Organ Cantatas', No. 172, was called for by circumstances already deduced in regard to No. 73.[7] In both, the organ obbligato is confined to a single movement, in No. 73 as a substitute for, in No. 172 to support, another instrument. The soprano-alto duet of the latter was scored originally for violoncello and violin *obbligati*, the violin sounding the Choral melody 'Komm, heiliger Geist, Herre Gott'. As Bach entrusts the obbligato of the preceding aria to all the violins and viola in unison, we judge that his players were not reliable. For that reason, it is probable, he altered his original scheme for the duet, and put both *obbligati* on the organ. It is the only unfigured movement in the cantata, and he probably took the organ himself.

---

[1] *Supra*, p. 158.   [2] B.-G. xxxiii, p. xxxi.   [3] *Supra*, p. 19.   [4] B.-J. 1908, p. 54.
[5] Cf. Terry, pp. 208, 212.   [6] Cf. *infra*, p. 175.   [7] *Supra*, p. 171.

In cantata No. 170, the second of the series, the organ is obbligato in the second and third of the three arias. In the second ('Wie jammern mich') its part is set out on two manuals and transposed down a tone. The movement is as original in its instrumentation as it is emotional in mood, and lacks an actual bass. In the third aria ('Mir ekelt mehr zu leben') the existence of an autograph traverso part seems to indicate a subsequent performance of the cantata.[1] The Positiv may have been used for the obbligato, for the part stands in the key of the aria.

So far Bach's experiments with an organ obbligato were tentative and simple: the organ functioned like any other wind instrument, contributing a single melodic line to the polyphonic structure. But in the third cantata of the series, No. 35, performed on the Twelfth Sunday after Trinity (12 August), the organ sounds in its full majesty. The cantata is in two parts, each prefaced by a movement of a Clavier Concerto in D minor, transformed into a Concerto for organ and orchestra.[2] That Leipzig had ever heard the organ in such conditions is improbable. To Bach himself the occasion must have been of exceptional interest, and the fact that no separate organ-part survives strengthens the agreeable belief that he played it himself. The organ is obbligato throughout, excepting the recitatives, and the form of the alto aria 'Geist und Seele wird verwirret' suggests that it is the middle movement of the original concerto.

Little more than a fortnight later (27 August), Bach gave St. Nicholas's another feast of concerted organ music. The occasion was of particular solemnity and pomp; for the burgomaster and councillors were present to inaugurate their year of office. Bach's normal orchestra, accordingly, was augmented by the trumpeter Reiche, his colleagues, and the drums. The cantata (No. 29) opened with the first movement of the Violin Concerto in E, adapted for organ and orchestra, an exhilarating sinfonia which, on its repetition eight years later, Their Magnificences applauded as 'clever and agreeable music' ('eine so künstlich als angenehme Music')![3] It is noteworthy that the organ is obbligato only in the opening sinfonia and last aria, and that the continuo is figured with particular care in the intervening movements. We infer that Bach was too concerned with the direction of his composition to displace Schneider altogether at the organ.

A fortnight later (9 September) the fifth of the organ cantatas (No. 27) was produced. Here the obbligato is confined to the alto aria 'Willkommen! will ich sagen'. The subject of the upper stave

[1] Cf. Spitta, ii. 453.   [2] Cf. B.-G. xvii, p. xx.   [3] Terry (4), p. 528.

is independent, on the lower the organ reinforces the continuo, a circumstance which, along with the fact that only the arias are unfigured, suggests that Bach himself took the organ for their performance. The score prescribes a harpsichord, though the organ part and the cover of the parts are marked 'organo obligato'.[1]

Again a fortnight intervened before Bach, in the same church, performed (23 September) the sixth of the organ cantatas (No. 169). He now borrowed and adapted the Clavier Concerto in E for the opening sinfonia and second aria. The organ is obbligato throughout, excepting the recitatives, alto arioso, and final Choral. Its part is so far unique, in that it contains both the obbligato and also the figured continuo, as is evident not only in the indication 'Organ obligato e Continuo', but also in the fact that the part is transposed down a tone in the score in every movement in which the organ is engaged.

On 7 October 1731, after another fortnight's interval, Bach produced the last but one (No. 49) of the eight. Its relationship to its predecessor is of the closest: the introductory sinfonia is the last movement of the same E major Clavier Concerto. Moreover, the organ obbligato and continuo are conjoined in the sinfonia, bass aria, and concluding duet. As in No. 169, also, the organ part is transposed down a tone in the score.

A week later (14 October), Bach conducted the last of the eight organ cantatas (No. 188). The date indicates that it was not performed in the same church as its immediate predecessors, and it is planned upon a smaller scale. The organ is obbligato only in the alto aria 'Unerforschlich ist die Weise'. But a note in the score (copy) directs that the first movement of the Clavier Concerto in D minor be played as an introductory sinfonia. The series ended, therefore, with music in which the organ displayed its full majesty.[2]

It has already been proposed that Bach's employment of an obbligato organ in 1731 was made possible by the transference of the School's Positiv to the churches during the building operations. Bach himself must have been seriously incommoded by them, since he was compelled to remove his family, furniture, and instruments while they were in progress. His unsettled conditions are evident in his choice of a libretto for the Passion music in 1731, and probably in his performance of the St. Luke Passion, an inferior work by another hand, in 1732. For similar reasons, while the school was excluded from its accustomed quarters, he appears to

---

[1] Cf. Spitta, ii. 451.
[2] Apart from the sinfonia, the authenticity of the cantata has been questioned. The hand of Friedemann Bach is suggested. Cf. Terry (4), p. 476.

have made large use of old material in his cantatas, or performed
solo anthems in which the choir's participation was confined to
the concluding Choral. Thus all three cantatas for the Whitsun
Festival 1731 are revisions of earlier material, as also is the Michaelmas cantata for that year. Those performed on the Nineteenth
and following three Sundays after Trinity are for a solo voice.[1]
It is a tenable proposition, therefore, that Bach's abnormal usage
of the organ in 1731 was invited by the disturbing conditions in
which he was placed. Nor can it be fortuitous that, with one exception in No. 49, all the arias having an organ obbligato are for an
alto voice. Did Bach draw upon arias already sung in the domestic
music-making he so much loved?

Only twice again, and in his latest years, Bach repeated the
experiments of 1731. For the wedding cantata *Herr Gott, Beherrscher aller Dinge* he adapted the first movement of the third Violin
Partita in E as a sinfonia for organ and orchestra. In cantata
No. 146 the opening sinfonia is an adaptation of the first movement
of the Clavier Concerto in D minor, which had done the same service
for No. 188 in 1731. The chorus that follows is an adaptation of
the slow movement of the concerto, and in both the organ is
obbligato. The authenticity of the rest of the cantata is suspect.
Carl Philipp Emanuel's hand is suggested, as is Friedemann's in
No. 188.[2] Is it only a coincidence that their father threw the same
ballast into both?

Not only in church did the conventions of Bach's period
require a keyboard accompaniment. In chamber and orchestral
music the organ's part was taken by the harpsichord. This is
self-evident in Bach's domestic vocal music: e.g. the secular
cantata *Amore traditore* has only a cembalo accompaniment; for
the 'Coffee cantata' (*Schweigt stille*) he wrote a cembalo part in
addition to the quartet of strings; for *O holder Tag* a part exists
inscribed 'La voce e Basso per il Cembalo', and another for violone,
the former figured. Even his elaborate cantatas written for open-
air performance require the harpsichord. Of the two continuo
parts of *Schleicht, spielende Wellen*, performed in Leipzig's market-
place on 7 October 1734, one is figured in his own hand.

In pure orchestral music the harpsichord was no less essential,
though the number of Bach's figured continuo parts that survive
is small.[3] Of the Brandenburg Concertos, he prescribes for the
second a 'Violone in Ripieno col Violoncello e Basso per il Cembalo'; for the third, 'tre Violoncelli col Basso per il Cembalo'; for
the fifth, 'Violoncello, Violone e Cembalo concertato'; and for the

[1] Cf. Terry, p. 209.   [2] Cf. Terry (4), p. 250.   [3] See Table XX.

sixth, 'due Viole da Gamba . . . e Cembalo'. The parts of all but the fifth have not survived, and, alone of the six, its continuo is figured. But the figuring is confined to the bars above which stands the instruction 'accompagnamento', that is, in which the cembalo is not 'concertato'. The score does not reveal whether the figured passages were played by a second cembalo.

Of the four Ouvertures, again, a part for 'Fagotto con Cembalo' was provided for the first, and the continuo of the first and second is figured throughout.

Turning to the concertos for harpsichord and orchestra: in the seven for a single clavier ('cembalo certato') Bach simply indicates 'continuo'. But for No. 4, in A, in addition to one for the violone, a second continuo part, completely figured, exists in his autograph, and an additional, accompanying, cembalo was certainly employed in them all. On the other hand, another cembalo was superfluous in the concertos for two, three, and four claviers with orchestra. Its addition, as Rust[1] remarks, would create 'a musical pleonasm of the most confusing character'. The concertos for violin and orchestra, however, needed a harpsichord accompaniment, and for two of them—No. II in E and No. III (double) in D minor—figured continuo parts exist. The Concerto in A minor for clavier, flute, violin, and orchestra reveals the same treatment of the cembalo as in the fifth Brandenburg: the part is figured only in those bars in which the upper manual is not engaged, i.e. in which the instrument is not 'concertato', but merely accompanying. As with the fifth Brandenburg, a second cembalo perhaps was employed.

In regard to Bach's music for a solo instrument and clavier, it must be borne in mind[2] that a 'Sonata for violin and clavier' was not the same as a 'Sonata for clavier and violin'. A 'Sonata for violin and clavier' represented solo music for the violin accompanied by a figured bass on the cembalo, while a 'Sonata for clavier and violin' treated the two instruments on a platform of equality. In our phraseology such a movement would be called a 'duet'. But Bach's epoch reckoned the obbligato parts, not the number of instruments engaged. Hence, if the cembalo part was written in two parts, as with Bach's sonatas is generally the case,[3] the piece was deemed a 'trio'. Thus the Sonatas (or Suites) for clavier and flute, for clavier and violin, for clavier and viola da gamba are in the category of trios. On the other hand, in a sonata for an instrument, or instruments, 'and continuo', the cembalo is an accompanying member, and its part is figured, as we find it in

[1] B.-G. xxi (2), p. vii.   [2] Cf. Schweitzer, i. 394.   [3] See Table XX.

Bach's Sonatas for flute, violin, and continuo; two violins and continuo; two flutes and clavier; flute and continuo; and violin and continuo.

The significance of Bach's continuo parts, and the need to use them as he intended, is expressed by Wilhelm Rust[1] in sentences with which this chapter can appropriately be brought to an end:

'Just as in pictures of historical scenes we need a background, however slight, on which to display the characters, so do Bach's polyphonic parts move freely, like persons passing on their lawful occasions, across a harmonic background. And as figures, lacking this pictorial background, lose their relationship to the whole design, even though their outline, colour, and character remain, so with Bach's music,[2] its full impression is not conveyed unless we hear it in its harmonic setting.'

[1] B.-G. xxii, p. xiv.   [2] 'Kirchenwerken.'

INDEX INSTRUMENTORUM

(The principal reference is indicated in figures of heavier type.)

INDEX NOMINUM

INDEX OPERUM

INDEX RERUM

THE TABLES

$c_{,,}$ $c_{,}$ c c' c'' c'''

TABLE I. THE TROMBA

NOTE. *The Instrument is in C unless the contrary is stated*

(A) CHURCH MUSIC

Cantata.	Date.	Movement.	Score.	Sounding Compass.
No. 5	1735	5. Aria (B.)	In Bb	$bb-bb''$
11	c. 1736	1. Coro	In D. 3 Tr.+Timp.	I $f♯'-e'''$
		11. Choral	,, ,, ,,	II $d'-d'''$
				III $a-f♯''$
15	1704	1. 4. Aria (B.)(T.)	3 Tr.+Timp.[1]	I $g'-b''$
		6. Terzetto	,, ,,	II $e'-b''$
		9. Coro and Choral	,, ,,	III $c'-c''$
19	1726	1. Coro	3 Tr.+Timp.	I $e'-c'''$
		7. Choral	,, ,,	II $c'-b''$
		5. Aria (T.)	Choral melody; obbl.	III $c'-a''$
20	c. 1725	8. Aria (B.)	...	$g-c''$
21	1714	11. Coro	3 Tr.+Timp.	I $e'-c'''$
				II $c'-a''$
				III $g-e''$
29	1731	1. Sinfonia	In D. 3 Tr.+Timp.	I $d'-d'''$
		2. Coro	,, ,, ,,	II $d'-b''$
		8. Choral	,, ,, ,,	III $a-c♯''$
30	1738	1. Coro	In D. 3 Tr.+Timp.	I $d'-d'''$
		12. Coro	,, ,, ,,	II $d'-b''$
				III $d'-f♯''$
31	1715	1. Sonata	3 Tr.+Timp.	I $g-e'''$
		2. Coro		II $g-bb''$
		9. Choral	Obbligato	III $g-a''$
34	1740–1	1. Coro	In D. 3 Tr.+Timp.	I $a'-e'''$
		5. Coro	,, ,, ,,	II $a'-c♯'''$
				III $d'-g♯''$
41	1736	1. Coro	3 Tr.+Timp.	I $g'-d'''$
		6. Choral	,, ,,	II $e'-b''$
				III $c'-g''$
43	c. 1735	1. Coro	3 Tr.+Timp.	I $c'-c'''$
		7. Aria (B.)	Solo	II $g'-bb''$
				III $c'-f''$
50	c. 1740	Coro	In D. 3 Tr.+Timp.	I $f♯'-e'''$
				II $d'-b''$
				III $a-g''$

[1] 2 Clarini and Principale.

Cantata.	Date.	Movement.	Score.	Sounding Compass.
No. 51	1731–2	1. Aria (S.) 5. Aria (S.)	...	c'–d'''
59	1716	1. Duetto (S.B.)	2 Tr.+Timp.	I c''–c''' II c'–a''
63	1723	1. Coro 7. Coro	4 Tr.+Timp. ,, ,,	I g'–d''' II e'–b'' III g–g'' IV g–g'
66	1731	1. Coro	In D	d'–e'''
69	1724	1. Coro 6. Choral	In D. 3 Tr.+Timp. ,, ,, ,,	I d'–d''' II d'–a'' III d'–a''
70	1716	1. Coro 2. Recit. (B.) 9. Recit. (B.) 10. Aria (B.)	... Choral melody. Obbl.	c'–c'''
71	1708	1. Coro 5. Aria (A.) 7. Coro	3 Tr.+Timp. ,, ,, ,, ,,	I c'–bb'' II c'–g'' III g–c''
74	1735	1. Coro	3 Tr.+Timp.	I e'–c''' II g'–b'' III c'–e''
75	1723	12. Aria (B.)	...	c'–c'''
76	1723	1. Coro 5. Aria (B.)	...	e'–c'''
77	c. 1725	5. Aria (A.)	Solo	g'–c'''
80	1730	1. Coro 5. Choral	In D. 3 Tr.+Timp. ,, ,, ,,	I d'–e''' II d'–c♯''' III d'–a''
90	c. 1740	3. Aria (B.)	In Bb	bb–bb''
110	post 1734	1. Coro 6. Aria (B.) 7. Choral	In D. 3 Tr.+Timp. ,, Choral melody; Tr. I. col. S.	I d'–e''' II d'–c♯''' III d'–a'' b'–f♯''
119	1723	1. Coro 4. Recit. (B.) 7. Coro	4 Tr.+Timp. ,, ,, ,, ,,	I c'–d''' II c'–c''' III c'–g'' IV g–c''
120	1730	2. Coro	In D. 3 Tr.+Timp.	I d'–d''' II d'–b'' III d'–e''
126	c. 1740	1. Coro	In D	a'–d'''
127	c. 1740	4. Recit. and Aria (B.)	...	c'–c'''
128	1735	3. Aria (B.)	In D	a'–d'''
129	1732	1. Coro 5. Choral	In D. 3 Tr.+Timp. ,, ,, ,,	I f♯'–d''' II f♯'–c♯'' III d'–a''
130	c. 1740	1. Coro 3. Aria (B.) 6. Choral	3 Tr.+Timp. ,, ,, ,, ,,	I c'–d''' II c'–c''' III g–a''
137	1732	1. Coro 5. Choral	3 Tr.+Timp. ,, ,,	I c''–d''' II g'–g'' III c'–e''

TABLE I. THE TROMBA 189

Work. Cantata.	Date.	Movement.	Score.	Sounding Compass.
No. 145	1729–30	2. Coro 5. Aria (B.)	In D ,,	d'–d'''
147	1716	1. Coro 9. Aria (B.)	...	c'–c'''
148	c. 1725	1. Coro	In D	$f\sharp'$–d'''
149	1731	1. Coro 7. Choral	In D. 3 Tr.+Timp. ,, C. ,, ,,	I d'–d''' II d'–a'' III d'–$f\sharp''$
171	c. 1730	1. Coro 6. Choral	In D. 3 Tr.+Timp. ,, ,, ,,	I d'–e''' II d'–b'' III d'–d''
172	1731	1. Coro 3. Aria (B.)	3 Tr.+Timp. ,, ,,	I c'–c''' II c'–bb'' III g–g''
175	1735	6. Aria (B.)	In D. 2 Tr.	I d''–e''' II d'–a''
181	c. 1725	5. Coro	In D	a'–d'''
190	1725	1. Coro 2. Choral 7. Choral	In D. 1 {3 Tr.+Timp. ,, 2 {Parts missing ,, 3 Tr.+Timp.	I d''–c''' II d''–c''' III d'–d''
191	1733	1. Coro 3. Coro	In D. 3 Tr.+Timp. ,, ,, ,,	I $f\sharp'$–e''' II d'–d''' III d'–b''
195	c. 1726	1. Coro 5. Coro	In D. 3 Tr.+Timp. ,, ,, ,,	I a'–e''' II d'–$c\sharp'''$ III d'–a''
197	1737	1. Coro	In D. 3 Tr.+Timp.	I d'–d''' II $f\sharp'$–a'' III d'–$f\sharp''$
Christmas Oratorio, Pt. I	1734	1. Coro 8. Aria (B.) 9. Choral	In D. 3 Tr.+Timp. ,, ,, 3 Tr.+Timp.	I a–d''' II d'–b'' III d'–a''
Christmas Oratorio, Pt. III	1734	1. Coro	In D. 3 Tr.+Timp.	I d''–d''' II $f\sharp'$–a'' III d'–e'''
Christmas Oratorio, Pt. VI	1734	1. Coro 11. Choral	In D. 3 Tr.+Timp. ,, ,, ,,	I d'–d''' II $f\sharp'$–b'' III d'–b''
Easter Oratorio	1736	1. Sinfonia 2 {Duetto (T.B.) {Coro 10. Coro	In D. 3 Tr.+Timp. ,, ,, ,, ,, ,, ,, ,, ,, ,,	I d'–d''' II d'–d''' III a–g''
Magnificat	1723	1. Coro 6. Coro 11. Coro	In D. 3 Tr.+Timp. ,, ,, ,, ,, ,, ,,	I $f\sharp'$–e''' II d'–d''' III a–b''
Hohe Messe	1733	4. Coro 6. Coro 11. Coro 13. Coro 17. Coro 19. Coro 20. Coro 21. Coro 24. Coro.	In D. 3 Tr.+Timp. ,,	I d'–e''' II d'–d''' III d'–$c\sharp'''$
Sanctus in C.	...	...	3 Tr.+Timp.	I c'–c''' II c'–g'' III c'–e''

(B) SECULAR CANTATAS

Work. Cantata.	Date.	Movement.	Score.	Sounding Compass.
Aeolus	1725	1. Coro 2. Recit. (B.) 11. Aria (B.) 15. Coro	In D. 3 Tr.+Timp. ,, ,, ,, ,, ,, ,, ,, ,, ,,	I d'–e''' II d'–c♯''' III a–b''
Phoebus und Pan	1731	1. Coro 15. Coro	In D. 3 Tr.+Timp. ,, ,, ,,	I d'–d''' II d'–a'' III d'–f♯''
Angenehmes Wiederau	1737	1. Coro 13. Coro	In D. 3 Tr.+Timp. ,, ,, ,,	I d'–d''' II d'–b'' III d'–f♯''
Schleicht, spielende Wellen	1734	1. Coro 11. Coro	In D. 3 Tr.+Timp. ,, ,, ,,	I d'–d''' II d'–c♯''' III d'–d'''
Preise dein' Glücke	1734	1. Coro 8. Recit. (S.T.B.) 9. Coro	In D. 3 Tr.+Timp. ,, ,, ,, ,, ,, ,,	I d'–e''' II d'–c♯''' III d'–g''
Tönet, ihr Pauken	1733	1. Coro 7. Aria (B.) 9. Coro	In D. 3 Tr.+Timp. ,, ,, 3 Tr.+Timp.	I a–d''' II d'–b'' III d'–a''
Vereinigte Zwietracht Auf, schmet- ternde Töne (omitting Nos. 1 and 7)	1726 1734	1. Marcia 2. Coro 7. Ritornello 11. Coro	In D. 3 Tr.+Timp. ,, 2 Tr. ,, ,, 2 Tr. ,, 3 Tr.+Timp.	I f♯'–d''' II d'–a'' III a–g''

(C) INSTRUMENTAL MUSIC

Sinfonia	...	...	In D. 3 Tr.+Timp.	I a–e''' II d'–d''' III a–a''
Ouverture in D (1)	...	...	In D. 3 Tr.+Timp.	I d'–d''' II d'–b'' III a–a''
Ouverture in D (2)	...	...	In D. 3 Tr.+Timp.	I d'–e''' II d'–c♯''' III d'–a''
Branden- burg Con- certo, No. 2	1721	...	In F	f–g'' or f'–g''''[1]

[1] See B.–J., 1916, pp. 1–7.

TABLE II. THE ZUGTROMPETE (TROMBA DA TIRARSI)[1]

Cantata. No.	Date.	Movement.	Score.	Sounding Compass.
3	c. 1740	6. Choral	'Corno' col S. (in C or A). Choral melody	$e'-d''$
5	1735	1. Coro	'Tromba da tirarsi' col S. (in C or B♭). Choral melody	$g'-f''$
		7. Choral	'Tromba da tirarsi' col S. (in C or B♭). Choral melody	$g'-f''$
8	c. 1725	1. Coro	'Corno' col S. (in C or A). Choral melody	$d\sharp'-e''$
		6. Choral	'Corno' col S. (in C or A). Choral melody	$d\sharp'-e''$
10	c. 1740	1. Coro	'Tromba' col S. and A. Choral melody	$c'-f''$
		5. Duetto (A.T.)	'Tromba' col Ob. I, II (in C or B♭). Choral melody, obbl.	$d'-c''$
		7. Choral	'Tromba' col. S. (in C or B♭). Choral melody	$g'-f''$
12	1724-5	6. Aria (T.)	'Tromba.' Choral melody, obbl.	$g'-bb''$
		7. Choral	'Oboe o Tromba.' Obbligato	$a'-c'''$
14	1735	1. Coro	'Corno di caccia.' Choral melody, obbl.	$f'-d''$
		5. Choral	'Corno di caccia' col S. (in C or B♭). Choral melody	$f'-d''$
16	1724	1. Coro	'Corno di caccia' col S. (in C). Choral melody	$e'-c''$
		6. Choral	'Corno di caccia' col S. (in C). Choral melody	$a'-e''$
20	c. 1725	1. Coro	'Tromba da tirarsi' col S. (in C). Choral melody	$f'-f''$
		7 & 11. Choral	'Tromba da tirarsi' col S. (in C). Choral melody	$f'-f''$
24	1723	3. Coro	'Clarino'	$d'-bb''$
		6. Choral	'Clarino.' Obbligato	$f-eb''$
26	c. 1740	1. Coro	'Corno' col S. (in C). Choral melody	$a'-f''$
		6. Choral	'Corno' col S. (in C). Choral melody	$a'-f''$
27	1731	1. Coro	'Corno' col S. (in C or B♭). Choral melody	$g'-ab''$
		6. Choral	'Corno' col S. (in C or B♭). Choral melody	$g'-f''$
40	1723	3. Choral	'Corno I' col S. (in C or B♭). Choral melody	$g'-d''$
		6. Choral	'Corno I' col S. (in C or B♭). Choral melody	$g'-f''$
		8. Choral	'Corno I' col S. (in C or B♭). Choral melody	$f'-f''$
43	c. 1735	11. Choral	'Tromba I, II' col S. (in C). Choral melody	I, II $g'-g''$
			'Tromba III' col A. (in C). Choral melody	III $b-b'$
46	c. 1725	1. Coro	'Tromba o Corno da tirarsi' col S. (in D)	$e'-a''$
		3. Aria (B.)	'Tromba o Corno da tirarsi.' Obbligato	$bb-bb''$

[1] Since the positions of the slide would have to be altered, at any rate slightly, for each key, when crooks were used, it is pertinent to remark that trombone players of the period had no difficulty in adjusting their slide-positions to an altered pitch.

Cantata. No.	Date.	Movement.	Score.	Sounding Compass.
46	c. 1735	6. Choral	'Tromba o Corno da tirarsi' col S. (in C). Choral melody	e'–d''
48	c. 1740	1. Coro	'Tromba.'[1] Choral melody, obbl.	g'–g''
		3. Choral	'Tromba' col S. (in C or B♭). Choral melody	f'–d''
		7. Choral	'Tromba' col S. (in C or B♭). Choral melody	d'–d''
60	1732	1. Duetto (A.T.)	'Corno.' Choral melody, obbl.	d'–d''
		5. Choral	'Corno' col S. (in D or C). Choral melody	a'–e''
62	c. 1740	1. Coro	'Corno' col S. (in D or C). Choral melody	a'–f♯''
		6. Choral	'Corno' col S. (in D or C). Choral melody	a'–f♯''
67	c. 1725	1. Coro	'Corno da tirarsi'	a–b''
		4. Choral	'Corno da tirarsi' col S. (in D). Choral melody	f♯'–f♯''
		7. Choral	'Corno da tirarsi' col S. (in D). Choral melody	g♯'–e''
68	1735	1. Coro	'Corno' col S. (in C). Choral melody	d'–g''
70	1716	7. Choral	'Tromba' col S. (in C). Choral melody	d'–e''
		11. Choral	'Tromba' col S. (in C). Choral melody	c'–d''
73	c. 1725	1. Coro	'Corno, ossia Organo obligato.' Mainly Choral melody	f'–e♭''
		5. Choral	'Corno' col S. (in C or B♭). Choral melody	g'–g''
74	1735	8. Choral	'Tromba I' col S. (in C). Choral melody	g'–e''
75	1723	8. Sinfonia	'Tromba' (in high G). Choral melody, obbl.	d''–e'''
76	1723	7 & 14. Choral	'Tromba.' Choral melody	c'–e''
77	c. 1725	1. Coro	'Tromba da tirarsi. Choral melody, obbl.	c'–c'''
78	c. 1740	1. Coro	'Corno' col S. (in C or B♭). Choral melody	f'–e♭''
		7. Choral	'Corno' col S. (in C or B♭). Choral melody	f'–e♭''
83	1724	5. Choral	'Corno I' col S. (in C). Choral melody	c'–d''
89	c. 1730	1. Aria (B.)	'Corno' [da caccia]. Obbligato	c'–f''
		6. Choral	'Corno' [da caccia] col S. (in C or B♭). Choral melody	g'–f''
95	1732	1. Coro	'Corno.' Choral melody col S. (in C) and obbligato	c'–a''
		6. Choral	'Corno' col S. (in C). Choral melody	d'–d''
96	c. 1740	1. Coro	'Corno e Trombone coll' Alto' (in C). Choral melody	d'–c''
		6. Choral	'Corno' col S. (in C or D). Choral melody	d'–c''
99	c. 1733	1. Coro	'Corno' col S. (in C). Choral melody	d'–e''
		6. Choral	'Corno' col S. (in C). Choral melody	d'–e''
103	1735	5. Aria (T.)	'Tromba'	d'–d'''
		6. Choral	'Tromba' col S. (in D or C). Choral melody	f♯'–e''

[1] Marked 'Clarino' on the parts.

TABLE II.   THE ZUGTROMPETE (TROMBA DA TIRARSI)   193

Cantata. No.	Date.	Movement.	Score.	Sounding Compass.
105	c. 1725	1. Coro 5. Aria (T.)	'Corno ed Oboe I' 'Corno'	d'–d''' f'–bb''
107	c. 1735	1. Coro 7. Choral	'Corno da caccia' col S. (in D or C). Choral melody 'Corno da caccia' col S. (in D or C). Choral melody	f#'–g'' f#'–f#''
109	c. 1731	1. Coro 6. Choral	'Corno da caccia' 'Corno da caccia' col S. (in C or D). Choral melody	c'–c''' d'–e''
114	c. 1740	1. Coro 7. Choral	'Corno' col S. (in C or Bb). Choral melody 'Corno' col S. (in C or Bb). Choral melody	f'–d'' f'–d''
115	c. 1740	1. Coro 6. Choral	'Corno' col S. (in C). Choral melody 'Corno' col S. (in C). Choral melody	g'–g'' g'–g''
116	1744	1. Coro 6. Choral	'Corno' col S. (in A or C). Choral melody 'Corno' col S. (in A or C). Choral melody	g#'–e'' g#'–e''
124	c. 1740	1. Coro 6. Choral	'Corno' col S. (in A or C). Choral melody 'Corno' col S. (in A or C). Choral melody	e'–f#'' e'–f#''
125	c. 1740	1. Coro 6. Choral	'Corno' col S. (in C). Choral melody 'Corno' col S. (in C). Choral melody	d'–e'' d'–e''
126	c. 1740	6. Choral	'Tromba' col S. (in C). Choral melody	g'–g''
137	1732	4. Aria (T.)	'Tromba.' Choral melody, obbl.	g'–g''
140	1731–42	1. Coro 7. Choral	'Corno' col S. (in C or Bb). Choral melody 'Corno' col S. (in C or Bb). Choral melody	eb'–g'' eb'–g''
147	1716	6 & 10. Choral	'Tromba' col S. (in C). Choral melody	g'–f''
162	1715	1. Aria (B.) 6. Choral	'Corno da tirarsi' 'Corno da tirarsi' col S. (in C). Choral melody	c'–c#'' e'–e''
167	c. 1725	5. Choral	'Clarino' col S. (in C). Choral melody	d'–d''
185	1715	1. Duetto (S.T.) 6. Choral	'Oboe (Tromba).' Choral melody, obbl. 'Tromba' col S. (? in D or A). Choral melody	e'–f#'' e'–f#''

TABLE III. THE CORNETT

Cantata.	Date.	Movement.	Score.	Sounding Compass.
No. 4	1724	2. Coro	Choral melody col S.[1]	$e'-g''$
		3. Duetto (S.A.)	,, ,, col S.	$d\sharp'-f\sharp''$
		8. Choral	,, ,, col S.[1]	$e'-f\sharp''$
23	1724	4. Choral	Choral melody col S.[1]	$bb'-f''$
25	c. 1731	1. Coro	Choral melody[1]	$d'-d''$
		6. Choral	,, ,, col S.[1]	$g'-a''$
28	c. 1736	2. Coro	Choral melody col S.[1]	$g'-g''$
		6. Choral	,, ,, ,, [1]	$a'-e''$
64	1723	1. Coro	Col S.[1]	$d\sharp'-a''$
		2. Choral	Choral melody col S.[1]	$d'-e''$
		4. Choral	,, ,, ,, [1]	$d'-e''$
		8. Choral	,, ,, ,, [1]	$e'-g''$
68	1735	5. Coro	Col S.[1]	$d'-a''$
101	c. 1740	1. Coro	Choral melody col S.[1]	$d'-f''$
		7. Choral	,, ,, ,, [1]	$d'-f''$
118	c. 1737	Coro	Mainly Choral melody[1]	$f'-d'''$
121	c. 1740	1. Coro	Choral melody col S.[1]	$e'-d''$
		6. Choral	,, ,, ,, [1]	$e'-d''$
133	1735-7	1. Coro	Choral melody col S.	$f\sharp'-e''$
		6. Choral	,, ,, ,,	$f\sharp'-e'$
135	c. 1740	6. Choral	Choral melody col S.	$d'-d''$
Sanctus in D		...	Col S.	$d'-a''$

[1] Associated with Trombones.

TABLE IV. THE TROMBONE 195

TABLE IV. THE TROMBONE

Cantata. No.	Date.	Movement.	Score.	Sounding Compass. Soprano. I	Alto. I, II	Tenor. II, III	Bass. III, IV
2	c. 1740	1. Coro	Tromb. I–IV col S.A.T.B. Choral Motet. No free instrumental parts except Continuo	f♯′–a″	d′–d″	f–a′	g–e♭′
3	c. 1740	6. Choral	Tromb. I–IV col S.A.T.B.	...	...	...	e–d″
4	1724	1. Coro	Tromb. col B. Choral melody	...	...	...	e͵–d″
		2. Coro	Tromb. I–III col A.T.B. Cornett col S. (Choral melody)	...	g–c♯″	c–f♯′	...
21	1714	3. Duetto	Tromb. I col A. Free Choral. Cornett col S.	...	a–c♯″	...	...
		8. Choral	Tromb. I–III col A.T.B. Cornett col S.	...	a–d″	d–a♭′	f–e♭′
		9. Coro	Tromb. I–IV col S.A.T.B. Choral. No free instrumental parts	d′–d″	...	d–g′	f–e♭′
23	1724	4. Choral	Tromb. I–III col A.T.B. Cornett col S.	...	c′–d″	...	...
25	c. 1731	1. Coro	Tromb. I–III + Cornett. Choral in four instrumental parts. Voices independent	...	g♯–b′	e–f′	e͵–a
28	c. 1736	6. Choral	Tromb. I–III col A.T.B. Cornett col S.	...	a–d″	d–g′	d–d′
38	c. 1740	6. Choral	Tromb. I–III col A.T.B. Cornett col S. Choral Motet	...	...	...	...
		1. Coro	Tromb. I–IV col S.A.T.B. No free instrumental parts except Continuo. Choral Motet	e–d″	a–d″	e–a′	g–e′
64	1723	6. Choral	Tromb. I–IV col S.A.T.B.	...	...	...	...
		1. Coro	Tromb. I–III col A.T.B. Cornett col S. No free instrumental parts except Continuo	...	b–d″	d–a′	g–e′
68	1735	2)4}8) Choral 5. Coro	Tromb. I–III col A.T.B. Cornett col S.	...	a–e″	d–a′	a͵–f♯′
96	c. 1740	1. Coro	Corno e Trombone col A. Choral melody	...	d′–c″	...	...
101	c. 1740	1. Coro	Tromb. I–III col A.T.B. Cornett col S. Choral Melody	...	a–c″	d–g′	g–e′
		7. Choral	Tromb. I–III + Cornett. Choral Motet	...	...	...	f♯–d′
118	c. 1737	1. Coro	Tromb. I–III col A.T.B. Cornett col S. No free instrumental parts except Continuo. Choral Motet	...	f–c″	d–g′	d–c′
121	c. 1740	1. Coro	Tromb. I–III col A.T.B. Cornett col S.	...	b–e″	e–a′	g–e′
135	c. 1740	6. Choral	Tromb. I–III col A.T.B. Cornett col S.	...	...	...	...
		1. Coro	Trombone col Continuo. Choral Melody	...	...	...	d–d″

TABLE V. THE WALDHORN (CORNO)

(A) CHURCH MUSIC

Work. Cantata.	Date.	Movement.	Key.	Sounding Compass.
No. 1	c. 1740	1. Coro	F	$\begin{cases} a-g'' \\ f-e'' \end{cases}$
		6. Choral	F	$\begin{cases} f'-f'' \\ f-c'' \end{cases}$
14	1735	1. Coro	F	$f'-d''$
		2. Aria (S.)	B♭	$bb-c'''$
40	1723	1. Coro	F	$\begin{cases} f-f'' \\ f-d'' \end{cases}$
		7. Aria (T.)	F	$\begin{cases} f-f'' \\ f-c'' \end{cases}$
52	c. 1730	1. Sinfonia	F	$\begin{cases} \text{I } c-f'' \\ \text{II } f-d'' \end{cases}$
		6. Choral		$\begin{cases} \text{I } f'-d'' \\ \text{II } f-a' \end{cases}$
79	1735	1. Coro	G	$\begin{cases} \text{I } g'-g'' \\ \text{II } g-d'' \end{cases}$
		3. Choral	G	$\begin{cases} \text{I } d'-g'' \\ \text{II } g-e'' \end{cases}$
		6. Choral	G	$\begin{cases} \text{I } a'-g'' \\ \text{II } d'-d'' \end{cases}$
83	1724	1. Coro	F	$\begin{cases} \text{I } a-f'' \\ \text{II } f-d'' \end{cases}$
88	1732	1. Aria (B.)	G	$\begin{cases} \text{I } d'-a''^* \\ \text{II } g-d' \end{cases}$
91	c. 1740	1. Coro	G	$\begin{cases} \text{I } g'-a'' \\ \text{II } b-f\sharp'' \end{cases}$
		6. Choral	G	$\begin{cases} \text{I } g'-g'' \\ \text{II } g-c'' \end{cases}$
100	c. 1735	1. Coro	G	$\begin{cases} \text{I } g-g'' \\ \text{II } g-f\sharp'' \end{cases}$
		6. Choral	G	$\begin{cases} \text{I } d'-g'' \\ \text{II } g-g'' \end{cases}$
112	1731	1. Coro	G	$\begin{cases} \text{I } g'-g'' \\ \text{II } g-e'' \end{cases}$
		5. Choral	G	$\begin{cases} \text{I } g'-d'' \\ \text{II } g-b' \end{cases}$
118	c. 1737	Coro	B♭ ('Lituus')	$\begin{cases} \text{I } f'-a'' \\ \text{II } bb-ab'' \end{cases}$
136	c. 1725	1. Coro	A	$a-a''$
		6. Choral	col S.	...
195	c. 1726	6. Choral	G	$\begin{cases} \text{I } g'-e'' \\ \text{II } g'-c'' \end{cases}$
Mass in F	c. 1736	Kyrie	F	$f'-d''$
Christmas Oratorio, Pt. IV	1734	1. Coro	F	$\begin{cases} \text{I } f-g'' \\ \text{II } f-e'' \end{cases}$
		7. Choral	F	$\begin{cases} \text{I } f-f'' \\ \text{II } f-c'' \end{cases}$
Three Wedding Chorals	(?) 1749	...	G	$\begin{cases} \text{I } d'-g'' \\ \text{II } g-e'' \end{cases}$

TABLE V.   THE WALDHORN (CORNO)   197

(B) SECULAR CANTATAS

Cantata.	Date.	Movement.	Key.	Sounding Compass.
Mer hahn en neue Oberkeet	1742	16. Aria (B.) 18. Aria (S.)	G D[1]	*g–e''* *d–a'*
Aeolus	1725	1. Coro	D	{ I *d–d''* { II *d–b'*
		2. Recit. (B.)	D	{ I *d–c♯'* { II *d–a'*
		11. Aria (B.)	D	{ I *f♯–d''* { II *d–c♯''*
		15. Coro	D	{ I *d–d''* { II *d–a'*

[1] The compass of the Horns in D is given in terms of the lower instrument.

TABLE VI.   THE JAGDHORN (CORNO DA CACCIA)

(A) CHURCH MUSIC

Work. Cantata.	Date.	Movement.	Key.	Sounding Compass.
No. 14	1735	2. Aria (S.)	B♭	*bb–c''*
16	1724	3. Coro&Aria(B.)	C	*c–c''*
65	1724	1. Coro	C	{ I *e–a'* { II *c–g'*
		6. Aria (T.)	C	{ I *c–c''* { II *c–bb'*
128	1735	1. Coro	G	{ I *g–a''* { II *g–g''*
		5. Choral	G	{ I *g'–g''* { II *g–c''*
143	1735	1. Coro	B♭	{ I *f'–bb''* { II *f'–g''* { III *bb–c''*
		5. Aria (B.)	B♭	{ I *bb–bb''* { II *bb–bb''* { III *bb–bb'*
		7. Choral	B♭	{ I *f'–ab''* { II *d'–g''* { III *f–bb'*
174	1729	1. Sinfonia	G	{ I *g–a''* { II *g–g''*
Hohe Messe	1733	10. Aria (B.)	D	*d–d''*

(B) SECULAR CANTATAS

Was mir behagt	1716	2. Aria (S.)	F	{ I *f–c''* { II *f–c''*
		11. Coro	F	{ I *f–d''* { II *f–bb'*
		15. Coro	F	{ I *f–d''* { II *f–bb'*
Hercules	1733	1. Coro	F	{ I *f–g''* { II *f–e''*
		13. Coro	F	{ I *f'–g''* { II *f–a'*

TABLE VI. THE JAGDHORN (CORNO DA CACCIA)

(C) INSTRUMENTAL MUSIC

Work.	Date.	Movement.	Key.	Sounding Compass.
Brandenburg Concerto, No. 1 in F	1721[1]	...	F[3]	$\begin{cases} \text{I } f\text{-}f'' \\ \text{II } c\text{-}d'' \end{cases}$
Sinfonia, in F	1721[2]	...	F[3]	$\begin{cases} \text{I } c\text{-}f'' \\ \text{II } f\text{-}d'' \end{cases}$

[1] The first movement serves as the Introduction to Cantata No. 52. But the horns used there are not indicated as Corni da caccia.
[2] Another score of the Brandenburg Concerto, No. 1 in F. In B.–G. xxxi (1).
[3] Perhaps a Jagdtrompete an octave higher.

TABLE VII. THE TIMPANI

(A) CHURCH MUSIC

Cantata.	Date.	Movement.	Key.	Score.	Tuning.
No. 11	c. 1736	1. Coro 11. Choral	D	3 Tr.+Timp. ,, ,,	d–a,
15	1704	1. Aria (B.) 4. Aria (T.) 6. Terzetto (A.T.B.) 8. Sonata 9. Quartetto and Choral	C	3 Tr.+Timp. ,, ,, :, ,, ,, ,, ,, ,,	c–g,
19	1726	1. Coro 7. Choral	C	3 Tr.+Timp. ,, ,,	c–g,
21	1714	11. Coro	C	3 Tr.+Timp.	no part
29	1731	1. Sinfonia 2. Coro 8. Choral	D	3 Tr.+Timp. ,, ,, ,, ,,	d–a,
30	1738	1. Coro 12. Coro	D	3 Tr.+Timp. ,, ,,	d–a,
31	1715	1. Sonata 2. Coro 9. Choral	C	3 Tr.+Timp. ,, ,, ,, ,,	c–g,
34	1740–1	1. Coro 5. Coro	D	3 Tr.+Timp. ,, ,,	d–a,
41	1736	1. Coro 6. Choral	C	3 Tr.+Timp. ,, ,,	c–g,
43	c. 1735	1. Coro	C	3 Tr.+Timp.	c–g,
50	c. 1740	Coro	D	3 Tr.+Timp.	d–a,
59	1716	1. Duetto (S.B.)	C	2 Tr.+Timp.	c–g,
63	1723	1. Coro 7. Coro	C	4 Tr.+Timp. ,, ,,	c–g,
69	1724	1. Coro 6. Choral	D	3 Tr.+Timp. ,, ,,	d–a,
71	1708	1. Coro 5. Aria (A.) 7. Coro	C	3 Tr.+Timp. ,, ,, ,, ,,	c–g,
74	1735	1. Coro	C	3 Tr.+Timp.	c–g,
79	1735	1. Coro 3 & 6. Choral	G	2 Cor.+Timp. ,, ,,	d–g,

TABLE VII.   THE TIMPANI   199

Work. Cantata.	Date.	Movement.	Key.	Score.	Tuning.
No. 80	1730	1. Coro 5. Choral	D	3 Tr.+Timp. ,, ,,	d–a,
91	c. 1740	1. Coro 6. Choral	G	2 Cor.+Timp. ,, ,,	d–g,
100	c. 1735	1. Coro 6. Choral	G	2 Cor.+Timp. ,, ,,	d–g,
110	post 1734	1. Coro	D	3 Tr.+Timp.	d–a,
119	1723	1. Coro 4. Recit. (B.) 7. Coro	C	4 Tr.+Timp. ,, ,, ,, ,,	c–g,
120	1730	2. Coro	D	3 Tr.+Timp.	d–a,
129	1732	1. Coro 5. Choral	D	3 Tr.+Timp. ,, ,,	d–a,
130	c. 1740	1. Coro 3. Aria (B.) 6. Choral	C	3 Tr.+Timp. ,, ,, ,, ,,	c–g,
137	1732	1. Coro 5. Choral	C	3 Tr.+Timp. ,, ,,	c–g,
143	1735	1. Coro 5. Aria (B.) 7. Choral	Bb	3 Cor. da caccia +Timp. ,, ,,	bb,–f,
149	1731	1. Coro 7. Choral	D	3 Tr.+Timp. ,, ,,	d–a,
171	c. 1730	1. Coro 6. Choral	D	3 Tr.+Timp. ,, ,,	d–a,
172	1731	1. Coro 3. Aria (B.)	C	3 Tr.+Timp. ,, ,,	c–g,
190	1725	1. Coro 2. Choral 7. Choral	D	3 Tr.+Timp. ,, ,, ,, ,,	d–a,
191	1733	1. Coro 3. Coro	D	3 Tr.+Timp. ,, ,,	d–a,
195	c. 1726	1. Coro 5. Coro 6. Choral	D G	3 Tr.+Timp. ,, ,, 2 Cor.+Timp.	d–a, d–g,
197	1737	1. Coro	D	3 Tr.+Timp.	d–a,
Christmas Oratorio, Pt. I III VI	1734	1. Coro 9. Choral 24. Coro 54. Coro 64. Choral	D	3 Tr.+Timp. ,, ,, ,, ,, ,, ,, ,, ,,	d–a,
Hohe Messe	1733	4. Coro 6. Coro 11. Coro 13. Coro 17. Coro 19. Coro 20. Coro 21. Coro 24. Coro	D	3 Tr.+Timp. ,, ,, ,, ,, ,, ,, ,, ,, ,, ,, ,, ,, ,, ,, ,, ,,	d–a,
Magnificat	1723	1. Coro 6. Coro 11. Coro	D	3 Tr.+Timp. ,, ,, ,, ,,	d–a,
Easter Oratorio	1736	1. Sinfonia 2. Duetto and Coro 10. Coro	D	3 Tr.+Timp. ,, ,, ,, ,,	d–a,
Sanctus in C	...	Coro	C	3 Tr.+Timp.	c–g,

TABLE VII. THE TIMPANI

(B) SECULAR CANTATAS

Work. Cantata.	Date.	Movement.	Key.	Score.	Tuning.
Aeolus	1725	1. Coro 2. Recit. (B.) 11. Aria (B.) 15. Coro	D	3 Tr.+Timp. ,,　,, ,,　,, ,,　,,	*d–a,*
Angenehmes Wiederau	1737	1. Coro 13. Coro	D	3 Tr.+Timp. ,,　,,	*d–a,*
Phoebus und Pan	1731	1. Coro 15. Coro	D	3 Tr.+Timp. ,,　,,	*d–a,*
Preise dein' Glücke	1734	1. Coro 8. Recit. (S.T.B.) 9. Coro	D	3 Tr.+Timp. ,,　,, ,,　,,	*d–a,*
Schleicht, spie- lende Wellen	1734	1. Coro 11. Coro	D	3 Tr.+Timp. ,,　,,	*d–a,*
Tönet, ihr Pauken	1733	1. Coro 9. Coro	D	3 Tr.+Timp. ,,　,,	*d–a,*
Vereinigte Zwietracht	1726	1. Marcia 2. Coro 11. Coro	D	3 Tr.+Timp. ,,　,, ,,　,,	*d–a,*

(C) INSTRUMENTAL MUSIC

Sinfonia in D	...	...	D	3 Tr.+Timp.	*d–a,*
Ouverture in D (1)	...	...	D	3 Tr.+Timp.	*d–a,*
Ouverture in D (2)	...	...	D	3 Tr.+Timp.	*d–a,*

TABLE VIII
THE FLÛTE À BEC (BLOCKFLÖTE: FLÛTE DOUCE)
(A) CHURCH MUSIC

Cantata.	Date.	Movement.	Score.	Sounding Compass.
No. 13	*c.* 1740	1. Aria (T.) 3. Choral (A.) 5. Aria (B.) 6. Choral	3. Unison col A. 5. Unison col Vn. obbl.	I *c'–e'''* II *c'–e♭'''*
18	1714	1. Sinfonia 3. Recit. (T.B.) and Coro 4. Aria (S.) 5. Choral	4. Unison 5. Col S.	I *e'–a'''* II *e'–g'''*
25	*c.* 1731	1. Coro 5. Aria (S.) 6. Choral	1. Unison 6. Col S.	1. *d''–d'''* 5. I *g'–g'''* 　II *g'–e'''* 6. III *f'–b♭''*
39	1732	1. Coro 5. Aria (S.) 6. Choral	5. Unison 6. Col S. in 8va	I *d'–f'''* II *d'–f'''*
46	*c.* 1725	1. Coro 2. Recit. (T.) 5. Aria (A.) 6. Choral	...	I *a'–g'''* II *f'–g'''*
65	1724	1. Coro 2. Choral 6. Aria (T.)	2. Unison col S..in 8va	I *f'–g'''* II *f'–g'''*

TABLE VIII. THE FLÛTE À BEC (BLOCKFLÖTE: FLÛTE DOUCE) 201

Work. Cantata.	Date.	Movement.	Score.	Sounding Compass.
No. 71	1708	1. Coro	...	1.{I $g'-g''$ {II $g'-g''$
		4. Arioso (B.)	...	4.{I $g-c'''$ {II $e'-g''$
		6. Coro	...	6.{I $eb'-ab''$ {II $eb'-ab''$
		7. Coro	...	7.{I $g'-a''$ {II $e'-b''$
81	1724	1. Aria (A.)	...	{I $g'-f'''$ {II $g'-c'''$
96	c. 1740	1. Coro (Flauto piccolo)	Col Violino piccolo	$f''-f''''$
103	1735	1. Coro (Fiauto piccolo)	Col Violino concertante or Fl. traverso	$e''-f\sharp''''$
106	(?) 1711	Sonatina, &c.	...	{I $eb'-d'''$ {II $eb'-d'''$
119	1723	1. Coro 4. Recit. (B.) 5. Aria (A.) 7. Coro	5. Unison	{I $f'-g'''$ {II $f'-g'''$
122	c. 1742	3. Recit. (S.)	...	{I $g''-g'''$ {II $c''-bb''$ {III $g'-g''$
127	c. 1740	1. Coro 3. Aria (S.) 5. Choral	5. Col S. in 8va	{I $a'-g'''$ {II $f'-g'''$
142	1712 or 1713	1. Concerto 2. Coro 7. Aria (A.) 8. Choral	... (?) authentic 7. Col Violini	{I $e'-e'''$ {II $e'-c'''$
152	1715	1. Concerto 4. Aria (S.) 6. Duet (S.B.)	6. Gli Stromenti all'unisono	$d'-e'''$
161	1715	1. Aria (A.) 4. Recit. (A.) 5. Coro 6. Choral	...	{I $ab'-g'''$ {II $f'-q'''$
175	1735	1. Recit. (T.) 2. Aria (A.) 7. Choral	...	{I $a'-g'''$ {II $a'-e'''$ {III $g'-c\sharp'''$
180	c. 1740	1. Coro 4. Recit. (A.) 5. Aria (S.)	...	{I $f'-g'''$ {II $f'-g'''$
182	1714 or 1715	1. Sonata 2. Coro 5. Aria (A.) 7. Choral 8. Coro	...	$e'-f\sharp''''$
Easter Oratorio	1736	6. Aria (T.)	...	{I $g'-e'''$ {II $g'-d'''$
St. Matthew Passion	1729	25. Recit. (T.) and Coro[1]	...	{I $g'-eb'''$ {I $f'-c'''$
Was mir behagt	1716	9. Aria (S.)	...	{I $a'-g'''$ {II $f'-eb'''$

[1] Wrongly indicated as Flauto transverso in the B.–G. Score. See B.–G. x, p. xxii.

THE FLÛTE À BEC (BLOCKFLÖTE: FLÛTE DOUCE)

(C) INSTRUMENTAL MUSIC

Work.	Date.	Movement.	Score.	Sounding Compass.
Clavier Concerto, No. 6 in F	...	...	...	{I $f'-f'''$ {II $f'-f'''$
Brandenburg Concerto, No. 2 in F	1721	...	...	$f'-g'''$
Brandenburg Concerto, No. 4 in G	1721	...	...	{I $g'-g'''$ {II $f'-g'''$

TABLE IX
THE TRANSVERSE (GERMAN) FLUTE (QUERFLÖTE)
(A) CHURCH MUSIC

Cantata.	Date.	Movement.	Score.	Sounding Compass.
No. 8	c. 1725	1. Coro 4. Aria (B.) 6. Choral	6. Col S.	$e'-a'''$
9	(?) 1731	1. Coro 5. Duetto (S.A.) 7. Choral	7. Col S.	$e'-f'''$
11	c. 1736	1. Coro 3. Recit. (B.) 6. Choral 8. Recit. (A.) 10. Aria (S.) 11. Choral	6. Col S. 10. Unis.	{I $d'-e'''$ {II $d'-e'''$
26	c. 1740	1. Coro 2. Aria (T.) 6. Choral	1. Col Ob. 1. 2. 'Solo' 6. Col S.	$c'-d'''$ [1]
30	1738	1. Coro 5. Aria (A.) 6. Choral 12. Coro	6. Col S.	{I $d'-e'''$ {II $d'-e'''$
34	1740 or 1741	3. Aria (A.)	...	{I $g\sharp'-f\sharp'''$ {II $e'-d'''$
45	c. 1740	1. Coro 5. Aria (A.) 7. Choral	1. Col Ob. 5. Solo	{I $d'-e'''$ [2] {II $b-c\sharp'''$
55	1731 or 1732	1. Aria (T.) 3. Aria (T.) 5. Choral	3. Solo 5. Col S.	$e'-eb'''$
67	c. 1725	1. Coro 4. Choral 6. Aria (B.) and Coro 7. Choral	4. Col S. 7. Col S.	$d'-f\sharp'''$
78	c. 1740	1. Coro 4. Aria (T.) 7. Choral	4. Solo 7. Col S. in 8va	$f'-g'''$

[1] See *supra*, p. 75.

[2] See *supra*, p. 76.

TABLE IX. THE TRANSVERSE (GERMAN) FLUTE (QUERFLÖTE) 203

Cantata.	Date.	Movement.	Score.	Sounding Compass.
No. 79	1735	1. Coro 2. Aria (A.) 3. Choral 6. Choral	1. Col Ob. 2. Or Oboe. Solo. 3. Col S.	{I $d'-c'''$ {II $c'-c'''$
94	1735	1. Coro 4. Aria (A.) 8. Choral	4. Solo 8. Col S. in 8va	$d'-g'''$
96	c. 1740	3. Aria (T.)	'Solo'	$d'-e'''$
99	c. 1733	1. Coro 3. Aria (T.) 5. Duetto (S.A.) 6. Choral	3. Solo 6. Col S. in 8va	$d'-g'''$
100	c. 1735	1. Coro 3. Aria (S.) 6. Choral	3. 'Solo'	$d'-g'''$
101	c. 1740	1. Coro 6. Duetto (S.A.) 7. Choral	7. Col S. in 8va	$e'-f'''$
102	1731	5. Aria (T.) 7. Choral	5. 'Solo.' Or Vn. pic- colo. 7. Col S. in 8va	$d'-e'''$
103	1735	3. Aria (T.) 6. Choral	3. Or Violin. Solo. 6. Col S.	$e'-d'''$
107	c. 1735	1. Coro 6. Aria (T.) 7. Choral	6. Unison. Obbl.	{I $d'-e'''$ {II $d'-e'''$
110	post 1734	1. Coro 2. Aria (T.) 7. Choral	1. Col Ob. 1. 2. Soli. 7. Col S.	{I $d'-e'''$ {II $d'-d'''$
113	c. 1740	5. Aria (T.)	5. Solo	$d'-f\sharp'''$
114	c. 1740	2. Aria (T.)	2. Obbl. 'Solo'	$d'-e'''$
115	c. 1740	1. Coro 4. Aria (S.) 6. Choral	6. Col S.	$d'-f\sharp'''$
117	c. 1733	1. Coro 7. Aria (A.)	...	{I$d'-e'''$ {II $d'-c'''$
123	c. 1740	1. Coro 5. Aria (B.) 6. Choral	5. 'Solo' 6. Col S. in 8va	{I $d'-e'''$ {II $f\sharp'-e'''$
125	c. 1740	1. Coro 2. Aria (A.) 6. Choral	6. Col S. in 8va	$e'-e'''$
129	1732	1. Coro 3. Aria (S.) 5. Choral	5. Col S. in 8va	$d'-e'''$
130	c. 1740	5. Aria (T.)	Solo	$d'-e'''$
145	1729 or 1730	5. Aria (B.)	...	$d'-a'''$
146	c. 1740	5. Aria (S.)	(?) authentic	$d'-e'''$
151	c. 1735–40	1. Aria (S.) 5. Choral	5. Col S.	$e'-e'''$

Work. Cantata.	Date.	Movement.	Score.	Sounding Compass.
157	1727	1. Duetto (T.B.) 4. Aria (B.) 5. Choral	5. Col S. in 8va	$d'-e'''$
164	1723 or 1724	3. Aria (A.) 5. Duetto (S.B.)	3. Soli	{I $c'-e'''$ [1] {II $c'-e'''$
173	1731	2. Aria (T.) 4. Duetto (S.B.) 6. Coro	2. Col Violini	{I $d'-d'''$ {II $d'-c'''$
180	c. 1740	2. Aria (T.)	2. Solo	$d'-e'''$
181	c. 1725	1. Aria (B.) 5. Coro	...	$d'-c'''$ [1]
184	1731	1. Recit. (T.) 2. Duetto (S.A.) 5. Choral 6. Coro	1. Soli 5. Col S.	{I $d'-d'''$ {II $d'-c'''$
189	c. 1707–10	1. Aria (T.) 5. Aria (T.)	(?) authentic	$bb'-d'''$
191	1733	1. Coro 2. Duetto (S.T.) 3. Coro	1. Col Ob.	{I $d'-e'''$ {II $d'-e'''$
192	c. 1732	1. Coro 2. Duetto (S.B.) 3. Choral	...	{I $c'-e'''$ [1] {II $a-d'''$
195	c. 1726	1. Coro 4. Recit. (S.) 5. Coro 6. Choral	1. Col Ob. 5. „ 6. Col S. in 8va	{I $d'-e'''$ {II $d'-e'''$
Ehre sei Gott	1728	4. Aria (A.)	4. Soli	{I $g'-e'''$ {II $g'-d'''$
Christmas Oratorio, Pt. I	1734	1. Coro 5. Choral 8. Aria (B.) 9. Choral	5. Col S. in 8va 9. „ „	{I $d'-e'''$ {II $d'-e'''$
Christmas Oratorio, Pt. II	1734	1. Sinfonia 3. Choral 6. Aria (T.) 8. Choral 10. Aria (A.) 12. Coro 14. Choral	3. Col S. in 8va 6. Solo 8. Col S. in 8va	{I $d'-e'''$ {II $d'-e'''$
Christmas Oratorio, Pt. III	1734	1. Coro 3. Coro 4. Recit. (B.) 5. Choral 9. Recit. (A.) 10. Choral 12. Choral	5. Col S. in 8va 10. „ „ 12. „ „	{I $d'-e'''$ {II $d'-d\sharp'''$
Easter Oratorio	1736	4. Aria (S.)	4. Or Vn. Solo.	$d\sharp'-d'''$
Magnificat	1723	1. Coro 3a. Coro 5. Duetto (A.T.) 6. Coro 8. Aria (A.) 11. Coro	5. Col Violini 8. Soli	{I $d'-f\sharp'''$ {II $d'-e'''$

[1] See *supra*, p. 76.

TABLE IX. THE TRANSVERSE (GERMAN) FLUTE (QUERFLÖTE) 205

Work.	Date.	Movement.	Score.	Sounding Compass.
Trauer-Ode	1727	1. Coro 4. Recit. (A.) 7. Coro 8. Aria (T.) 9. Recit. (B.) 10. Coro	...	{I $d'-f\sharp'''$ {II $d'-d'''$
Mass in A	*c.* 1737	1. Coro 2. Coro 4. Aria (S.) 6. Coro	4. Soli	{I $e'-f\sharp'''$ {II $d'-f\sharp'''$
Hohe Messe	1733	7. Duetto (S.T.) and choruses	24. Col Ob.	{I $d'-g'''$ 1 {II $c\sharp'-g'''$
St. John Passion	1723	13. Aria (S.) 62. Arioso (T.) 63. Aria (S.) and Choruses and Chorals	1. &c. Col Ob. 13. Solo	{I $c'-f\sharp'''$ 1 {II $d'-f\sharp'''$
St. Matthew Passion	1729	9. Recit. (A.) 10. Aria (A.) 12. Aria (S.) 26. Aria (T.) and Coro 33. Duetto (S.A.) and Coro 36. Aria (A.) and Coro 58. Aria (S.) 65. Recit. (B.) and Choruses and Chorals	9. Soli 10. ,, 36. Col Ob.	I{I $a-g'''$ 2 {II $d'-g'''$ II{I $a-e'''$ {II $d'-e'''$

(B) SECULAR CANTATAS

Work.	Date.	Movement.	Score.	Sounding Compass.
Aeolus	1725	1. Coro 2. Recit. (B.) 10. Recit. (S.B.) 13. Duetto (A.T.) 15. Coro	10. Soli 13. Obbl.	{I $d'-g'''$ {II $d'-g'''$
Angenehmes Wiederau	1737	11. Aria (T.)	A version of Cantata No. 30. Excepting the Tenor Aria flutes do not appear to be in the score	$c\sharp'-g''$ 2
Die Freude reget sich	*c.* 1733	1. Coro 5. Aria (A.) 7. Aria (S.)	7. Solo	$d'-e'''$
Durchlaucht'ster Leopold	? 1718	2. Aria (S.) 4. Duetto (S.B.) 6. Aria (S.) 8. Coro	2. Col Vn. I.	{I $d'-e'''$ {II $d'-e'''$
Ich bin in mir vergnügt	*c.* 1730	6. Aria (S.) 8. Aria (S.)	6. Solo	$d'-e'''$
Mer hahn en neue Oberkeet	1742	14. Aria (S.)	...	$e'-d'''$

1 See *supra*, p. 77.   2 See *supra*, p. 78.

Work. Cantata.	Date.	Movement.	Score.	Sounding Compass.
Non sa che sia dolore	...	1. Sinfonia 3. Aria (S.) 5. Aria (S.)	...	$d'-e'''$
O holder Tag (O angenehme Melodei)	1746	6. Aria (S.) 9. Recit. (S.) 10. Aria (S.)	6. Solo	$d'-f\sharp'''$
Phoebus und Pan	1731	1. Coro 5. Aria (B.) 13. Aria (A.) 15. Coro	13. Soli	$\begin{cases} \text{I } d'-f\sharp''' \\ \text{II } d'-f\sharp''' \end{cases}$
Preise dein' Glücke	1734	1. Coro 6. Recit. (S.) 7. Aria (S.) 8. Recit. (S.T.B.) 9. Coro	6. Soli 7. Solo	$\begin{cases} \text{I } d'-e''' \\ \text{II } d'-e''' \end{cases}$
Schleicht, spielende Wellen	1734	1. Coro 9. Aria (S.) 11. Coro	9. Soli	$\begin{cases} \text{I } d'-e''' \\ \text{II } d'-d''' \\ \text{III } d'-a'' \end{cases}$
Schweigt stille	1732	4. Aria (S.) 10. Coro	4. Solo	$d'-e'''$
Tönet, ihr Pauken	1733	1. Coro 3. Aria (S.) 8. Recit. (B.) 9. Coro	3. Soli	$\begin{cases} \text{I } d'-f\sharp''' \\ \text{II } d'-f\sharp''' \end{cases}$
Vereinigte Zwietracht (Auf, schmetternde Töne)	1726	2. Coro 9. Aria (A.) 11. Coro	.. ...	$2\begin{cases} \text{I } a-g\sharp'' \\ \text{II } a-e'' \end{cases}$ $9\begin{cases} \text{I } d'-e''' \\ 11\end{cases} \text{II } d'-d'''$

(C) INSTRUMENTAL MUSIC

Sonata I, in B mi., for Clavier and Flute[1]	...	...	...	$e'-g'''$
Sonata II, in E♭ ma.	...	...	...	$d'-d'''$
Sonata III, in A ma.	...	...	...	$d'-e'''$
Sonata IV (Trio), in G ma.	...	...	...	$d'-e'''$
Sonata for 2 Flutes and Clavier, in G ma.	...	...	...	$\begin{cases} \text{I } d'-d''' \\ \text{II } d'-d''' \end{cases}$
Clavier Concerto VIII in A mi.[2]	...	...	...	$d'-e'''$
Brandenburg Concerto, No. 5, in D ma.	1721	...	...	$d'-d'''$
Ouverture in B mi.[3]	...	...	...	$d'-f\sharp'''$
Sonata I for flute and Clavier, in C ma.[4]	...	...	...	$d'-e'''$
Sonata II, in E mi.[4]	...	...	...	$d'-g'''$
Sonata III, in E ma.[4]	...	...	...	$e'-e'''$
Trio and Canon, in C mi.[5]	1747	...	...	$d'-e♭'''$

[1] The five Sonatas are in B.-G. ix.
[2] In B.-G. xvii.   [3] In B.-G. xxxi (1).   [4] In B.-G. xliii (1).
[5] In B.-G. xxxi (2): 'Musicalisches Opfer'.

207

TABLE X. THE OBOE (HAUTBOIS)
(A) CHURCH MUSIC

Cantata.	Date.	Movement.	Score.	Sounding Compass.
No. 2	c. 1740	1. Coro 5. Aria (T.) 6. Choral	5. Col Vn. I	{I g–d''' [1] {II g–d'''
5	1735	1. Coro 4. Recit. (A.) 5. Aria (B.) 7. Choral	4. Choral obbligato 5. Col Vn. I	{I c'–d''' {II c'–bb''
6	1736	1. Coro 6. Choral	1. Ob. da caccia as Taille	{I d'–bb'' {II c'–bb''
10	c. 1740	1. Coro 2. Aria (S.) 5. Duetto (A.T.) 7. Choral	5. Col Tromba. Choral obbligato	{I c'–d''' {II bb–d'''
11	c. 1736	1. Coro 6. Choral 10. Aria (S.) 11. Choral	...	{I d'–d''' {II d'–$c\sharp'''$
12	1724–5	1. Sinfonia 2. Coro 4. Aria (A.) 7. Choral	4. Obbligato 7. Or Tromba; obbligato	c'–c'''
14	1735	1. Coro 4. Aria (B.) 5. Choral	4. 2 Ob.+Cont.	{I c'–c''' {II c'–bb''
16	1724	1. Coro 3. Coro and Aria (B.) 6. Choral	1. Col Violini 3. ,, ,,	{I a–c''' {II g–a''
17	c. 1737	1. Coro 7. Choral	...	{I $c\sharp'$–b'' {II a–$c\sharp'''$
19	1726	1. Coro 7. Choral	1. Col Violini 7. ,, ,,	{I d'–b' {II b–a'' {III c–d'' [2]
20	c. 1725	1. Coro 5. Aria (B.) 7. Choral 8. Aria (B.) 11. Choral	5. 3 Ob.+Cont. 8. Col Violini and Viola	{I c'–d''' {II c'–a'' {III c'–f''
21	1714	1. Sinfonia 2. Coro 3. Aria (S.) 6. Coro 9. Coro 11. Coro	3. Obbligato	bb–d'''
22	1723	1. Coro 2. Aria (A.) 5. Choral	2. 'Solo'	c'–c'''
23	1724	1. Duetto (S.A.) 2. Recit. (T.) 3. Coro 4. Choral	1. 2 Ob.+Cont. 2. 2 Ob. col Vn. I	{I c'–c''' {II c'–c'''
24	1723	3. Coro 6. Choral	3. Col Violini 6. ,, ,,	{I c'–d''' {II bb–bb''

[1] For this and other examples of an abnormal Oboe compass see *supra*, p. 98.
[2] Cf. Nos. 31, 35, 36, 122, 186, and p. 99, note 5, *supra*.

Cantata.	Date.	Movement.	Score.	Sounding Compass.
No. 25	c. 1731	1. Coro 5. Aria (S.) 6. Choral	1. Col Violini 5. ,, ,,	{I c'-d''' {II a-a''
26	c. 1740	1. Coro 4. Aria (B.) 6. Choral	4. 3 Ob.+Org. and Cont.	{I c'-d''' {II c'-c''' {III c'-c'''
27	1731	1. Coro 6. Choral	...	{I c'-c''' {II c'-a''
28	c. 1736	1. Aria (S.) 2. Coro 6. Choral	...	{I e'-b'' {II c'-g'' {III f-d''
29	1731	1. Sinfonia 2. Coro 5. Aria (S.) 8. Choral	1. Col Violini 2. ,, ,, 8. ,, ,,	{I g-c''' {II g-a''
30	1738	1. Coro 6. Choral 7. Recit. (B.) 12. Coro	7. 2 Ob.+Org. and Cont. 12. Ob. I col Fl. I	{I d'-d''' {II c♯'-d'''
31	1715	1. Sonata 2. Coro 8. Aria (S.) 9. Choral	8. Oboes with Fagotto foundation	{I b-b♭'' {II b-g'' {III a-d'' {IV d-c''
32	c. 1740	1. Aria (S.) 5. Duetto (S.B.) 6. Choral	...	d'-d'''
33	c. 1740	1. Coro 5. Duetto (T.B.) 6. Choral	5. 2 Ob.+Org. and Cont.	{I c'-d''' {II c'-c'''
34	1740-1	1. Coro 5. Coro	...	{I d'-d''' {II c♯'-b''
35	1731	1. Sinfonia 2. Aria (A.) 5. Sinfonia 7. Aria (A.)	...	{I b♭-d''' {II b-d''' {III e-e''
38	c. 1740	1. Coro 3. Aria (T.) 6. Choral	3. 2 Ob.+Cont.	{I c'-c''' {II c'-g''
39	1732	1. Coro 3. Aria (A.) 7. Choral	3. Ob.+Vn. Solo+ Cont.	{I c'-c''' {II c'-a''
40	1723	1. Coro 3. Choral 4. Aria (B.) 6. Choral 7. Aria (T.) 8. Choral	7. 2 Ob.+2 Cor.+ Cont.	{I c'-d''' {II c'-c'''
41	1736	1. Coro 2. Aria (S.) 6. Choral	2. 3 Ob.+Org. e Cont.	{I d♯'-d''' {II c'-a'' {III c'-a''
42	1731	1. Sinfonia 3. Aria (A.) 7. Choral	...	{I d'-c♯''' {II c'-a''
43	c. 1735	1. Coro 5. Aria (S.) 9. Aria (A.) 11. Choral	1. Col Violini 5. ,, ,, 9. 2 Ob.+Cont.	{I g-e''' {II g-d'''

TABLE X. THE OBOE (HAUTBOIS) 209

Cantata.	Date.	Movement.	Score.	Sounding Compass.
No. 44	c. 1725	1. Coro (T.B.) 2. Coro 3. Aria (A.) 6. Aria (S.) 7. Choral	2. Col Violini 3. Ob.+Fag. e Cont. 6. Col Violini	I c′–d‴ II g–bb″
45	c. 1740	1. Coro 7. Choral	1. Col Flauti	I d′–c♯‴ II a–c♯‴
47	1720	1. Coro 4. Aria (B.) 5. Choral	4. Ob.+Vn.+Cont.	I c′–d‴ II c′–c‴
48	c. 1740	1. Coro 3. Choral 4. Aria (A.) 6. Aria (T.) 7. Choral	4. 'Solo'+Cont. 6. Col Vn. I	I c′–c‴ II d′–bb″
50	c. 1740	Coro	...	I e′–d‴ II e′–b″ III a–g♯″
52	c. 1730	1. Sinfonia 5. Aria (S.) 6. Choral	1. Oboes with Fagotto foundation 5. 3 Ob.+Cont.	I c′–d‴ II c′–a″ III c′–f″
55	1731–2	5. Choral	5. Col Sop.	...
56	1731	1. Aria (B.) 3. Aria (B.) 5. Choral	1. Col Violini and Viola 3. 'Solo'	I c′–d‴ II bb–ab″ III d–e″
57	c. 1740	1. Aria (B.) 8. Choral	1. Col Violini and Viola	I d′–c‴ II c′–g″ Taille f–eb′
58	1733	1. Duetto (S.B.) 5. Duetto (S.B.)	1. Col Violini and Viola 5. ,, ,,	I c′–d‴ II c′–g″ III g–f″
62	c. 1740	1. Coro 2. Aria (T.) 6. Choral	2. Col Violini	I d′–c‴ II d′–a″
63	1723	1. Coro 3. Duetto (S.B.) 6. Recit. (B.) 7. Coro	1. Oboes with Fagotto foundation 3. 'Solo'	I e′–c‴ II c′–a″ III c′–f♯″
66	1731	1. Coro 3. Aria (B.)	3. Oboes with Fagotto foundation	I d′–d‴ II d′–d‴
68	1735	1. Coro 2. Aria (S.) 4. Aria (B.) 5. Coro	1. Col Violini and Viola 4. 3 Ob.+Cont. 5. Col Violini and Viola	I c′–d‴ II c′–g♯″ III f–d″
69	1724–30	1. Coro 3. Aria (A.) 6. Choral	1. Oboes with Fagotto foundation 3. Oboe+Vn.+Cont.	I d′–d‴ II d′–a″ III d′–b″
70	1716	1. Coro 2. Recit. (B.) 7. Choral 8. Aria (T.) 11. Choral	8. Col Vn. I	g–c‴
71	1708	1. Coro 4. Arioso (B.) 6. Coro 7. Coro	1–7. Oboes have Fagotto foundation	I c′–c‴ II c′–g″

Cantata.	Date.	Movement.	Score.	Sounding Compass.
No. 72	c. 1726	1. Coro 4. Aria (S.) 5. Choral	...	{I $c'-d'''$ {II $c'-c'''$
73	c. 1725	1. Coro 2. Aria (T.) 5. Choral	2. Ob.+Cont.	{I $c'-c'''$ {II $c'-bb''$
74	1735	1. Coro 6. Recit. (B.) 7. Aria (A.) 8. Choral	1–7. Ob. da caccia as Taille	{I $c'-d'''$ {II $c'-b''$
75	1723	1. Coro 3. Aria (T.) 7. Choral 14. Choral	7. Col Violini 14. ,, ,,	{I $d'-d'''$ {II $c'-c'''$
76	1723	1. Coro	1. Col Violini	{I $c'-d'''$ {II $g-b''$
77	c. 1725	3. Aria (S.)		{I $e'-c'''$ {II $c'-b''$
78	c. 1740	1. Coro 6. Aria (B.) 7. Choral	6. Obbligato	{I $c'-d'''$ {II $c'-d'''$
79	1735	1. Coro 2. Aria (A.) 3. Choral 6. Choral	1. Col Flauti 2. 'Solo'; or Fl.	{I $d'-c'''$ {II $c'-c'''$
80	1730	1. Coro 2. Duetto (S.B.) 5. Choral (?)	...	{I $d'-f\sharp''$ {II $d'-f\sharp''$ {III $g-d''$
82	c. 1731	1. Aria (B.) 5. Aria (B.)	...	$c'-db'''$
83	1724	1. Aria (A.) 5. Choral	...	{I $d'-c'''$ {II $c'-a''$
84	1731–2	1. Aria (S.) 3. Aria (S.) 5. Choral	3. Ob.+Vn. Solo+Cont.	$d'-d'''$
85	1735	1. Aria (B.) 3. Choral (S.) 6. Choral	3. 2 Ob.+Cont.	{I $c'-c'''$ {II $c'-c'''$
86	c. 1725	3. Choral (S.)	3. 2 Ob.+Cont.	{I $b-a''$ {II $b-a''$
87	1735	1. Aria (B.) 7. Choral	1. Col Violini and Viola. Ob. da caccia as Taille	{I $d'-c'''$ {II $bb-bb''$
88	1732	1. Aria (B.)	1. Taille. Col Viola	$c-e''$
89	c. 1730	1. Aria (B.) 5. Aria (S.) 6. Choral	5. Ob.+Cont.	{I $c'-d'''$ {II $c'-d'''$
91	c. 1740	1. Coro 3. Aria (T.) 6. Choral	3. 3 Ob.+Cont.	{I $d'-d'''$ {II $c'-c'''$ {III $c'-g''$
93	1728	1. Coro 6. Aria (S.) 7. Choral	6. Ob.+Cont.	{I $c'-d'''$ {II $c'-c'''$

TABLE X.   THE OBOE (HAUTBOIS)   211

Cantata.	Date.	Movement.	Score.	Sounding Compass.
No. 94	1735	1. Coro 3. Recit. and Choral (T.) 8. Choral	1. Col Violini 3. 2 Ob.+Cont.	$\begin{cases} \text{I } a\text{–}d''' \\ \text{II } b\text{–}a'' \end{cases}$
95		See Table XII		
96	c. 1740	1. Coro 5. Aria (B.) 6. Choral	…	$\begin{cases} \text{I } d'\text{–}d''' \\ \text{II } c'\text{–}c''' \end{cases}$
97	1734	1. Coro 8. Aria (S.) 9. Choral	1. Oboes have Fagotto foundation 8. 2 Ob.+Cont.	$\begin{cases} \text{I } c'\text{–}c''' \\ \text{II } c'\text{–}d''' \end{cases}$
98	c. 1732	1. Coro 3. Aria (S.)	3. 'Solo'+Cont.	$\begin{cases} \text{I } c'\text{–}b\flat'' \\ \text{II Col A.} \\ \text{III Col T.} \end{cases}$
101	c. 1740	1. Coro 4. Aria (B.) 7. Choral	4. 3 Ob.+Cont.	$\begin{cases} \text{I } d'\text{–}d''' \\ \text{II } c'\text{–}b'' \\ \text{III } f\text{–}d'' \end{cases}$
102	1731	1. Coro 3. Aria (A.) 7. Choral	3. Ob.+Cont.	$\begin{cases} \text{I } c'\text{–}d''' \\ \text{II } c'\text{–}b\flat'' \end{cases}$
104	c. 1725	1. Coro	…	$\begin{cases} \text{I } d'\text{–}c''' \\ \text{II } c'\text{–}a'' \\ \text{III } g\text{–}e'' \end{cases}$
105	c. 1725	1. Coro 3. Aria (S.)	1. Col Violini	$\begin{cases} \text{I } c'\text{–}d''' \\ \text{II } g\text{–}f'' \end{cases}$
109	c. 1731	1. Coro 5. Aria (A.) 6. Choral	5. 2 Ob.+Cont.	$\begin{cases} \text{I } c'\text{–}c''' \\ \text{II } c'\text{–}c''' \end{cases}$

110	post 1734	1. Coro
		6. Aria (B.)
		7. Choral
			1. Oboes have Fagotto
			    foundation
			6. Col Violini and
			    Viola. Ob. da
			    caccia as Taille
				$\begin{cases} \text{I } c\sharp'\text{–}d''' \\ \text{II } d'\text{–}b'' \\ \text{III } c'\text{–}g'' \end{cases}$

111	c. 1740	1. Coro 5. Recit. (S.) 6. Choral	5. 2 Ob.+Cont.	$\begin{cases} \text{I } e'\text{–}d''' \\ \text{II } c'\text{–}c''' \end{cases}$
113	c. 1740	1. Coro	…	$\begin{cases} \text{I } e'\text{–}b'' \\ \text{II } c\sharp'\text{–}g'' \end{cases}$
114	c. 1740	1. Coro 5. Aria (A.) 7. Choral	…	$\begin{cases} \text{I } c'\text{–}c''' \\ \text{II } d'\text{–}c''' \end{cases}$
117	c. 1733	1. Coro	…	$\begin{cases} \text{I } d'\text{–}d''' \\ \text{II } d'\text{–}c''' \end{cases}$
119[1]	1723	1. Coro 7. Coro	…	$\begin{cases} \text{I } d'\text{–}c''' \\ \text{II } c'\text{–}a'' \\ \text{III } c'\text{–}a'' \end{cases}$
122	c. 1742	1. Coro 6. Choral	1. Col Violini and Viola	$\begin{cases} \text{I } d'\text{–}c''' \\ \text{II } c'\text{–}a'' \\ \text{III } d\text{–}e\flat'' \end{cases}$
125	c. 1740	1. Coro 6. Choral	…	$c'\text{–}c'''$
126	c. 1740	1. Coro 2. Aria (T.) 6. Choral	2. 2 Ob.+Cont.	$\begin{cases} \text{I } c'\text{–}d''' \\ \text{II } c'\text{–}d''' \end{cases}$

[1] An alternative score of No. 118 introduces an oboe.

Cantata.	Date.	Movement.	Score.	Sounding Compass.
No. 127	*c.* 1740	1. Coro 3. Aria (S.) 5. Choral	...	{I *c′–d‴* {II *c′–c‴*
128	1735	1. Coro 5. Choral	1. Col Violini. Ob. da caccia col Viola	{I *d′–e‴* {II *b–g″*
129	1732	1. Coro 5. Choral	...	{I *d′–d‴* {II *c♯′–a″*
130	*c.* 1740	1. Coro 6. Choral	...	{I *g′–d‴* {II *d′–b″* {III *c′–a″*
131	1707–8	1. Coro 2. Duetto (S.B.) 3. Coro 5. Coro	2. Ob.+Cont.	*c′–d‴*
132	1715	1. Aria (S.)	...	*b–b″*
134	1731	2. Aria (T.) 6. Coro	...	{I *c′–c‴* {II *c′–c‴*
135	*c.* 1740	1. Coro 3. Aria (T.) 6. Choral	3. 2 Ob.+Cont.	{I *e′–c‴* {II *c′–b″*
136	*c.* 1725	1. Coro 6. Choral	1. Ob. II is a d'amore 6. Ob. II col S.	I *c♯′–d‴*
137	1732	1. Coro 3. Duetto (S.B.) 5. Choral	3. 2 Ob.+Cont.	{I *e′–c♯‴* {II *c′–a″*
140	1731–42	1. Coro 6. Duetto (S.B.) 7. Choral	6. 'Solo'+Cont.	{I *c′–bb″* {II *c′–g″* {III *f–eb″*
141	1721–2	1. Coro 2. Aria (T.)	? Authentic	{I *d′–b″* {II *c′–b″*
142	1712–13	1. Concerto 2. Coro 5. Aria (T.) 8. Choral	? Authentic 5. 2 Ob.+Cont. 8. Col Violini	{I *e′–c‴* {II *d′–c‴*
146	*c.* 1740	1. Sinfonia 7. Duetto (T.B.)	? Authentic (exc. Sinfonia)	{I *c′–d‴* {II *c′–d‴* {III *f–e″*
147	1716	1. Coro 6. Choral 9. Aria (B.) 10. Choral	1. Col Vn. I 6. „ „ 9. Col Violini 10. Col Vn. I	{I *c′–c‴* {II *a–c‴*
148	*c.* 1725	4. Aria (A.)	4. 3 Ob.+Cont.	{I *b–a″* {II *b–f♯″* {III *g–d″*
149	1731	1. Coro 7. Choral	1. Oboes have Fagotto foundation	{I *d′–d‴* {II *c♯′–a″* {III *d′–f♯″*
152	1715	1. Concerto 2. Aria (B.) 6. Duetto (S.B.)	2. Ob.+Cont. 6. Col Fl. and Viole	*a–a″*
154	1724	3. Choral 8. Choral	Col Soprano	...
156	1729–30	1. Sinfonia 4. Aria (A.) 6. Choral	4. Ob.+Vn.+Cont.	*c′–d‴*

TABLE X. THE OBOE (HAUTBOIS)   213

Cantata.	Date.	Movement.	Score.	Sounding Compass.
No. 157	1727	1. Duetto (T.B.) 5. Choral	...	$b-a''$
158	1708–17	2. Duetto (S.B.)	2. Col S.	...
159	1729	2. Duetto (S.A.) 4. Aria (B.) 5. Choral	2. Col S.	$c'-c'''$
164	1723–4	5. Duetto (S.B.) 6. Choral	5. Col Violini and Flauti	{I $c'-c'''$ II $c'-c'''$
166	c. 1725	1. Aria (B.) 2. Aria (T.) 5. Aria (A.)	2. Ob.+Cont.	$c'-c'''$
167	c. 1725	5. Choral	...	$c'-d'''$
169	1731	1. Sinfonia 7. Choral	1. Col Violini	{I $a-b''$ II $g\sharp-a''$ III $f-d''$
171	c. 1730	1. Coro 5. Recit. (B.) 6. Choral	5. 2 Ob.+Cont.	{I $d'-d'''$ II $c\sharp'-g''$
174	1729	1. Sinfonia 2. Aria (A.) 5. Choral	2. 2 Ob.+Cont.	{I $d'-d'''$ II $c'-a''$ III $g-d\sharp''$
176	1735	1. Coro 5. Aria (A.) 6. Choral	5. 2 Ob.+Ob. da caccia (all unison)+ Cont.	{I $c'-a''$ II $c'-f''$
177	1732	1. Coro 5. Choral	...	{I $d'-b\flat''$ II $c'-c'''$
178	c. 1740	1. Coro 7. Choral	...	{I $d'-d'''$ II $c'-d'''$
179	1724	3. Aria (T.) 6. Choral	3. Col Vn, I	{I $c'-d'''$ II $c'-d'''$
180	c. 1740	1. Coro 5. Aria (S.)	Ob. II da caccia	I $d'-d'''$
181	c. 1725	1. Aria (B.) 5. Coro	...	$d'-c'''$
185	1715	1. Duetto (S.T.) 3. Aria (A.) 6. Choral	1. Ob. (or Tromba)+ Cont.	$b-b''$
186	1723	1. Coro 6. Choral 10. Duetto (S.A.)	1. Col Violini	{I $c'-d'''$ II $c'-b\flat''$ III $c-e\flat''$
187	1732	1. Coro 3. Aria (A.) 5. Aria (S.) 7. Choral	3. Ob. I col Vn. I 5. 'Solo'+Cont.	{I $c'-d'''$ II $d'-b\flat''$
188	1731	1. Aria (T.)	...	$c'-d'''$
189	1707–10	1. Aria (T.) 5. Aria (T.)	...	$f'-b\flat''$
190	1725	1. Coro 2. Choral 7. Choral	...	No parts exc. for No. 7
191	1733	1. Coro 3. Coro	1. Col Flauti	{I $d'-d'''$ II $d'-c\sharp'''$

Work. Cantata.	Date.	Movement.	Score.	Sounding Compass.
No. 192	c. 1732	1. Coro 2. Duetto (S.B.) 3. Choral	2. Ob. I col Vn. I and Fl. I 3. Col Violini and Flauti	{I c'–e''' {II a–d'''
193	c. 1740	1. Coro 3. Aria (S.) 5. Aria (A.) 7. Coro	5. Ob.+Cont.	{I a–d''' {II d'–d'''
194	1723	1. Coro 3. Aria (B.) 6. Choral 10. Duetto (S.B.) 12. Choral	1. Oboes have Fagotto foundation 10. 2 Ob.+Cont.	{I c'–c''' {II c'–bb'' {III c'–bb''
195	c. 1726	1. Coro 5. Coro 6. Choral	1. and 5. Col. Flauti 5. Ob. II d'amore	{I d'–b'' {II d'–a''
197	1737	1. Coro 6. Aria (B.) 9. Recit. (B.)	...	{I d'–d''' {II d'–a''
Mein Herze schwimmt	1714	2. Aria (S.) 8. Aria (S.)	2. Ob.+Cont.	bb–ab''
Easter Oratorio	1736	1. Sinfonia 2. Duetto (T.B.) and Coro 10. Coro	...	{I d'–d''' {II d'–d'''
Christmas Oratorio, Pt. I	1734	1. Coro 5. Choral 7. Duetto S.B. 9. Choral	7. Ob.+Ob. d'amore +Cont.	{I b–c#''' {II b–b''
Christmas Oratorio, Pt. III	1734	1. Coro 5. Choral 10. Choral 12. Choral	...	{I f#'–d''' {II d'–b''
Christmas Oratorio, Pt. IV.	1734	1. Coro 4. Aria (S.) 7. Choral	4. 'Solo'+Cont.	{I c'–d''' {II c'–a''
Christmas Oratorio, Pt. VI	1734	1. Coro 6. Choral 11. Choral	...	{I d'–d''' {II c#'–d'''
St. Matthew Passion	1729	Excepting No. 40 (Recit. Tenor) the Oboe is scored only in the Choruses and simple Chorals	Coro I 40. 2 Ob.+Cont. Coro II	{I c'–d''' {II c'–c''' {I c'–c#''' {II c'–c'''
St. John Passion	1723	Excepting No. 11 (Aria, Alto) the Oboe is scored only in the Choruses and simple Chorals	11. 2 Ob.+Cont.	{I c'–c''' {II c'–c'''
Hohe Messe	1733–	The Oboe is scored only in the Choruses	3rd Oboe only in the 'Sanctus'	{I d'–d''' {II a–c#''' {III d'–g#''
Mass in F	c. 1736	4. Aria (S.) and 3 Choruses	4. 'Solo'+Cont.	{I c'–d''' {II c'–g'''
Mass in G mi.	c. 1737	4. Aria (A.) 5. Aria (T.) and 3 Choruses	5. Ob.+Cont.	{I c'–d''' {II c'–d'''

TABLE X. THE OBOE (HAUTBOIS) 215

Work.	Date.	Movement.	Score.	Sounding Compass.
Mass in G ma.	c. 1738	5. Aria (T.) and 3 Choruses	5. 'Solo' + Cont.	{I c'–c''' {II c'–c'''
Magnificat	1723	The Oboe is scored only in the Choruses	...	{I d'–d''' {II c♯'–a''
Sanctus in C	...	...	...	{I c'–c''' {II c'–a''
Sanctus in G ma.	...	...	...	{I d'–d''' {II d'–c'''

(B) SECULAR CANTATAS

Work.	Date.	Movement.	Score.	Sounding Compass.
Aeolus	1725	1. Coro 2. Recit. (B.) 3. Aria (B.) 15. Coro	3. Col Vn. I	{I b–d''' {II c♯'–d''
Angenehmes Wiederau	1737	See Cantata, No. 30		
Hercules	1733	1. Coro 7. Aria (T.) 13. Coro	7. Ob. + Vn. + Cont.	{I c'–d''' {II c'–a''
Ich bin in mir vergnügt	c. 1730	2. Aria (S.) 8. Aria (S.)	2. 2 Ob. + Cont. 8. Col Violini	{I g–d''' {II g–b♭''
Mit Gnaden bekröne	? 1722	1. Aria (T.) 7. Coro	...	{I c'–c''' {II c'–c'''
Phoebus und Pan	1731	1. Coro 15. Coro	...	{I d'–d''' {II d'–b''
Preise dein' Glücke	1734	1. Coro 2. Recit. (T.) 5. Aria (B.) 8. Recit. (S.T.B.) 9. Coro	2. 2 Ob. + Cont.	{I c♯'–d''' {II c♯'–b''
Schleicht, spielende Wellen	1734	1. Coro 11. Coro	11. Col Flauti	{I d'–d''' {II d'–a''
Tönet, ihr Pauken	1733	1. Coro 5. Aria (A.) 8. Recit. (B.) 9. Coro	5. 2 Ob. (unison) + Cont. 8. Fl. unis. + 2 Ob. + Cont.	{I a–d''' {II a–b''
Trauer-Ode	1727	4. Recit. (A.) 9. Recit. (B.)	...	{I f♯'–e'' {II c'–c♯''
Vereinigte Zwietracht	1726	2. Coro 7. Ritornello 10. Recit. (S.A.T.B.) 11. Coro	3rd Oboe	g♯–d''
Was mir behagt	1716	7. Aria (B.) 11. Coro 15. Coro	7. 3 Ob. + Cont. 11. Col Violini and Viola 15. Oboes have Fagotto foundation	{I c'–c''' {II b–a'' {Taille f–d''
Weichet nur	1717–22	1. Aria (S.) 7. Aria (S.) 9. Aria (S.)	7. Ob. + Cont.	d'–b''

TABLE X. THE OBOE (HAUTBOIS)

(C) INSTRUMENTAL MUSIC

Work.	Date.	Movement.	Score.	Sounding Compass.
Brandenburg Concerto, No. 1, in F ma.	1721	...	'ē Bassono'	I c'-d''' II c'-b'' III c'-g''
Brandenburg Concerto, No. 2, in F ma.	1721	...	...	c'-d'''
Sinfonia in D ma.[1]	...	...	...	I d'-d''' II d'-a''
Ouverture in C ma.	...	...	...	I d'-d''' II c'-d'''
Ouverture in D ma.	...	...	...	I d'-d''' II c#'-d'''
Ouverture in D ma.	...	...	...	I d'-d''' II d'-b'' III c'-g''
Sinfonia in F ma.[2]	...	...	...	I c'-d''' II c'-bb'' III c'-f''
Trio (Violin, Oboe, Continuo) in F ma.[3]	...	...	Fragment	c'-b''

[1] B.-G. xxi (1), p. 65.
[2] Brandenburg Concerto, No. I.
[3] B.-G. xxix, p. 250.

TABLE XI.   THE OBOE DA CACCIA
(ENGLISH HORN: HAUTBOIS DE CHASSE)
(A) CHURCH MUSIC

Cantata.	Date.	Movement.	Score.	Sounding Compass.
No. 1	c. 1740	1. Coro 3. Aria (S.) 6. Choral	3. Ob.+Cont.	I f-f'' II f-f''
6	1736	1. Coro 2. Aria (A.) 6. Choral	1. As Taille 2. Ob.+Cont.	f-f''
13	c. 1740	1. Aria (T.) 3. Choral (A.)	3. Col A.	f-eb''
16	1724	5. Aria (T.)	5. Or Violetta+Cont.	f-d''
27	1731	3. Aria (A.)	3. Ob.+Org. obbl.+ Cont.	f-eb''
46	c. 1725	1. Coro 5. Aria (A.)	5. 2 Fl.+2 Ob. in unison	I f-eb'' II f-eb''
65	1724	1. Coro 2. Choral 4. Aria (B.) 6. Aria (T.)	4. 2 Ob.+Cont.	I g-e'' II f-e''

TABLE XI. THE OBOE DA CACCIA 217

Work. Cantata.	Date.	Movement.	Score.	Sounding Compass.
No. 74	1735	1. Coro 2. Aria (S.) 6. Recit. (B.) 7. Aria (A.) 8. Choral	1. As Taille 2. Ob.+Cont. 6. As Taille 7. ,, ,,	g–f''
80	1730	7. Duetto (A.T.)	7. Ob.+Vn.+Cont. Transposed	f♯–f♯''
87	1735	1. Aria (B.) 3. Aria (A.) 7. Choral	1. As Taille col Viola 3. 2 Ob.+Cont.	{ I f–e♭'' { II f–b''
101	c. 1740	6. Duetto (S.A.)	6. Fl.+Ob.+Cont.	f–e''
110	post 1734	6. Aria (B.) 7. Choral	6. Col Viola 7. Col T and Viola	e'–d''
119	1723	3. Aria (T.) 4. Recit. (B.)	3. 2 Ob.+Cont.	{ I g–d'' { II g–d''
128	1735	1. Coro 5. Choral	1. As Taille	f♯–e''
147	1716} 1727}	8. Recit. (A.)	8. 2 Ob.+Cont.	{ I a–e'' { II f–d''
167	c. 1725	3. Duetto (S.A.)	3. Ob.+Cont.	g–f''
176	1735	1. Coro 5. Aria (A.) 6. Choral	1. As Taille 5. 2 Ob. and Ob. da caccia in unison+ Cont.	f–f''
177	1732	3. Aria (S.)	3. 'Solo'+Cont.	f–f''
179	1724	5. Aria (S.)	5. 2 Ob.+Cont.	{ I f–d'' { II f–d''
180	c. 1740	1. Coro 5. Aria (S.)	1. As 2nd Oboe 5. ,, ,,	g–f''
183	1735	1. Recit. (B.) 3. Recit. (A.) 4. Aria (S.) 5. Choral	1. With 2 Ob. d'amore and Cont. 3. As No. 1 with strings 4. Unison	{ I g–f'' { II g–f''
186	1723	5. Aria (T.)	5. Ob.+Cont.	d–e''[1]
Christmas Oratorio, Pt. II	1734	1. Sinfonia 3. Choral 5. Recit. (B.) 8. Choral 9. Recit. (B.) 10. Aria (A.) 12. Coro 14. Choral	5. With 2 Ob. d'amore +Cont. 9. As No. 5 10. Col Vn. II and Viola	{ I g–e'' { II g–c♯''
St. Matthew Passion	1729	25. Recit. (T.) and Coro 57. Recit. (S.) 58. Aria (S.) 69. Recit. (A.) 70. Aria (A.) and Coro 75. Aria (B.)	57. 2 Ob.+Cont. 58. Fl.+2 Ob. 69. As No. 57 75. Col Violini	{ I g–f'' { II f–f''
St. John Passion	1723	62. Arioso (T.) 63. Aria (S.)	63. 2 Fl.+2 Ob. unison +Cont.	{ I f–d♭'' { II f–d♭''

[1] For this abnormal compass see supra, p. 104.

(B) INSTRUMENTAL MUSIC

See *Christmas Oratorio* (supra), No. 1.

TABLE XII. THE OBOE D'AMORE
(HAUTBOIS D'AMOUR: LIEBESOBOE)
(A) CHURCH MUSIC

Cantata.	Date.	Movement.	Score.	Sounding Compass.
No. 3	c. 1740	1. Coro 5. Duetto (S.A.) 6. Choral	5. Col Violini	$\{$ I a–b'' $\{$ II b–b''
7	c. 1740	1. Coro 6. Aria (A.) 7. Choral	6. Col Vn. I	$\{$ I b–c''' $\{$ II b–c'''
8	c. 1725	1. Coro 2. Aria (T.) 6. Choral	2. Ob.+Cont.	$\{$ I a–b'' $\{$ II a–b''
9	? 1731	1. Coro 5. Duetto (S.A.) 7. Choral	5. Fl.+Ob.+Cont.	a–b''
19	1726	3. Aria (S.)	3. 2 Ob.+Cont.	$\{$ I b–b'' $\{$ II a–b''
24	1723	5. Aria (T.)	5. 2 Ob.+Cont. Soprano C Clef	$\{$ I a–a'' $\{$ II a–f''
30	1738	8. Aria (B.)	...	d'–b''
36	c. 1730	1. Coro 2. Choral (S.A.) 3. Aria (T.) 4. Choral 6. Choral (T.) 8. Choral	2. Col S.A. 3. 'Solo'+Cont. 6. 2 Ob.+Cont.	$\{$ I a–b'' $\{$ II a–b''
37	c. 1727	1. Coro 5. Aria (B.) 6. Choral	...	$\{$ I c♯'–b'' $\{$ II b–b''
49	1731	1. Sinfonia 4. Aria (S.) 6. Duetto (S.B.)	1. Col Violino I 4. Ob.+Vcello piccolo +Cont. 6. Col Violino I	a–c♯'''
55	1731–2	1. Aria (T.)	...	d'–c'''
60	1732	1. Duetto (A.T.) 3. Duetto (A.T.) 5. Choral	Transposed	$\{$ I a–b'' $\{$ II a–b''
64	1723	7. Aria (A.)	7. Ob.+Cont.	a–a''
67	c. 1725	1. Coro 2. Aria (T.) 4. Choral 6. Aria (B.) and Coro 7. Choral	...	$\{$ I c♯'–b'' $\{$ II a–b''
69	c. 1730	5. Aria (B.)	Transposed	b–a''
75	1723	5. Aria (S.)	5. Ob.+Cont.	c'–a''
76	1723	8. Sinfonia 12. Aria (A.)	12. Ob.+Va. da gamba +Cont.	a–a''
80	1730	5. Choral	5. With Taille	$\{$ I g♯–b''[1] $\{$ II a–b''
81	1724	5. Aria (B.) 7. Choral	...	$\{$ I c'–a'' $\{$ II a–a''

[1] See p. 108, *supra*.

TABLE XII. THE OBOE D'AMORE   219

Cantata.	Date.	Movement.	Score.	Sounding Compass.
No. 88	1732	1. Aria (B.) 3. Aria (T.) 5. Duetto (S.A.) 7. Choral	1. Col Violini and Viola 5. Col Violini	{I *a–b''* {II *a–b''*
92	*c.* 1740	1. Coro 4. Choral (A.) 8. Aria (S.) 9. Choral	4. 2 Ob.+Cont.	{I *a–b''* {II *a–b''*
94	1735	7. Aria (S.)	7. 'Solo'+Cont.	*b–b''*
95	1732	1. Coro 2. Recit. (S.) 4. Aria (T.) 6. Choral	1. Ord. Oboes for last 53 bars 2. Ob. (unis.)+Cont.	{I *a–b''* {II *a–a''*
99	*c.* 1733	1. Coro 5. Duetto (S.A.) 6. Choral	5. Fl.+Ob.+Cont.	*a–b''*
100	*c.* 1735	1. Coro 5. Aria (A.) 6. Choral	5. Ob.+Cont. Transposed throughout	*a–b''*
103	1735	1. Coro 5. Aria (T.) 6. Choral	5. Col Vn. I	{I *g–d'''* {II *g–d'''*
104	*c.* 1725	3. Aria (T.) 5. Aria (B.)	3. 2 Ob.+Cont. 5. Col Vn. I	{I *g–b''* {II *a–f♯''*
107	*c.* 1735	1. Coro 2. Recit. (B.) 5. Aria (S.) 7. Choral	2. 2 Ob.+Cont. 5. 2 Ob.+Cont. 7. Col Violini	{I *c♯'–b''* {II *b–b''*
108	1735	1. Aria (B.) 4. Coro 6. Choral	4. Col Violini	{I *a–b''* {II *b–e''*
110	*post* 1734	4. Aria (A.)	4. 'Solo'+Cont.	*a–a''*
112	1731	1. Coro 2. Aria (A.) 5. Choral	2. 'Solo'+Cont.	{I *a–b''* {II *c'–a''*
113	*c.* 1740	3. Aria (B.)	3. 2 Ob.+Cont.	{I *a–b''* {II *a–g''*
115	*c.* 1740	1. Coro 2. Aria (A.) 6. Choral	...	*a–c'''*
116	1744	1. Coro 2. Aria (A.) 6. Choral	2. 'Solo'+Cont.	{I *a–b'* {II *a–b''*
117	*c.* 1733	3. Aria (T.)	3. 2 Ob.+Cont.	{I *b–a''* {II *a–f♯''*
120	1730	1. Aria (A.) 2. Coro	2. Col Violini	{I *a–d'''* {II *a–a''*
121	*c.* 1740	1. Coro 2. Aria (T.) 6. Choral	1. Col S. 2. 'Solo'+Cont.	*a–a''*
123	*c.* 1740	1. Coro 3. Aria (T.) 6. Choral	3. 2 Ob.+Cont.	{I *b–b''* {II *a-b''*
124	*c.* 1740	1. Coro 3. Aria (T.) 6. Choral	1. Ob. concertante	*a–b''*

Cantata.	Date.	Movement.	Score.	Sounding Compass.
No. 125	c. 1740	2. Aria (A.)	2. Fl.+Ob.+Cont.	a–b″
128	1735	4. Duetto (A.T.)	4. Ob.+Cont.	a–a″
129	1732	4. Aria (A.)	4. Ob.+Cont.	a–b″
133	1735–7	1. Coro 2. Aria (A.) 6. Choral	1. Col Vn. II and Va. 2. 2 Ob.+Cont.	{I b–b″ {II a–f♯″
136	c. 1725	1. Coro 3. Aria (A.)	1. Ob. I is not d'amore 3. Ob.+Cont. Transposed	{I a–g♯″ {II a–a″
138	c. 1740	1. Coro 3. Choral and Recit. (S.A.T.B.) 7. Choral	...	{I e′–a″ {II a–f♯″
139	c. 1740	1. Coro 4. Aria (B.) 6. Choral	...	{I a–b″ {II a–b″
144	c. 1725	5. Aria (S.)	5. Ob.+Cont.	a–a″
145	1729–30	5. Aria (B.)	5. Generally col Violini Transposed	{I d′–c♯‴ {II d′–c♯‴
146	c. 1740	5. Aria (S.)	? Authentic	{I b–b″ {II a–f″
147	1716} 1727}	3. Aria (A.)	3. Ob.+Cont. Transposed	a–g″
151	1735–40	1. Aria (S.) 3. Aria (A.) 5. Choral	1. Col Vn. I 3. Ob.+Violini and Viola (unis.) + Cont.	a–b″
154	1724	4. Aria (A.) 7. Duetto (A.T.)	4. Ob.+Violini and Viola (unis.) + Cont. 7. Col Violini	{I a–a″ {II a–g♯″
157	1727	2. Aria (T.)	2. Ob.+Cont.	a–a″
163[1]	1715	1. Aria (T.)	...	a–c‴
168	c. 1725	2. Recit. (T.) 3. Aria (T.) 6. Choral	2. 2 Ob.+Cont. 3. 2 Ob.+Cont.	{I a–a″ {II a–a″
170	1731	1. Aria (A.) 5. Aria (A.)	1. Col Vn. I 5. ,,　,,	a–b″
178	c. 1740	4. Choral (T.)	4. 2 Ob.+Cont.	{I b–b″ {II a–f♯″
183	1735	1. Recit. (B.) 3. Recit. (A.) 5. Choral	1. 2 Ob.+2 Ob. da caccia+Cont. 3. ,,　,,　+Strings	{I a′–a″ {II c♯′–e″
190	1725	5. Duetto (T.B.)	5. Ob.+Cont.	a–g♯″
195	c. 1726	3. Aria (B.) 4. Recit. (S.) 5. Coro	3. Col Violini 4. 2 Fl.+2Ob.+Cont. 5. Ob. II only is d'amore	{I b–d‴ {II g–d‴
197	1737	3. Aria (A.) 8. Aria (S.)	8. Vn. Solo+2 Ob.+ Cont.	{I a–a″ {II a–e″
Ehre sei Gott	1728	6. Aria (B.)	6. 'Solo'+Cont.	a–a″

[1] In its extant state the Cantata belongs to the Leipzig period.

TABLE XII. THE OBOE D'AMORE   221

Work.	Date.	Movement.	Score.	Sounding Compass.
Sanctus in D ma.[1]	...	...	...	{I d′–f♯″ {II d′–f♯″
Easter Oratorio	1736	8. Aria (A.)	...	a–b″
Christmas Oratorio, Pt. I	1734	3. Recit. (A.) 4. Aria (A.) 7. Choral (S.B.)	3. 2 Ob.+Cont. 4. Col Vn. I+Cont. 7. Ob.+Ob. d'amore+ Cont.	{I g–a″ {II a–a″
Christmas Oratorio, Pt. II	1734	1. Sinfonia 3. Choral 5. Recit. (B.) 8. Choral 9. Recit. (B.) 10. Aria (A.) 12. Coro 14. Choral	1. With 2 Ob. da caccia 5. +2 Ob. da caccia and Cont. 9. As No. 5 10. With 2 Ob. da caccia 12. ,, ,, 14. ,, ,,	{I a–b″ {II a–a″
Christmas Oratorio, Pt. III	1734	3. Coro 6. Duetto (S.B.)	3. Col S.A. 6. 2 Ob.+Cont.	{I c♯′–a″ {II a–a″
Christmas Oratorio, Pt. V	1734	1. Coro 3. Coro 4. Choral 5. Aria (B.) 10. Recit. (A.) 11. Choral	3. Col Violini 5. 'Solo'+Cont. 10. 2 Ob.+Cont.	{I a–b″ {II a–a″
Christmas Oratorio, Pt. VI	1734	4. Aria (S.) 8. Recit. (T.) 9. Aria (T.)	8. 2 Ob.+Cont. 9. ,, ,,	{I a–b″ {II a–b″
St. Matthew Passion	1729	18. Recit. (S.) 19. Aria (S.) 35. Choral 36. Coro 47. Coro	18. 2 Ob.+Cont. 19. ,, ,, 36. Col Fl. I	{I a–d‴ {II a–b″
St. John Passion	1723	42. Coro 44. Coro 46. Coro 54. Coro	42. 2nd Oboe is d'amore col A. 44. ,, ,, 46. 2 Ob. is d'amore col Vn. II 54. ,, ,,	g♯–f♯″
Hohe Messe	1733–	1. Coro 3. Coro 9. Aria (A.) 14. Duetto (S.A.) 18. Aria (B.)	3. Col Violini 18. 2 Ob.+Cont.	{I b–c‴ {II a–b″
Magnificat	1723	3. Aria (S.) 3a. Coro	3. 'Solo'+Cont. Transposed	{I a–a″ {II b–g♯″

(B) SECULAR CANTATAS

Work.	Date.	Movement.	Score.	Sounding Compass.
Aeolus	1725	7. Aria (A.)	7. Ob.+Cont.	a–a″
Angenehmes Wiederau	1737	7. Aria (B.) 11. Aria (T.)	...	a–b″
Hercules	1733	5. Aria (A.)	5. Ob. +Cont.	a–a″
O holder Tag (O angenehme Melodei)	1746	2. Aria (S.) 4. Aria (S.) 8. Aria (S.) 9. Recit. (S.) 10. Aria (S.)	2. Col Violino I 4. Ob.+Vn.+Cont.	a–c♯‴

1 B.–G. xli. 177.

Cantata.	Date.	Movement.	Score.	Sounding Compass.
Phoebus und Pan	1731	5. Aria (B.) 9. Aria (T.)	9. 'Solo'+Cont.	a–c♯'''
Preise dein' Glücke	1734	3. Aria (T.)	3. Unison. Col Vn. I	a–a''
Schleicht, spielende Wellen	1734	7. Aria (A.)	7. 2 Ob.+Cont. Transposed	{ I a–a'' II a–a''
Schwingt freudig	1730–4	1. Coro 3. Aria (T.) 9. Coro	3. Ob.+Cont.	a–b''
Trauer-Ode	1727	1. Coro 6. Recit. (T.) 7. Coro 8. Aria (T.) 10. Coro	6. 2 Ob.+Cont.	{ I b–b'' II a–b''
Vereinigte Zwietracht	1726	2. Coro 4. Aria (T.) 7. Ritornello 10. Recit. (S.A.T.B.) 11. Coro	2. Col Flauti 7. Col Taille 10. Col Violini	{ I a–b'' II a–g''

(C) INSTRUMENTAL MUSIC

See *Vereinigte Zwietracht* (supra), No. 7; *Christmas Oratorio*, Pt. II, No. 1; Cantata No. 49, No. 1, and Cantata No. 76, No. 8.

TABLE XIII. THE BASSOON (FAGOTTO)

(A) CHURCH MUSIC

Cantata.	Date.	Movement.	Score.	Sounding Compass.
No. 12	1724–5 (? Weimar)	1. Sinfonia 2. Coro 3. Recit. (A.) 7. Choral	...	c,–b♭
18	1714	1. Sinfonia 2. Recit. (B.) 3. Recit. (T.B.) and Coro 5. Choral	5. Col Bassi	c,–e♭'
21	1714	1. Sinfonia 2. Coro 4. Recit. (T.) 5. Aria (T.) 6. Coro 7. Recit. (S.B.) 9. Coro 11. Coro	...	c,–e♭'
31	1715	1. Sonata 2. Coro 9. Choral	1. With four Oboes	g„–d'

TABLE XIII.   THE BASSOON (FAGOTTO)   223

Cantata.	Date.	Movement.	Score.	Sounding Compass.

No. 42	1731	1. Sinfonia
		2. Recit. (T.)
		  and all other
		  movements
			1. With two Oboes
			4. 'Fagotto e Violoncello'
			  obbligato
				$b\sharp_{,,}-a'$

44	c. 1725	1. Coro and all movements	...	$c_,-f'$
52	c. 1730	1. Sinfonia and all movements	1. With three Oboes	$c_,-e'$
61	1714	1. Coro 6. Choral	6. Col Bassi	$c_,-e'$
63	1723	1. Coro 6. Recit. (B.) 7. Coro	With three Oboes	$c_,-e'$
66	1731	1. Coro 3. Aria (B.)	'Bassono oblig.'	$c\sharp_,-f\sharp'$
69	c. 1730	1. Coro 2. Recit. (S.) and every movement	1. With three Oboes	$b_{,,}-f\sharp'$
70	1716	1. Coro and every movement	...	$c_,-e'$
71	1708	1. Coro 4. Arioso (B.) 6. Coro 7. Coro	With two Oboes	$b\flat_{,,}-c'$
75	1723	1. Coro	Fagotti	$d_,-f\sharp'$
97	1734	1. Coro	Fagotti	$c_,-g'$
110[1]	post 1734	1. Coro 2. Aria (T.)	...	$c_,-f\sharp'$
131	1707–8	1. Coro 3. Coro 5. Coro	Transposed	$c_,-e\flat'$
143	1735	1. Coro 4. Aria (T.) 5. Aria (B.) 6. Aria (T.) 7. Choral	6. Obbligato	$c_,-f'$
147	1716} 1727}	1. Coro	...	$d_,-e'$
149	1731	1. Coro 6. Duetto (A.T.) 7. Choral	6. Obbligato 7. Col Bassi	$d_,-g'$
150	c. 1712	1. Sinfonia 2. Coro 4. Coro 5. Terzetto (A.T.B.) 6. Coro 7. Coro	5. Obbligato 6. ,,	$c_,-f'$
155	1716	2. Duetto (A.T.)	Obbligato	$b_{,,}-d'$
159	1729	2. Duetto (S.A.)	Fagotti	$d_,-e\flat'$
160	1714	1. Aria (T.) 3. Aria (T.) 5. Aria (T.)	...	$d_,-d'$
162	1715	1. Aria (B.) 6. Choral	6. Col Bassi	$c_,-d'$

[1] Apparently bassoons supported the continuo in No. 119.

Work. Cantata.	Date.	Movement.	Score.	Sounding Compass.
No. 165	1724	1. Aria (S.) 4. Recit. (B.) 6. Choral	6. Col Bassi	$c_{,}-c'$
172	1731	1. Coro 3. Aria (B.) 6. Choral	...	$c_{,}-d'$
174	1729	1. Sinfonia	...	$c_{,}-e'$
177	1732	4. Aria (T.) 5. Choral	4. Obbligato	$e\flat_{,}-g'$
185	1715	2. Recit. (A.) 3. Aria (A.) 4. Recit. (B.) 5. Aria (B.) 6. Choral	6. Col Bassi	$c\sharp_{,}-d'$
186	1716⎫ 1723⎭	1. Coro	...	$c_{,}-f'$
194	1723	1. Coro	1. With three oboes. Fagotti	$c_{,}-f'$
197	1737	6. Aria (B.)	Obbligato	$d_{,}-e'$
Mein Herze schwimmt	1714	1. Recit. (S.) 3. Recit. (S.) 4. Aria (S.) 7. Recit. (S.) 8. Aria (S.)	...	$c_{,}-f'$
Sanctus in D[1]	...	...	...	$d_{,}-f\sharp'$
Easter Oratorio	1736	1. Sinfonia 2. Duetto (T.B.) and Coro and every movement	1. 'Solo'	$c\sharp_{,}-f\sharp'$
Christmas Oratorio, Pt. I	1734	1. Coro and every movement	...	$c_{,}-c'$
St. John Passion	1723	1. Coro	'Continuo pro Bassono grosso'	$c_{,}-f$
Mass in F	c. 1736	1. Kyrie	Fagotti. Col Bassi	$f_{,}-c'$
Magnificat	1723	...	No parts	
Hohe Messe	1733–	10. Aria (B.) and Choruses of 'Kyrie' and 'Gloria'	Fagotti 10. 2 Fagotti obbl.	⎰ I $c\sharp_{,}-a'$ ⎱ II $c\sharp_{,}-f\sharp'$

(B) SECULAR CANTATAS

Work. Cantata.	Date.	Movement.	Score.	Sounding Compass.
Durchlaucht'ster Leopold	? 1718	7. Aria (B.)	Obbligato col 'Cello	$d\sharp_{,}-f\sharp'$
Was mir behagt	1716	11. Coro 15. Coro	Fagotti. Generally col Violoncello	$c_{,}-e'$

(C) INSTRUMENTAL MUSIC

Work. Cantata.	Date.	Movement.	Score.	Sounding Compass.
Brandenburg Concerto, No. 1 in F	1721	...	...	$c_{,}-e\flat'$
Ouverture in C	...	...	...	$c_{,}-f'$
Sinfonia in F	...	...	In the first Trio, two Oboes and Fagotti	$c_{,}-e\flat'$

[1] B.–G. xli. 177.

TABLE XIV. THE VIOLINO PICCOLO

Work. Cantata.	Date.	Movement.	Score.	Sounding Compass.
No. 96	c. 1740	1. Coro	Col Flauto piccolo	f'–f'''
102	1731	5. Aria (T.)	Or Flauto traverso	d'–e''
140	1731	1. Coro 3. Duetto (S.B.) 5. Recit. (B.) 7. Choral	1 & 5. Col Violino I 3. Obbligato. Solo 7. Col S. in 8va	1 & 5. a–d''' 3. bb–eb'''
Brandenburg Concerto, No. 1	1721	…	…	bb–eb'''

TABLE XV. THE VIOLETTA

Work. Cantata.	Date.	Movement.	Score.	Sounding Compass.
No. 16	1724	5. Aria (T.)	Or Oboe da caccia	f–d''
157	1727	3. Recit. (T.) 5. Choral	5. Col T.	e–b'
Preise dein' Glücke	1734	7. Aria (S.)	Col Violini	g–e''

TABLE XVI. THE VIOLA D'AMORE

Work. Cantata.	Date.	Movement.	Sounding Compass.
No. 152	1715	1. Concerto 4. Aria (S.) 6. Duetto (S.B.)	b,–f#''
St. John Passion	1723	31. Arioso (B.) 32. Aria (T.)	{I g–bb'' {II f–c'''
Aeolus	1725	5. Aria (T.)	c#'–c♮'''
Schwingt freudig	1730–4	7. Aria (S.)	a–c#'''

TABLE XVII. THE VIOLA DA GAMBA

Work. Cantata.	Date.	Movement.	Sounding Compass.
No. 76	1723	8. Sinfonia 9. Recit. (B.) 10. Aria (T.) 11. Recit. (A.) 12. Aria (A.)	8 & 12. $b,-c''$ 9–11. $c,-g'$
106	1707–11	1. Sonatina 2. Coro 3. Duetto (A.B.) 4. Choral	$\{$I $c-c''$ $\{$II $d,-bb'$
152	1715	1. Concerto	$d,-g'$
St. Matthew Passion	1729	65. Recit. (B.) 66. Aria (B.)	$a,,-c''$
St. John Passion	1723	58. Aria (A.)	$c\sharp,-c''$
Aeolus	1725	5. Aria (T.)	$c\sharp-b'$
Trauer-Ode	1727	1. Coro 4. Recit. (A.) 5. Aria (A.) 7. Coro 8. Aria (T.) 10. Coro	$\{$I $f\sharp,-e''$ $\{$II $f\sharp,-b'$
Sonata I¹ in G ma.	c. 1720	...	$b,-d''$
Sonata II in D ma.	c. 1720	...	$b,,-c\sharp''$
Sonata III in G mi.	c. 1720	...	$f\sharp,-d''$
Brandenburg Concerto, No. 6	1721	...	$\{$I $a,-c''$ $\{$II $bb,-bb'$

¹ Sonatas I–III are in B.–G. ix.

TABLE XVIII. THE VIOLONCELLO PICCOLO

Cantata.	Date.	Movement.	Sounding Compass.
No. 6	1736	3. Choral (S.)	$g,-c''$
41	1736	4. Aria (T.)	$c,-b'$
49	1731	4. Aria (S.)	$d-b'$
68	1735	2. Aria (S.)	$c,-bb'$
85	1735	2. Aria (A.)	$g,-bb'$
115	c. 1740	4. Aria (S.)	$c\sharp,-c''$
175	1735	4. Aria (T.)	$f\sharp,-a'$
180	c. 1740	3. Recit. (S.) and Arioso	$c-b'$
183	1735	2. Aria (T.)	$g,-c''$

TABLE XIX. THE LUTE

Work.	Date.	Movement.	Sounding Compass.
St. John Passion	1727	31. Arioso (B.)	$c_{,}-b\flat'$
Trauer-Ode	1727	1. Coro 4. Recit. (A.) 5. Aria (A.) 7. Coro 8. Aria (T.) 10. Coro	$\{$I $b_{,,}-b'$ $\{$II $b_{,,}-f\sharp'$
Suite in E ma.[1]	...	...	$a_{,,}-e''$
Suite in E mi.[2]	...	...	$c_{,}-c''$
Suite in C mi.[3]	...	...	$a\flat_{,,}-f''$
Prelude in C mi.[4]	...	...	$d_{,}-c''$
Prelude and Fugue in E flat ma.[5]	...	...	$a\flat_{,,}-e\flat''$
Fugue in G mi.[6]	...	...	$g_{,}-f''$
Suite in G mi.[7]	...	...	$g-d''$

[1] For Clavier, B.-G. xlii. 16; for Violin, B.-G. xxvii (1) 48.
[2] For Clavier, B.-G. xlv (1) 149.
[3] For Clavier, B.-G. xlv (1) 156.
[4] For Clavier, B.-G. xxxvi. 119.
[5] For Clavier, B.-G. xlv (1) 141.
[6] For Violin, B.-G. xxvii (1) 4; for Organ, in D minor, B.-G. xv. 149.
[7] For Violoncello, in C minor, B.-G. xxvii (1) 81.

TABLE XX. THE CONTINUO

TABLE XX. THE CONTINUO

(The Score column indicates the completeness, or reverse, of the Continuo figuring)

(A) CHURCH MUSIC

Cantata.	Date.	Key.	Continuo Unfigured.	Continuo Figured.	Score Unfigured.	Score Figured.	Organ Obbligato.	Cembalo.
No. 1	c. 1740	F	F	Eb	...	only first Coro		
2	c. 1740	G mi.	G	F	...	almost complete		
3	c. 1740	A.	A	A	unfigured			
4	1724	E mi.	G F?	E D	"			
5	1735	G mi.	C	F	...	Tenor Aria unfigured		figured
6	1736	C mi.		C Bb	...	complete		
7	c. 1740	E mi.	D	E	...	"		
8	c. 1725	E and D[1]	E	C	...	Duet unfigured	...	
9	? 1731			D	...	complete		
10	c. 1740	G mi.		G F	unfigured			
11	c. 1736	D	D		...	only Sinfonia		
12	1724–5	F mi.	F	C	...	complete		
13	c. 1740	D mi.	D D	F	...	"		
14	1735	G mi.	G	C B	unfigured	very incomplete		
15	1704	C		G	...	T. Aria unfigured		
16	1724	A mi.	A		unfigured			
17	c. 1737	A.		G	...	only Sinfonia and first Recit.		
18	1714	G mi.	...	G	...	complete		
19	1726	C	no indication		...	"		
20	c. 1725	F	F	Eb	...	"		
21	1714	C mi.	C C	C	unfigured			
22	1723	G mi.	no parts					
23	1724	C mi.		A	...	complete		
24	1723	F	F F	Eb	unfigured			
25	c. 1731	A mi.	A G		...	very incomplete		
26	c. 1740	A mi.	A	G	...	T. Aria unfigured		

1 The version in D is a later text.

TABLE XX. THE CONTINUO 229

No.	Date	Key	C	B♭	Fig.	Completeness	Alto Aria	Alto Aria¹ (orig. version)
27	1731	C mi.	C	...	...	both Arias unfigured		Alto Aria
28	c. 1736	A mi.	A A G	...	...	very incomplete	Alto Aria	
29	1731	D	D D	C	...	complete		
30	1738	D	D D	C	...	"		
31	1715}1731}	C	C	C B♭	...	"		
32	c. 1740	E mi.	D D	...	...	only Recits.		
33	c. 1740	A mi.	...	A G	...	complete		
34	1740–1	D	D	...	unfigured	Alto Recit.		
35	1731	D mi.	D	...	...	complete	throughout (no part)	
36	c. 1730	D	D D	C	...	"		
37	c. 1727	A	A	G	...	Pt. II, unfigured		
38	c. 1740	E mi.	...	E D	...	complete		
39	1732	G mi.	G	F	...	Recits. only		
40	1723	F	F F	F E♭	...	complete		
41	1736	C	C	B♭	...	except two Recits.		
42	1731	D	D	D C C	...	only first two movts.		
43	c. 1735	C	C C	B♭	...			
44	c. 1725	G mi.	...	F G	...	except Alto Aria, and final Choral		
45	c. 1740	E	D	...	unfigured	except S. Aria		
46	c. 1725	D mi.	...	D C	...	very incomplete		
47	1720	G mi.	G G	F	...	...	S. Aria (autograph)	
48	c. 1740	G mi.	G G	...	...	complete	Coro, Bass Aria, Duet	
49	1731	E	E E²	...	unfigured			
50	c. 1740	D	C C	no parts	"	complete		
51	1731–2	C	F E♭	B♭	...			
52	c. 1730	F		...	"	complete (copy score)		
53	c. 1723–34	E	no parts	...	...			
54	c. 1723–34	E♭	no parts	...	"	complete		
55	1731–2	G mi.	G G F	...	unfigured	except last two movts.		
56	1731	G mi.	G F	F	"			
57	c. 1740	G mi.	G G	B♭	...			
58	1733	C	C C	B♭?	unfigured			
59	1716}1735}	C	C?		...			

¹ Cf. Spitta, ii. 451, note.

² The continuo and organ parts in the score are in D.

Cantata	Date	Key	Continuo Unfigured	Continuo Figured	Score Unfigured	Score Figured	Organ Obbligato	Cembalo
60	1732	D mi.	D	C	…	incomplete		
61	1714	A mi.	B B	no parts	unfigured	complete		
62	c. 1740	B mi.	C B♭	A	…	"		
63	1723	C	E D	B♭	…			
64	1723	E mi.		…	unfigured			
65	1724	C	A	no parts	"	complete		
66	1731	D	D	no parts	…	"		
67	1735	A	D	A G	…			
68	c. 1725	D mi.		C	unfigured	complete		
69	1724 / 1730	D		…	…			
70	1716	C	C	B♭	…	complete		
71	1708	C	D D	C	…	"		
72	c. 1726	A mi.	A	G	…	"		
73	c. 1725	G mi.	C	F	…	"		
74	1735	C	C	B♭	…	only a few bars		
75	1723	E mi.	no part	no parts	unfigured	complete	first Coro (or Horn)	
76	c. 1725	C	no part	no parts	…			
77	c. 1740	G mi.	G	…	"	very incomplete (copy score)		
78	1735	G	G G	no parts	unfigured	complete		
79	1730	D			…	"		
80	1724	E mi.	E	D E	…			
81	c. 1731	C mi.	C C	B♭	…	only Recits.		
82	1724	F	F	E♭	…			
83	1731–2	E mi.	E	D	unfigured			
84	1735	C mi.	C B♭	…	"	only Recits.		
85	c. 1725	E	D	no parts	…			
86	1735	D mi.	D C	C	unfigured	except Recits.		
87	1732	D	C	…	unfigured			
88	c. 1730	C mi.		B♭	…	complete		
89	c. 1740	D mi.	G	no parts	…	except both Arias		
90	c. 1740	G	B	F	…	complete		
91	c. 1740	B mi.	C	A	…			
92	1728	C mi.		C B♭	…			

TABLE XX.   THE CONTINUO   231

No.	Date	Key			Figured	Completeness	Notes
94	1735	D	DD	C	⋮	except three Arias	'Cont. pro Cembalo' in D. figd.
95	1732	G	G	F	⋮	except T. Aria ('senza l'Organo')	
96	c. 1740	F	F	F	⋮	complete	
97	1734	Bb	Bb Bb	Ab G	⋮	only first Coro	
98	c. 1732	Bb	Bb Bb	F	⋮	„	
99	c. 1733	G	G	F F F	⋮	complete	
100	c. 1735	D mi.	D	C	⋮	except the Arias	
101	c. 1740	G mi.		G F F	⋮	complete	
102	1731	B mi.	B B	F	unfigured	complete	
103	1735	G	G	G	⋮	except S. Aria	
104	c. 1725	G mi.	no part	no part	⋮	a few bars	
105	c. 1725	Eb	no parts		⋮		
106	1707 / 1711				⋮		
107	c. 1735	B mi.	B	A	⋮	only three movements (partial)	⋮
108	1735	A	A A	G	⋮	complete	
109	c. 1731	D mi.	D	C D	⋮	„	
110	p. 1734	D	D	C	⋮	only first Coro (partial) and B. Recit.	
111	c. 1740	A mi.	A G	G	⋮	except B. Aria	
112	1731	G		F	unfigured	complete	
113	c. 1740	B mi.		G F	⋮	complete (copy score)	
114	c. 1740	G mi.	A G		practically unfigured	complete	
115	c. 1740	G	no parts		unfigured		
116	1744	A	no parts		practically unfigured		
117	c. 1733	G	no parts		unfigured	complete	
118	1737	Bb			practically unfigured	only Recits.	
119	1723	C			unfigured	first Coro and Recits.	
120	1730	A	E	D	⋮	complete	
121	c. 1740	E mi.	G	F	⋮	except A. Aria	
122	c. 1742	G mi.	B	A	⋮	complete	
123	c. 1740	B mi.	E	D	⋮		
124	c. 1740	E	E E	D	⋮		
125	c. 1740	E mi.		D	⋮		
126	c. 1740	A mi.	A	G	⋮	complete	

Cantata	Date	Key	Continuo Unfigured	Continuo Figured	Score Unfigured	Score Figured	Organ Obbligato	Cembalo
127	c. 1740	F	F	E♭	...	only Recits.		
128	1735	G	G	F	...	complete		
129	1732	D	D D	C	...	,,		
130	c. 1740	C	no part	no part	practically unfigured	...		
131	1707–8	G mi.	no parts		...	complete (score)		
132	1715	A	A	C	...	a few bars		
133	1735–7	B♭	D D	A♭ A♭	...	complete		
134	1731	A mi.	B♭ B♭		...	only Recits.		
135	c. 1740	A	A	A G	...	complete (copy score)		
136	c. 1725	C	C	B♭	...	complete		
137	1732	B mi.			...	,,		
138	c. 1740	E	E	D	...	exc. first Recit. and Arias		
139	c. 1740	E♭	E♭	D♭	...	complete		
140	1731	G		no parts	unfigured			
141	1721–2	A mi.		no parts	,,			
142	1712–13	B♭		no parts	...	incomplete (copy score)		
143	1735	B mi.		no parts	unfigured			
144	c. 1725	D		no parts	,,			
145	1729–30	D mi.		no parts	...	incomplete (copy score)		
146	c. 1740	D mi.		no parts	unfigured	...		
147	1716 / c. 1727	C		C B♭	...	except Chorals	Sinfonia and first Coro	
148	c. 1725	D	D	no parts	...	incomplete		
149	1731	D		C	...	except Terzet		
150	c. 1712	B mi.	D	no parts	...	only Recits.		
151	1735–40	G		F	...	,, (score)		
152	1715	E mi.	E	D	...	complete		
153	1727	E mi.	B	A	...	,,		
154	1724	B mi.			...		...	
155	1716	D mi.	F F	no parts	unfigured	only first Recit. (score)		
156	1729–30	F	B	A	...	complete		
157	1727	B mi.	D	C	...	,,		
158	1708–17 Leipzig	D						A. Aria 'Jesu, lass dich'

TABLE XX.   THE CONTINUO   233

No.	Date	Key	Organ	Other parts	Figuring	Completeness	Remarks
159	1729	C mi.	C	B♭	,,	, complete (copy score)	
160	1714	C	no parts		,,	complete	
161	1715	A mi.	C	B♭	,,	,,	
162	1715	B mi.	A	A¹	,,		
163	1715		no parts		practically unfigured	only Recits.	
164	{1723-4 / ?1715}	G mi.	G	F	,,	except Arias (copy score)	Sinfonia and A. Arias / A. Arias
165	1724	G	no parts		,,	only first two movts.	
166	c. 1725	B♭	A♭	B♭	,,	complete	
167	c. 1725	G	G	F	,,	,,	
168	c. 1725	B mi.	B	A	,,	,,	
169	1731	D	D	D	,,	,,	
170	1731	D	D	C	,,	a few bars	
171	c. 1730	D	no parts		,,	,,	
172	{1724-5 / 1731}	C	C C	B♭	,,	except S. A. Duet	S. A. Duet (or Violin and Violoncello)
173	1731	D	no parts		unfigured	complete	
174	1729	G	G	F	,,	only Recits.	
175	1735	C mi.	G	F	,,	complete	
176	1735	G mi.	G	C B♭	,,	,,	
177	1732	A mi.	A A	F	,,	incomplete	
178	c. 1740	G	no part	G	unfigured	,,	
179	1724	F	no parts	no part	,,	complete	
180	c. 1740	E mi.	E	D	,,	very incomplete (score)	
181	c. 1725	G	G G G			only first movement	
182	1714-15	A mi.	A G		unfigured	(copy score)	
183	1735	G	G F	D	,,	complete (orig. score)	
184	1731	F♯ mi.	F♯ F	F²	,,	complete	
185	1715	G mi.	G G G	F	unfigured	only B. Recit.	
186	1723(1716)	G mi.	no parts		,,	only Nos. 2-4	
187	1732	F	no parts				
188	1731	B♭	no part	no part			
189	1707-10	D	no parts				
190	1725	D					A. Aria
191	1733	D	no parts		unfigured ,,		

¹ The cantata appears to have been given at Leipzig by raising the other instruments to the pitch of the organ.
² Later orchestral parts in G mi. exist.

Work	Date	Key	Continuo Unfigured	Continuo Figured	Score Unfigured	Score Figured	Organ Obbligato	Cembalo
192	c. 1732	G	G G	F	unfigured	complete		
193	c. 1740	D	no part	no part	…	incomplete; only first Coro and S. Recit.		
194	1723	Bb	Ab Bb Bb	G	…			
195	c. 1726	D	D	D D	…	very incomplete		
196	1708	C		no parts	unfigured			
197	1737	D.		no parts	unfigured			
198	1727	B mi.		no parts	unfigured			
(Trauer-Ode)	1714	C mi.	D D	D D	,,	complete		
'Mein Herze schwimmt'.	1728	G		no parts				
'Ehre sei Gott'	p. 1734	D	D	C	…	incomplete	Sinfonia	
'O ewiges Feuer'.	p. 1734	D	D D	C	…	complete		
'Herr Gott, Beherrscher'.	1734	D	D D	F	…	,,		
Christmas Oratorio, Pt. I	1734	D	G G	C	…	,,		
,, ,, II	1734	D	D D	F Eb	…	,,		
,, ,, III	1734	F	F	G	…	,,		
,, ,, IV	1734	A	A A	C C	…			
,, ,, V	1734	D	D D	C	…			
,, ,, VI	1736	E mi.	{E E / E E}	{D / D}	…	incomplete		
Easter Oratorio	1729	G mi.	G G	F	…	complete		
St. Matthew Passion	1723	D		no parts	…	,,	…	
St. John Passion	1723	D		no parts	unfigured			
Magnificat	…	C	C C	Bb	,,	complete (copy score)		
Sanctus in D[1]	…	D.	D D	C	…	complete		
,, D .	…	D mi.	D	G F	…			
,, D mi.	…	G.	G	B	…			
,, G .	…	B mi.			…	only 'Kyrie' and 'Gloria'		
Hohe Messe .	1733	D.	'Missa' B / 'Sanctus' D D C					
Mass in F .	c. 1736	F		? G	unfigured	complete		
,, A .	c. 1737	A.	no part	no parts	…	complete		
,, G mi.	1737	G mi.		no parts	…			
,, G .	c. 1738	G		no parts	unfigured	complete (other scores)	…	'Continuo pro Cembalo' figd. and unfigd.

[1] B.–G. xli. 177.

TABLE XX. THE CONTINUO   235

(B) SECULAR CANTATA

			no parts Cembalo	accomp.	unfigured		...	'Cembalo obbligato'
Aeolus	1725	D				...	...	
Amore traditore	...	A mi.						
Angenehmes Wiederau	1737	D						
Die Freude reget sich	c. 1733	D	D	no parts	,,	some Recits. only		
Durchlaucht'ster Leopold	1718	D		no parts	unfigured			
Hercules	1733	F	F	no parts	,,			
Ich bin in mir vergnügt	c. 1730	B♭		no parts	,,			
Mer hahn en neue Oberkeet	1742	A		no parts	,,			
Mit Gnaden bekröne	? 1722	D mi.		no parts	,,			
Non sa che sia dolore	...	B mi.		no parts	,,			
O angenehme Melodei	c. 1749}	A	A	A	...	very incomplete	...	Cembalo
O holder Tag	1746}							
Phoebus und Pan	1731	D	D					
Preise dein' Glücke	1734	D	D D	D D	unfigured	complete		
Schleicht, spielende Wellen	1734	D		D·D				
Schweigt stille	1732	G	G	G	...	complete except four Recits.	...	Cembalo obbl.
Schwingt freudig	c. 1730–4	D	D					
Tönet, ihr Pauken	1733	D	D	no parts	unfigured			
Vereinigte Zwietracht	1726}	D	D D D D		,,			
Auf, schmetternde Töne	1734}	D	D					
Vergnügte Pleissenstadt	1728	C		no parts	unfigured			
Was mir behagt	1716	F		no parts	,,			
Weichet nur	1717–22	G		no parts	...	very incomplete		

(C) ORCHESTRAL MUSIC

Work	Date	Key	Continuo — Unfigured	Continuo — Figured
Concertos for Clavier and Orchestra I	…	D mi.	unfigured	
„ „ II	…	E	„	
„ „ III	…	D	„	
„ „ IV	…	A	…	complete
„ „ V	…	F mi.	unfigured	
„ „ VI	…	F	„	
„ „ VII	…	G mi.	„	
Concerto for Clavier, Flute, Violin, and Orchestra	…	A mi.	…	complete[1]
Brandenburg Concerto I	1721	F	unfigured	
„ „ II	1721	F	practically unfigured	
„ „ III	1721	G	unfigured	
„ „ IV	1721	G	unfigured	
„ „ V	1721	D	…	complete[1]
„ „ VI	1721	Bb	unfigured	
Sinfonia in D (Violin and Orchestra)	…	D	unfigured	
Concertos for Violin and Orchestra I	…	A mi.	unfigured	
„ „ II	…	E	„	
„ „ III	…	D mi.	„	
„ „ IV	…	D	„	
Concertos for two Claviers and Orchestra I	…	C mi.	…	complete
„ „ II	…	C	…	„
„ „ III	…	C mi.	unfigured	
Ouverture I	…	C	unfigured	
„ II	…	B mi.	„	
„ III	…	D	„	
„ IV[2]	…	D	„	
Sinfonia in F	…	F	unfigured	
Concerto for three Claviers and Orchestra I	…	D mi.	…	complete
„ „ II	…	C	unfigured	
Concerto for four Claviers and Orchestra	…	C	…	„

[1] The concerted Cembalo part alone is figured.

[2] B.–G. xlv (1), p. 190, prints an unauthenticated Ouverture for strings and cembals in G mi.

TABLE XX. THE CONTINUO   237

(D) CHAMBER MUSIC

Work.	Key.	State of Cembalo part.
Sonatas for Cembalo and Flute I	B mi.	Generally two-part. Unfigured. Autograph score.
" " " II	E♭	Two-part. Unfigured. Copy score.
" " " III	A	Two-part. Unfigured. Autograph score.
Suite for Cembalo and Violin	A	Generally two-part. Unfigured. Autograph parts.
Sonatas for Cembalo and Violin I	B mi.	Generally two-part. Figured where upper part is silent.
" " " II	A	" " " "
" " " III	E	Two part. No figuring.
" " " IV	C mi.	" " No figuring.
" " " V	F mi.	Generally two-part. Figuring as in No. I.
" " " VI	G	" " " " ⎫ Copy score. Partly autograph parts.
Sonatas for Cembalo and Viola da gamba I	D	Two part. Unfigured. Autograph parts.
" " " II	G mi.	Generally two-part. Figuring where upper part is silent. Copy score.
" " " III	G	Two-part. Figuring where upper part is silent. Autograph parts.
Sonata for Flute, Violin, and Continuo	C mi.	Figured continuo. Autograph parts (?).
Trio " " "	C mi.	Figured continuo (in the *Musicalisches Opfer*).
Canon " " "	C	Figured continuo. Copies.
Sonata for two Violins and Continuo	G	Figured continuo. Cembalo part autograph.
Sonata for two Flutes and Cembalo	G mi.	Cembalo two-part. Figured where upper part is silent. Copy score.
Sonata for Cembalo and Violin	C	Figured continuo. Cembalo three-part in Menuetto I. Copies.
Sonatas for Flute and Continuo I	E mi.	Copies.
" " " II	E	Copies.
" " " III	E mi.	Copy score.
Sonata for Violin and Continuo	G	Autograph.
Fuga for Violin and Continuo	G mi.	Copy.
Sonata for two Cembali	F	Each generally in two parts. Unfigured. Copy parts.

238

TABLE XXI

THE CANTATAS IN ALPHABETICAL ORDER
(with a précis of their scores)

The sign + indicates that the instruments following it are in addition to the normal strings and continuo. When no instruments are named, strings are to be inferred. Obsolete instruments are invariably mentioned, excepting the violone, which must normally be associated with the continuo. Wind instruments named in italic type are merely auxiliary and dispensable. Though more than one species of oboe is frequently prescribed in a score, the number of instruments indicated almost invariably exaggerates the number of players required.

Bach's instrumentation should be observed, if possible, for it brings us closer to his mind and meaning. Unfortunately many of his instruments are obsolete, and others are not easily obtainable. The following substitutions are recommended by Professor Whittaker[1] out of his unique experience:

For	Substitute
Violino piccolo	Violin
Violetta	Viola
Viola d'amore	Viola or muted violin
Viola da gamba	Violoncello
Violoncello piccolo	Violoncello or viola, or both
Violone	Contrabass
Flute à bec	Flute
Oboe d'amore	Oboe
Oboe da caccia	Cor anglais
Corno da caccia	Horn or Trumpet
Corno da tirarsi	Horn or Trumpet
Cornetto	Trumpet
Tromba da tirarsi	Trumpet
Tromba, Clarino, Principale	Trumpet

	NO.	SCORE
Ach Gott, vom Himmel sieh' darein	2	+2 Ob., 4 *Trombones*
Ach Gott, wie manches Herzeleid	3	+*Cor.*, *Trombone*, 2 Ob. d'am.
Ach Gott, wie manches Herzeleid	58	+3 Ob.
Ach Herr, mich armen Sünder	135	+*Cornett*, *Trombone*, 2 Ob.
Ach, ich sehe	162	+Cor. da tirarsi, Fag.
Ach, lieben Christen, seid getrost	114	+Cor., Fl., 2 Ob.
Ach wie flüchtig	26	+*Cor.*, Fl., 3 Ob.
Aergre dich, o Seele, nicht	186	+3 Ob., Ob. da cacc., Fag.
Allein zu dir, Herr Jesu Christ	33	+2 Ob.
Alles nur nach Gottes Willen	72	+2 Ob.
Also hat Gott die Welt geliebt	68	+*Cor.*, *Cornett*, 3 *Trombones*, 3 Ob., Vcello piccolo
Am Abend aber desselbigen Sabbaths	42	+2 Ob., Fag., Vcello
Amore traditore	—	Cembalo
Angenehmes Wiederau	—	+3 Tr., Timp., 2 Fl., 2 Ob., Ob. d'am.
Auf Christi Himmelfahrt allein	128	+Tr., 2 Cor. da caccia, 2 Ob., Ob. d'am., Ob. da caccia
Auf, schmetternde Töne	—	+3 Tr., Timp., 2 Fl., 2 Ob. d'am., Ob.
Aus der Tiefe rufe ich, Herr	131	+Ob., Fag.
Aus tiefer Noth schrei' ich zu dir	38	+2 Ob., 4 *Trombones*
Barmherziges Herze	185	+[Tr.], Ob., Fag.
Bereitet die Wege	132	+Ob., Fag.
Bisher habt ihr nichts gebeten	87	+2 Ob., 2 Ob. da cacc.
Bleib' bei uns, denn es will Abend werden	6	+2 Ob., Ob. da cacc., Vcello piccolo
Brich dem Hungrigen dein Brod	39	+2 Fl., 2 Ob.
Bringet dem Herrn Ehre	148	+Tr., 3 Ob.

[1] *Fugitive Notes on Bach's Cantatas* (1924), p. 254.

TABLE XXI. THE CANTATAS IN ALPHABETICAL ORDER 239

	NO.	SCORE
Christ lag in Todesbanden . . .	4	+Cornett, 3 Trombones
Christ unser Herr zum Jordan kam . .	7	+2 Ob. d'am.
Christen, ätzet diesen Tag . . .	63	+4 Tr., Timp., 3 Ob., Fag.
Christum wir sollen loben schon . .	121	+Cornett, 3 Trombones, Ob. d'am.
Christus, der ist mein Leben . . .	95	+Cor., 2 Ob., 2 Ob. d'am.
Das ist je gewisslich wahr . . .	141	+2 Ob.
Das neugebor'ne Kindelein . . .	122	+3 Fl., 3 Ob.
Dazu ist erschienen der Sohn Gottes .	40	+2 Cor., 2 Ob.
Dem Gerechten muss das Licht . .	195	+3 Tr., Timp., 2 Cor., 2 Fl., 2 Ob., 2 Ob. d'am.
Denn du wirst meine Seele nicht in der Hölle lassen	15	+3 Tr., Timp.
Der Friede sei mit dir	158	Vn., Ob., Cont.
Der Herr denket an uns . . .	196	
Der Herr ist mein getreuer Hirt . .	112	+2 Cor., 2 Ob. d'am.
Der Himmel lacht, die Erde jubiliret .	31	+3 Tr., Timp., 4 Ob., Fag.
Der Streit zwischen Phoebus und Pan .	—	+3 Tr., Timp., 2 Fl., 2 Ob., Ob. d'am.
Der zufriedengestellte Aeolus . . .	—	+3 Tr., Timp., 2 Cor., 2 Fl., 2 Ob., Ob. d'am., Va. d'am., Va. da gamba
Die Elenden sollen essen . . .	75	+Tr., 2 Ob., Ob. d'am., Fagotti
Die Freude reget sich	—	+Fl.
Die Himmel erzählen die Ehre Gottes .	76	+Tr., 2 Ob., Ob. d'am., Va. da gamba
Die Wahl des Herkules	—	+2 Cor. da caccia, 2 Ob., Ob. d'am.
Du Friedefürst, Herr Jesu Christ . .	116	+Cor., 2 Ob. d'am.
Du Hirte Israel, höre	104	+3 Ob., 2 Ob. d'am.
Du sollst Gott, deinen Herren, lieben .	77	+Tr. da tirarsi, 2 Ob.
Du wahrer Gott und Davids Sohn . .	23	+Cornett, 3 Trombones, 2 Ob.
Durchlaucht'ster Leopold . . .	—	+2 Fl., Fag., Vcello, Cembalo
Ehre sei dir, Gott, gesungen (Part V. Christmas Oratorio)	—	+2 Ob. d'am.
Ehre sei Gott in der Höhe (incomplete) .	—	2 Fl., Ob. d'am., Vcello, Cont.
Ein Herz, das seinen Jesum lebend weiss .	134	+2 Ob.
Ein ungefärbt Gemüthe	24	+Tr., 2 Ob., 2 Ob. d'am.
Ein' feste Burg ist unser Gott . .	80	+3 Tr., Timp., 3 Ob., 2 Ob. d'am., Ob. da cacc.
Er rufet seinen Schafen	175	+2 Tr., 3 Fl., Vcello piccolo
Erforsche mich, Gott	136	+Cor., 2 Ob., 2 Ob. d'am.
Erfreut euch, ihr Herzen . . .	66	+Tr., 2 Ob., Fag.
Erfreute Zeit im neuen Bunde . . .	83	+2 Cor., 2 Ob.
Erhalt' uns, Herr, bei deinem Wort . .	126	+Tr., 2 Ob.
Erhöhtes Fleisch und Blut . . .	173	+2 Fl.
Erschallet, ihr Lieder . . .	172	+3 Tr., Timp., Fag., Org. (or Vn. and Vcello)
Erwünschtes Freudenlicht . . .	184	+2 Fl.
Es erhub sich ein Streit . . .	19	+3 Tr., Timp., 3 Ob., 2 Ob. d'am.
Es ist das Heil uns kommen her . .	9	+Fl., Ob. d'am.
Es ist dir gesagt, Mensch . . .	45	+2 Fl., 2 Ob.
Es ist ein trotzig	176	+2 Ob., Ob. da cacc.
Es ist euch gut, dass ich hingehe . .	108	+2 Ob. d'am.
Es ist nichts Gesundes an meinem Leibe .	25	+Cornett, 3 Trombones, 3 Fl., 2 Ob.
Es reifet euch ein schrecklich Ende . .	90	+Tr.
Es wartet Alles auf dich	187	+2 Ob.
Fallt mit Danken (Part IV. Christmas Oratorio)	—	+2 Cor., 2 Ob.
Falsche Welt, dir trau' ich nicht . .	52	+2 Cor., 3 Ob., Fag.
Freue dich, erlöste Schaar . . .	30	+3 Tr., Timp., 2 Fl., 2 Ob., Ob. d'am.

	NO.	SCORE
Geist und Seele wird verwirret	35	+3 Ob., Org.
Gelobet sei der Herr, mein Gott	129	+3 Tr., Timp., Fl., 2 Ob., Ob. d'am.
Gelobet seist du, Jesu Christ	91	+2 Cor., Timp., 3 Ob.
Gleich wie der Regen und Schnee	18	4 Ve., Vcello, 2 Fl., Fag., Cont.
Gloria in excelsis Deo	191	+3 Tr., Timp., 2 Fl., 2 Ob.
Gott, der Herr, ist Sonn' und Schild	79	+2 Cor., Timp., 2 Fl., 2 Ob.
Gott fähret auf mit Jauchzen	43	+3 Tr., Timp., 2 Ob.
Gott ist mein König	71	+3 Tr., Timp., 2 Fl., 2 Ob., Fag.
Gott ist unsre Zuversicht	197	+3 Tr., Timp., 2 Ob., 2 Ob. d'am., Fag.
Gott, man lobet dich in der Stille	120	+3 Tr., Timp., 2 Ob. d'am.
Gott soll allein	169	+3 Ob., Org.
Gott, wie dein Name	171	+3 Tr., Timp., 2 Ob.
Gottes Zeit ist die allerbeste Zeit	106	2 Fl., 2 Va. da gamba, Cont.
Gottlob! nun geht das Jahr zu Ende	28	+Cornett, 3 Trombones, 3 Ob.
Halt' im Gedächtniss Jesum Christ	67	+Cor. da tirarsi, Fl., 2 Ob. d'am.
Herr Christ, der ein'ge Gottes-Sohn	96	+Cor., Trombone, Vn. piccolo, Fl., Fl. piccolo, 2 Ob.
Herr, deine Augen sehen	102	+Fl. (or Vn. piccolo), 2 Ob.
Herr, gehe nicht in's Gericht	105	+Cor., 2 Ob.
Herr Gott, Beherrscher (incomplete)	—	+3 Tr., Timp., 2 Ob., 2 Ob. d'am., Org.
Herr Gott, dich loben alle wir	130	+3 Tr., Timp., Fl., 3 Ob.
Herr Gott, dich loben wir	16	+Cor. da cacc., 2 Ob., Ob. da cacc. or Violetta
Herr Jesu Christ, du höchstes Gut	113	+Fl., 2 Ob., 2 Ob. d'am.
Herr Jesu Christ, wahr'r Mensch und Gott	127	+Tr., 2 Fl., 2 Ob.
Herr, wenn die stolzen Feinde (Part VI. Christmas Oratorio)	—	+3 Tr., Timp., 2 Ob., 2 Ob. d'am.
Herr, wie du willst	73	+Cor. (or Org. obblig.), 2 Ob.
Herrscher des Himmels (Part III. Christmas Oratorio)	—	+3 Tr., Timp., 2 Fl., 2 Ob., 2 Ob. d'am.
Herz und Mund und That	147	+Tr., 2 Ob., Ob. d'am., 2 Ob. da cacc., Fag.
Himmelskönig, sei willkommen	182	+Fl.
Höchsterwünschtes Freudenfest	194	+3 Ob., Fagotti
Ich armer Mensch	55	+Fl., Ob., Ob. d'am.
Ich bin ein guter Hirt	85	+2 Ob., Vcello piccolo
Ich bin in mir vergnügt	—	+Fl., 2 Ob.
Ich bin vergnügt mit meinem Glücke	84	+Ob.
Ich elender Mensch	48	+Tr., 2 Ob.
Ich freue mich in dir	133	+Cornett, 2 Ob. d'am.
Ich geh' und suche mit Verlangen	49	+Ob. d'am., Org., Vcello piccolo
Ich glaube, lieber Herre	109	+Cor. da caccia, 2 Ob., Cembalo
Ich habe genug	82	+Ob.
Ich hab' in Gottes Herz und Sinn	92	+2 Ob. d'am.
Ich habe meine Zuversicht	188	+Ob., Org., Vcello
Ich hatte viel Bekümmerniss	21	+3 Tr., 4 Trombones, Timp., Ob., Fag.
Ich lasse dich nicht	157	+Fl., Ob., Ob. d'am., Violetta
Ich liebe den Höchsten	174	+2 Cor. da caccia, 3 Ob., Fag.
Ich ruf' zu dir	177	+2 Ob., Ob. da caccia, Fag.
Ich steh' mit einem Fuss im Grabe	156	+Ob.
Ich weiss, dass mein Erlöser lebt	160	Vn., Fag., Cont.
Ich will den Kreuzstab gerne tragen	56	+3 Ob. (or Str.), Vcello
Ihr, die ihr euch	164	+2 Fl., 2 Ob.
Ihr Menschen, rühmet Gottes Liebe	167	+Tr., Ob., Ob. da cacc.
Ihr Pforten zu Zion (incomplete)	193	+2 Ob.
Ihr werdet weinen und heulen	103	+Tr., Fl. (or Vn.), Fl. piccolo, 2 Ob. d'am.
In allen meinen Thaten	97	+2 Ob., Fagotti
Jauchzet, frohlocket (Part I. Christmas Oratorio).	—	+3 Tr., Timp., 2 Fl., 2 Ob., 2 Ob. d'am., Fag.

TABLE XXI. THE CANTATAS IN ALPHABETICAL ORDER 241

	NO.	SCORE
Jauchzet Gott in allen Landen . .	51	+Tr.
Jesu, der du meine Seele . . .	78	+Cor., Fl., 2 Ob.
Jesu, nun sei gepreiset	41	+3 Tr., Timp., 3 Ob., Vcello piccolo
Jesus nahm zu sich die Zwölfe . . .	22	+Ob.
Jesus schläft, was soll ich hoffen . .	81	+2 Fl., 2 Ob. d'am.
Komm, du süsse Todesstunde . .	161	+2 Fl.
Kommt, eilet und laufet (Easter Oratorio) .	—	+3 Tr., Timp., 2 Fl., 2 Ob., Ob. d'am., Fag.
Lass, Fürstin, lass noch einen Strahl (Trauer-Ode)	198	+2 Fl., 2 Ob.,2 Ob. d'am.,2 Lutes, 2 Va. da gamba
Leichtgesinnte Flattergeister . . .	181	+Tr., Fl., Ob.
Liebster Gott, wann werd' ich sterben .	8	+Cor., Fl., 2 Ob. d'am., Cembalo
Liebster Immanuel, Herzog der Frommen.	123	+2 Fl., 2 Ob. d'am.
Liebster Jesu, mein Verlangen . .	32	+Ob.
Lobe den Herrn, den mächtigen König .	137	+3 Tr., Timp., 2 Ob.
Lobe den Herrn, meine Seele . . .	69	+3 Tr., Timp., 3 Ob., Ob. d'am., Fag.
Lobe den Herrn, meine Seele . . .	143	+3 Cor. da caccia, Timp., Fag.
Lobet Gott in seinen Reichen . . .	11	+3 Tr., Timp., 2 Fl., 2 Ob.
Mache dich, mein Geist, bereit . .	115	+Cor., Fl., Ob. d'am., Vcello piccolo
Man singet mit Freuden vom Sieg . .	149	+3 Tr., Timp., 3 Ob., Fag.
Mein Gott, wie lang', ach lange . .	155	+Fag.
Mein Herze schwimmt im Blut . .	—	+Ob., Fag.
Mein liebster Jesus ist verloren . .	154	+2 Ob., 2 Ob. d'am, Cembalo
Meine Seel' erhebt den Herren . .	10	+Tr., 2 Ob.
Meine Seele rühmt und preist . .	189	Fl., Ob., Vn., Cont.
Meine Seufzer, meine Thränen . .	13	+2 Fl., Ob. da cacc.
Meinen Jesum lass' ich nicht . . .	124	+Cor., Ob. d'am.
Mer hahn en neue Oberkeet . . .	—	+Cor., Fl.
Mit Fried' und Freud' ich fahr' dahin .	125	+Cor., Fl., Ob., Ob. d'am.
Mit Gnaden bekröne der Himmel die Zeiten	—	+2 Ob.
Nach dir, Herr, verlanget mich . .	150	+2 Vn., Fag., Cont.
Nimm von uns, Herr	101	+Cornett, 3 Trombones, Fl., 3 Ob., Ob. da cacc.
Nimm, was dein ist	144	+Ob. d'am.
Non sa che sia dolore	—	+Fl.
Nun danket Alle Gott (incomplete) .	192	+2 Fl., 2 Ob.
Nun ist das Heil und die Kraft . .	50	+3 Tr., Timp., 3 Ob.
Nun komm, der Heiden Heiland . .	61	+Fag.
Nun komm, der Heiden Heiland . .	62	+Cor., 2 Ob.
Nur Jedem das Seine	163	+Ob. d'am., Vcello
O angenehme Melodei	—	+Fl., Ob. d'am., Cembalo
O ewiges Feuer, o Ursprung der Liebe .	34	+3 Tr., Timp., 2 Fl., 2 Ob.
O ewiges Feuer (incomplete) . .	—	+3 Tr., Timp., 2 Fl., 2 Ob.
O Ewigkeit, du Donnerwort . .	20	+Tr. da tirarsi, 3 Ob.
O Ewigkeit, du Donnerwort . .	60	+Cor., 2 Ob. d'am.
O heil'ges Geist und Wasserbad . .	165	+Fag.
O holder Tag	—	+Fl., Ob. d'am., Cembalo
O Jesu Christ, mein's Lebens Licht .	118	2 Litui, Cornett, 3 Trombones (or +2 Litui, Ob., Fag.)
Preise dein' Glücke	—	+3 Tr., Timp., 2 Fl., 2 Ob., 2 Ob. d'am., Violetta
Preise, Jerusalem, den Herrn . .	119	+4 Tr., Timp., 2 Fl., 3 Ob., 2 Ob. da caccia

	NO.	SCORE
Schau', lieber Gott.	153	
Schauet doch und sehet .	46	+Tr. (or Cor.) da tirarsi, 2 Fl., 2 Ob. da cacc.
Schlage doch, gewünschte Stunde	53	+Campanella
Schleicht, spielende Wellen	—	+3 Tr., Timp., 2 Fl., 2 Ob., 2 Ob. d'am.
Schmücke dich, o liebe Seele .	180	+2Fl.,Ob.,Ob. da caccia,Vcello picc.
Schweigt stille, plaudert nicht .	—	+Fl., Cembalo
Schwingt freudig euch empor .	36	+2 Ob. d'am.
Schwingt freudig euch empor .	—	+Ob. d'am., Va. d'amore
Sehet, welch' eine Liebe	64	+Cornett, 3 Trombones, Ob. d'am.
Sehet, wir geh'n hinauf .	159	+Ob., Fagotti
Sei Lob und Ehr' dem höchsten Gut	117	+2 Fl., 2 Ob., 2 Ob. d'am.
Selig ist der Mann	57	+3 Ob.
Sie werden aus Saba Alle kommen	65	+2 Cor. da caccia, 2 Fl., 2 Ob. da cacc.
Sie werden euch in den Bann thun	44	+2 Ob., Fag.
Sie werden euch in den Bann thun	183	+2 Ob. d'am., 2 Ob. da caccia, Vcello piccolo
Siehe, ich will viel Fischer aussenden	88	+2 Cor., 2 Ob. d'am., Ob.
Siehe zu, dass deine Gottesfurcht	179	+2 Ob., 2 Ob. da caccia
Singet dem Herrn .	190	+3 Tr., Timp., 3 Ob., Ob. d'am.
So du mit deinem Munde	145	+Tr., Fl., 2 Ob. d'am.
Süsser Trost, mein Jesus kommt	151	+Fl., Ob. d'am.
Thue Rechnung! Donnerwort	168	+2 Ob. d'am.
Tönet, ihr Pauken!	—	+3 Tr., Timp., 2 Fl., 2 Ob.
Trauer-Ode. See 'Lass, Fürstin'.		
Tritt auf die Glaubensbahn	152	Fl., Ob., Va. d'am., Va. da gamba, Cont.
Und es waren Hirten (Part II. Christmas Oratorio)	—	+2 Fl., 2 Ob. d'am., 2 Ob. da caccia
Uns ist ein Kind geboren	142	+2 Fl., 2 Ob.
Unser Mund sei voll Lachens .	110	+3 Tr., Timp., 2 Fl., 3 Ob., Ob. d'am., Ob. da caccia., Fag.
Vereinigte Zwietracht	—	+3 Tr., Timp., 2 Fl., 2 Ob. d'am., Ob.
Vergnügte Pleissen-Stadt	—	[2 Fl., Ob., Vcello, Cembalo]
Vergnügte Ruh'	170	+Ob. d'am., Org.
Wachet auf, ruft uns die Stimme	140	+Cor., 3 Ob., Vn. piccolo
Wachet, betet, seid bereit	70	+Tr., Ob., Fag., Vcello
Wär' Gott nicht mit uns diese Zeit	14	+Cor. da cacc., 2 Ob.
Wahrlich, ich sage euch .	86	+2 Ob.
Warum betrübst du dich	138	+2 Ob. d'am.
Was frag' ich nach der Welt	94	+Fl., 2 Ob., Ob. d'am.
Was Gott thut, das ist wohlgethan	98	+3 Ob.
Was Gott thut, das ist wohlgethan	99	+Cor., Fl., Ob. d'am.
Was Gott thut, das ist wohlgethan	100	+2 Cor., Timp., Fl., Ob. d'am.
Was mein Gott will	111	+2 Ob.
Was mir behagt	—	+2 Cor., 2 Cor. da caccia, 2 Fl., 3 Ob., Fagotti, Violone grosso
Was soll ich aus dir machen, Ephraim?	89	+Cor. da caccia, 2 Ob.
Was willst du dich betrüben	107	+Cor. da cacc., 2 Fl., 2 Ob. d'am.
Weichet nur, betrübte Schatten	—	+Ob.
Weinen, Klagen, Sorgen, Zagen	12	+Tr., Ob., Fag.
Wer da glaubet und getauft wird	37	+2 Ob. d'am.
Wer Dank opfert, der preiset mich	17	+2 Ob.
Wer mich liebet .	59	+2 Tr., Timp.
Wer mich liebet .	74	+3 Tr., Timp., 2 Ob., Ob. da cacc.
Wer nur den lieben Gott lässt walten	93	+2 Ob.
Wer sich selbst erhöhet .	47	+2 Ob., Org.
Wer weiss, wie nahe mir mein Ende	27	+Cor., 2 Ob., Ob. da cacc., Org.

TABLE XXI.   THE CANTATAS IN ALPHABETICAL ORDER   243

TABLE XXII

THE CANTATAS IN THE NUMERICAL ORDER OF THEIR PUBLICATION BY THE BACHGESELLSCHAFT

The dates indicate the year to which each volume belongs. Figures in brackets date the Preface when publication was delayed. Page references to the text of the present volume follow the titles

I. CHURCH CANTATAS

JAHRGANG I

1851. ED. MORITZ HAUPTMANN

NO.
1. Wie schön leuchtet der Morgenstern .   47, 105, 150.
2. Ach Gott, vom Himmel sieh' darein .   40, 95, 98, 122, 150.
3. Ach Gott, wie manches Herzeleid   .   35, 39, 40, 111, 150, 162, 170.
4. Christ lag in Todesbanden   .   .   39, 40, 101, 123, 150, 162.
5. Wo soll ich fliehen hin   .   .   .   27, 29, 30, 31, 32, 36, 124, 150, 153, 154.
6. Bleib' bei uns, denn es will Abend   99, 107, 139, 140, 150, 153, 162.
    werden
7. Christ unser Herr zum Jordan kam .   111, 150, 153, 162.
8. Liebster Gott, wann werd' ich sterben   8, 36, 81, 84, 85, 150, 164, 168.
9. Es ist das Heil uns kommen her   .   81, 91, 111, 150.
10. Meine Seel' erhebt den Herren   .   33, 35, 97, 150, 162.

JAHRGANG II

1852. ED. MORITZ HAUPTMANN

NO.
11. Lobet Gott in seinen Reichen   .   .   81, 87, 88, 90, 92, 150, 162, 168.
12. Weinen, Klagen, Sorgen, Zagen   .   33, 97, 113, 116, 123, 150, 162.
13. Meine Seufzer, meine Thränen   .   63, 67, 105, 122, 150, 153, 168.
14. Wär' Gott nicht mit uns diese Zeit   .   35, 42, 44, 150.
15. Denn du wirst meine Seele nicht in der   2, 23, 52, 60, 150.
    Hölle lassen
16. Herr Gott, dich loben wir   .   .   35, 36, 44, 46, 98, 105, 127, 128, 150.
17. Wer Dank opfert, der preiset mich   .   95, 97, 150, 162.
18. Gleich wie der Regen und Schnee vom   5, 64, 67, 113, 116, 122, 124, 150.
    Himmel fällt
19. Es erhub sich ein Streit   .   .   80, 99, 150.
20. O Ewigkeit, du Donnerwort   .   26, 30, 33, 36, 102, 150.

JAHRGANG V (1)

1855. ED. WILHELM RUST

NO.
21. Ich hatte viel Bekümmerniss   .   .   5, 40, 41, 51, 97, 98, 113, 116, 153, 168.
22. Jesus nahm zu sich die Zwölfe .   .   102.
23. Du wahrer Gott und Davids Sohn   .   40, 165, 166, 168.
24. Ein ungefärbt Gemüthe   .   .   23, 33, 34, 35, 95, 96, 109, 122, 153.
25. Es ist nichts Gesundes an meinem   40, 41, 64, 68, 95, 154, 162.
    Leibe
26. Ach wie flüchtig, ach wie nichtig   .   35, 75, 80, 84, 86, 102, 122, 168.
27. Wer weiss, wie nahe mir mein Ende .   164, 171, 173.
28. Gottlob! nun geht das Jahr zu Ende .   40, 95, 153, 154, 162.
29. Wir danken dir, Gott, wir danken dir   88, 95, 98, 122, 168, 171, 173.
30. Freue dich, erlöste Schaar   .   84, 85, 95, 108, 122, 153, 168.

TABLE XXII. THE CANTATAS IN NUMERICAL ORDER   245

JAHRGANG VII
1857. ED. WILHELM RUST

NO.
31.	Der Himmel lacht, die Erde jubiliret	5, 26, 27, 95, 97, 99, 113, 114, 116, 123, 153, 155.
32.	Liebster Jesu, mein Verlangen . .	122, 162.
33.	Allein zu dir, Herr Jesu Christ .	162, 168.
34.	O ewiges Feuer, o Ursprung der Liebe	84, 85, 95, 162.
35.	Geist und Seele wird verwirret . .	95, 97, 99, 162, 171, 173.
36.	Schwingt freudig euch empor . .	122, 131, 153, 168.
37.	Wer da glaubet und getauft wird .	—
38.	Aus tiefer Noth schrei' ich zu dir .	40, 162.
39.	Brich dem Hungrigen dein Brod .	63, 68, 82, 122.
40.	Dazu ist erschienen der Sohn Gottes	44, 47, 153, 162.

JAHRGANG X
1860. ED. WILHELM RUST

NO.
41.	Jesu, nun sei gepreiset . . .	80, 102, 138, 139, 140, 168.
42.	Am Abend aber desselbigen Sabbaths	113, 114, 115, 117, 124, 135, 153, 162, 168.
43.	Gott fähret auf mit Jauchzen . .	80, 95, 97, 98, 153.
44.	Sie werden euch in den Bann thun .	95, 98, 162.
45.	Es ist dir gesagt, Mensch, was gut ist	76, 80, 81, 82, 95, 97, 162.
46.	Schauet doch und sehet, ob irgend ein Schmerz sei	8, 27, 30, 33, 34, 36, 68, 70, 107, 162, 168.
47.	Wer sich selbst erhöhet, der soll erniedriget werden	97, 153, 171.
48.	Ich elender Mensch, wer wird mich erlösen?	23, 33, 35, 97, 153, 154, 162.
49.	Ich geh' und suche mit Verlangen .	108, 111, 112, 139, 140, 162, 171, 174, 175.
50.	Nun ist das Heil und die Kraft .	80, 95, 168.

JAHRGANG XII (2)
1862 [1863]. ED. WILHELM RUST

NO.
51.	Jauchzet Gott in allen Landen . .	29, 101, 122, 153.
52.	Falsche Welt, dir trau' ich nicht .	102, 116, 154, 162, 168.
53.	Schlage doch, gewünschte Stunde .	101
54.	Widerstehe doch der Sünde . .	101, 123.
55.	Ich armer Mensch, ich Sündenknecht	75, 82, 83, 88, 90, 108, 153, 154, 162.
56.	Ich will den Kreuzstab gerne tragen .	99, 124, 135, 154, 162.
57.	Selig ist der Mann	95, 122, 153, 168.
58.	Ach Gott, wie manches Herzeleid .	122, 153.
59.	Wer mich liebet, der wird mein Wort halten	5, 51, 60.
60.	O Ewigkeit, du Donnerwort . .	110, 122.

JAHRGANG XVI
1866 [1868]. ED. WILHELM RUST

NO.
61.	Nun komm, der Heiden Heiland .	5, 113, 122, 123, 168.
62.	Nun komm, der Heiden Heiland .	35, 122, 153, 168.
63.	Christen, ätzet diesen Tag . .	23, 26, 56, 80, 113, 153, 154, 168.
64.	Sehet, welch' eine Liebe hat uns der Vater erzeiget	40, 153, 154, 162, 168.
65.	Sie werden aus Saba Alle kommen .	8, 44, 46, 67, 104, 106, 107.
66.	Erfreut euch, ihr Herzen . . .	27, 115, 117, 122.
67.	Halt' im Gedächtniss Jesum Christ .	8, 30, 34, 36, 80, 81, 153, 162, 168.
68.	Also hat Gott die Welt geliebt .	40, 95, 102, 138, 139, 140.
69.	Lobe den Herrn, meine Seele .	51, 80, 110, 114, 162.
70.	Wachet, betet, seid bereit allezeit .	5, 27, 28, 40, 95, 98, 113, 124, 153.

JAHRGANG XVIII
1868 [1870].   ED. WILHELM RUST

NO.

71. Gott ist mein König . . . 2, 54, 60, 66, 67, 96, 113, 114, 153, 168.
72. Alles nur nach Gottes Willen . . 34.
73. Herr, wie du willst, so schick's mit 171, 172.
mir
74. Wer mich liebet, der wird mein Wort 26, 80, 99, 106, 122.
halten
75. Die Elenden sollen essen . . . 29, 33, 108, 109, 113.
76. Die Himmel erzählen die Ehre Gottes 28, 29, 98, 108, 109, 111, 112, 122, 133,
134, 153.
77. Du sollst Gott, deinen Herren, lieben . 29, 30, 33, 36.
78. Jesu, der du meine Seele . . . 35, 75, 80, 81, 82, 84, 151, 168.
79. Gott, der Herr, ist Sonn' und Schild . 51, 52, 76, 80, 81, 82, 162.
80. Ein' feste Burg ist unser Gott . . 34, 54, 80, 102, 104, 105, 108, 110, 122,
168.

JAHRGANG XX (1)
1870 [1872].   ED. WILHELM RUST

NO.

81. Jesus schläft, was soll ich hoffen? . 8, 68, 111, 153, 162.
82. Ich habe genug . . . . 153, 168.
83. Erfreute Zeit im neuen Bunde . . 122.
84. Ich bin vergnügt mit meinem Glücke 122.
85. Ich bin ein guter Hirt . . . 122, 138, 139, 140, 154, 162.
86. Wahrlich, ich sage euch . . . 95, 97, 122.
87. Bisher habt ihr nichts gebeten in mei- 99, 106, 107.
nem Namen
88. Siehe, ich will viel Fischer aussenden 47, 111, 154, 162.
89. Was soll ich aus dir machen, Ephraim? 35.
90. Es reifet euch ein schrecklich Ende . 27, 29, 101.

JAHRGANG XXII
1872 [1875].   ED. WILHELM RUST

NO.

91. Gelobet seist du, Jesu Christ . . 51, 52, 80, 91, 102.
92. Ich hab' in Gottes Herz und Sinn . —
93. Wer nur den lieben Gott lässt walten 153, 162.
94. Was frag' ich nach der Welt . . 82, 83, 95, 98, 111, 153, 168.
95. Christus, der ist mein Leben . . 96, 102, 109, 168.
96. Herr Christ, der ein'ge Gottes Sohn . 35, 40, 63, 66, 82, 86, 126, 153, 162.
97. In allen meinen Thaten . . . 114, 122, 153, 165, 166, 168.
98. Was Gott thut, das ist wohlgethan . 153.
99. Was Gott thut, das ist wohlgethan . 82, 83, 91, 111.
100. Was Gott thut, das ist wohlgethan . 50, 51, 52, 82, 86, 108, 110, 153, 168,
169.

JAHRGANG XXIII
1873 [1876].   ED. WILHELM RUST

NO.

101. Nimm von uns, Herr, du treuer Gott 40, 75, 81, 91, 102, 122, 123.
102. Herr, deine Augen sehen nach dem 75, 79, 82, 83, 84, 86, 97, 126, 162.
Glauben
103. Ihr werdet weinen und heulen . . 33, 34, 63, 65, 66, 68, 82, 83, 108, 111,
122, 162.
104. Du Hirte Israel, höre . . . 95, 108, 111.
105. Herr, gehe nicht in's Gericht . 97, 98, 168.
106. Gottes Zeit ist die allerbeste Zeit . 5, 65, 69, 122, 134.
107. Was willst du dich betrüben . 35, 81, 82, 84, 168.
108. Es ist euch gut, dass ich hingehe . 122, 153.
109. Ich glaube, lieber Herre . . . 35, 153, 162, 164.
110. Unser Mund sei voll Lachens . . 29, 80, 81, 82, 95, 99, 102, 110, 168.

TABLE XXII. THE CANTATAS IN NUMERICAL ORDER 247

JAHRGANG XXIV
1874 [1876]. ED. ALFRED DÖRFFEL

NO.
111.	Was mein Gott will, das g'scheh' allzeit	152, 168.
112.	Der Herr ist mein getreuer Hirt .	47, 148, 152, 153.
113.	Herr Jesu Christ, du höchstes Gut .	82, 95.
114.	Ach, lieben Christen, seid getrost .	35, 75, 82, 86, 152, 162.
115.	Mache dich, mein Geist, bereit . .	35, 81, 84, 86, 87, 135, 138, 139, 140.
116.	Du Friedefürst, Herr Jesu Christ .	35, 152, 154, 162.
117.	Sei Lob und Ehr' dem höchsten Gut	80, 81, 84, 85, 122.
118.	O Jesu Christ, mein's Lebens Licht .	22, 37, 40, 41, 47, 122, 123, 168.
119.	Preise, Jerusalem, den Herrn . .	8, 23, 26, 56, 58, 60, 67, 82, 151.
120.	Gott, man lobet dich in der Stille .	55, 80, 108, 111, 122.

JAHRGANG XXVI
1876 [1878]. ED. ALFRED DÖRFFEL

NO.
121.	Christum wir sollen loben schon .	40, 111, 152.
122.	Das neugebor'ne Kindelein . .	64, 69, 99, 152.
123.	Liebster Immanuel, Herzog der Frommen	81, 82, 84, 86, 152.
124.	Meinen Jesum lass' ich nicht . .	35, 152, 154, 168.
125.	Mit Fried' und Freud' ich fahr' dahin	35, 81, 88, 90, 111, 152, 153, 168, 169.
126.	Erhalt' uns, Herr, bei deinem Wort .	28, 35, 152, 154.
127.	Herr Jesu Christ, wahr'r Mensch und Gott	28, 69, 152.
128.	Auf Christi Himmelfahrt allein .	28, 44, 46, 95, 97, 99, 102, 110, 152.
129.	Gelobet sei der Herr, mein Gott .	81, 84, 86, 95, 122, 152, 153, 168.
130.	Herr Gott, dich loben alle wir . .	60, 61, 82, 83.

JAHRGANG XXVIII
1878 [1881]. ED. WILHELM RUST

NO.
131.	Aus der Tiefe rufe ich, Herr, zu dir .	96, 113, 114, 123.
132.	Bereitet die Wege, bereitet die Bahn .	5, 97, 122, 124, 155.
133.	Ich freue mich in dir . . .	38, 153.
134.	Ein Herz, das seinen Jesum lebend weiss	153, 154.
135.	Ach Herr, mich armen Sünder . .	38, 40, 41, 153.
136.	Erforsche mich, Gott, und erfahre mein Herz	95, 97, 110, 153, 162.
137.	Lobe den Herren, den mächtigen König der Ehren	33, 51, 80, 122.
138.	Warum betrübst du dich, mein Herz?	109, 110.
139.	Wohl dem, der sich auf seinen Gott .	122, 168, 169.
140.	Wachet auf, ruft uns die Stimme .	97, 122, 126.

JAHRGANG XXX
1880 [1884]. ED. PAUL COUNT WALDERSEE

NO.
141.	Das ist je gewisslich wahr . .	—
142.	Uns ist ein Kind geboren . .	66, 82.
143.	Lobe den Herrn, meine Seele . .	44, 46, 51, 52, 60, 80, 101, 115, 118.
144.	Nimm, was dein ist, und gehe hin .	—
145.	So du mit deinem Munde bekennest Jesum	8, 28, 88, 90, 108, 109.
146.	Wir müssen durch viel Trübsal in das Reich Gottes eingehen	75, 88, 175.
147.	Herz und Mund und That und Leben	5, 28, 29, 102, 104, 110, 113, 122, 162.
148.	Bringet dem Herrn Ehre seines Namens	28, 95, 102, 122.
149.	Man singet mit Freuden vom Sieg .	80, 95, 114, 115, 118.
150.	Nach dir, Herr, verlanget mich .	5, 113, 114, 116, 118, 122, 123, 155.

JAHRGANG XXXII
1882 [1886].   Ed. Ernst Naumann

NO.
151. Süsser Trost, mein Jesus kommt . 88, 89, 111.
152. Tritt auf die Glaubensbahn . . 5, 63, 65, 69, 80, 82, 95, 97, 122, 130, 131, 134, 153, 155.
153. Schau', lieber Gott, wie meine Feind' 101.
154. Mein liebster Jesus ist verloren . 111, 164, 168.
155. Mein Gott, wie lang', ach lange . 5, 113, 114, 118, 155.
156. Ich steh' mit einem Fuss im Grabe . 122, 162.
157. Ich lasse dich nicht, du segnest mich 8, 84, 86, 91, 95, 96, 108, 109, 122, 127, denn 128.
158. Der Friede sei mit dir . . . 5, 122, 123.
159. Sehet, wir geh'n hinauf gen Jerusalem 97, 113.
160. Ich weiss, dass mein Erlöser lebt . 5, 113, 122, 123.

JAHRGANG XXXIII
1883 [1887].   Ed. Franz Wüllner

NO.
161. Komm, du süsse Todesstunde . . 5, 66, 69, 168.
162. Ach, ich sehe, jetzt da ich zur Hochzeit 5, 30, 34, 36, 113, 168. gehe
163. Nur Jedem das Seine . . . 5, 110, 124.
164. Ihr, die ihr euch von Christo nennet . 8, 75, 76, 82, 91.
165. O heil'ges Geist und Wasserbad . 101.
166. Wo gehest du hin? . . . . 122, 162.
167. Ihr Menschen, rühmet Gottes Liebe . 23, 35.
168. Thue Rechnung! Donnerwort . . 111.
169. Gott soll allein mein Herze haben . 95, 98, 99, 162, 171, 174.
170. Vergnügte Ruh', beliebte Seelenlust . 111, 124, 168, 171, 173.

JAHRGANG XXXV
1885 [1888].   Ed. Alfred Dörffel

NO.
171. Gott, wie dein Name, so ist auch dein 80, 95, 122, 123. Ruhm
172. Erschallet, ihr Lieder . . . 60, 80, 101, 122, 123, 124, 135, 153, 171, 172.
173. Erhöhtes Fleisch und Blut . . 80, 81, 84, 86, 91, 101.
174. Ich liebe den Höchsten von ganzem 44, 47, 96, 116, 122, 124, 154, 168. Gemüthe
175. Er rufet seinen Schafen mit Namen . 64, 70, 71, 82, 101, 138, 139, 140.
176. Es ist ein trotzig und verzagt Ding . 99, 104, 162.
177. Ich ruf' zu dir, Herr Jesu Christ . 106, 114, 115, 119, 122, 168, 169.
178. Wo Gott der Herr nicht bei uns hält 122, 153.
179. Siehe zu, dass deine Gottesfurcht nicht 106. Heuchelei sei
180. Schmücke dich, o liebe Seele . . 70, 75, 81, 82, 106, 135, 138, 139, 140.

JAHRGANG XXXVII
1887 [1891].   Ed. Alfred Dörffel

NO.
181. Leichtgesinnte Flattergeister . . 8, 28, 82, 88, 91.
182. Himmelskönig, sei willkommen . 5, 66, 70, 82, 122, 123, 153.
183. Sie werden euch in den Bann thun . 106, 111, 138, 139, 140, 154, 162.
184. Erwünschtes Freudenlicht . . 80, 81, 91, 92, 101, 122, 154, 162.
185. Barmherziges Herze der ewigen Liebe 5, 33, 96, 97, 113, 153, 154, 155.
186. Aergre dich, o Seele, nicht . . 99, 104, 106, 113, 154.
187. Es wartet Alles auf dich . . . 153, 168.
188. Ich habe meine Zuversicht . . 124, 135, 171, 174, 175.
189. Meine Seele rühmt und preist . . 5, 66, 75, 78, 81, 88, 91, 122, 123.
190. Singet dem Herrn ein neues Lied . 80.

TABLE XXII. THE CANTATAS IN NUMERICAL ORDER 249

JAHRGANG XLI
1891 [1894]. ED. ALFRED DÖRFFEL

NO.
191. Gloria in excelsis . . . . 50, 80, 81, 92.
192. Nun danket Alle Gott . . . 76, 78, 81, 91, 97, 98, 153.
193. Ihr Pforten zu Zion . . . 96, 98.
Ehre sei Gott in der Höhe . . 84, 86, 119, 122, 123.
O ewiges Feuer, o Ursprung der —
Liebe
Herr Gott, Beherrscher aller Dinge . 80, 153, 175.

JAHRGANG XXIX
1879 [1881]. ED. PAUL COUNT WALDERSEE

NO.
194. Höchsterwünschtes Freudenfest . 97, 153, 154, 165, 166, 167.
Mit Gnaden bekröne der Himmel die 6.
Zeiten —
O angenehme Melodei

JAHRGANG XIII (1)
1863 [1864]. ED. WILHELM RUST

NO.
195. Dem Gerechten muss das Licht . 8, 51, 52, 80, 81, 92, 108, 111, 153, 162.
196. Der Herr denket an uns . . . 66, 168.
197. Gott ist unsre Zuversicht . . 26, 80, 115, 119, 122.
Three Wedding Chorals . . . . 21.

JAHRGANG V (2)
1855 [1856] ED. WILHELM RUST

Weihnachts-Oratorium (Christmas Oratorio):
Part I. . . . . . . 29, 54, 55, 91, 96, 98, 108, 111, 153, 154, 168.
II. . . . . . . 79, 80, 82, 88, 91, 104, 105, 111, 112, 133, 154.
III. . . . . . . 92, 111, 153, 154, 168.
IV. . . . . . . 102, 111, 153, 154, 162, 168.
V. . . . . . . 111, 153, 154, 168.
VI. . . . . . . 26, 80, 96, 102, 111, 153, 154, 168.

JAHRGANG XXI (3)
1871 [1874]. ED. WILHELM RUST

Kommt, eilet und laufet (Easter Oratorio) . 60, 70, 79, 83, 84, 115, 116, 122.

JAHRGANG XIII (3)
1863 [1865]. ED. WILHELM RUST

NO.
198. Trauer-Ode . . . . . 22, 81, 88, 89, 92, 93, 134, 142, 143, 154, 161, 164.

II. SECULAR CANTATAS
JAHRGANG XI (2)
1861 [1862]. ED. WILHELM RUST

Der Streit zwischen Phoebus und Pan . 61, 82, 88, 89, 108.
Weichet nur, betrübte Schatten . . 6, 21, 122.
Amore traditore . . . . . 122, 175.
Ich bin in mir vergnügt . . . 75, 82, 88, 89, 98, 122.
Der zufriedengestellte Aeolus . . 8, 26, 46, 61, 92, 93, 96, 97, 98, 122, 123, 128, 131, 133, 134, 135.

JAHRGANG XX (2)
1870 [1873]. ED. WILHELM RUST

Schleicht, spielende Wellen . . .	61, 81, 82, 110, 122, 175.
Auf, schmetternde Töne	—
Vereinigte Zwietracht der wechselnden Saiten	54, 78, 84, 88, 111, 112, 122.

JAHRGANG XXIX
1879 [1881]. ED. PAUL COUNT WALDERSEE

Was mir behagt	43, 46, 70, 71, 102, 113, 121, 122, 153, 167.
Non sa che sia dolore	79, 84, 85.
O holder Tag	21, 82, 88, 90, 93, 108, 111, 175.
Schweigt stille, plaudert nicht . .	21, 82, 175.
Mer hahn en neue Oberkeet . . .	46, 84, 85.

JAHRGANG XXXIV
1884 [1887]. ED. PAUL COUNT WALDERSEE

Die Wahl des Herkules	44, 46, 96, 123.
Durchlaucht'ster Leopold . . .	6, 75, 81, 84, 85, 91, 113, 116, 117, 124.
Schwingt freudig euch empor . . .	128, 131.
Die Freude reget sich	82, 84, 85, 131.
Tönet, ihr Pauken!	54, 55, 82, 84, 92, 96, 154.
Preise dein' Glücke, gesegnetes Sachsen .	61, 82, 84, 87, 92, 96, 97, 111, 127, 128, 168.
Angenehmes Wiederau	77, 88.
Auf, schmetternde Töne der muntern Trompeten	—

CANTATAS PUBLISHED SUBSEQUENT TO 1900

Mein Herze schwimmt im Blut (Neue Bachgesellschaft)	5, 97, 113.
Vergnügte Pleissen-Stadt (Schlesinger) .	21.
Was sind das für grosse Schlösser (Neue Bachgesellschaft)	—